LION CITY

LION CITY

SINGAPORE AND THE INVENTION
OF MODERN ASIA

JEEVAN VASAGAR

PEGASUS BOOKS
NEW YORK LONDON

LION CITY

Pegasus Books, Ltd.
148 West 37th Street, 13th Floor
New York, NY 10018

First Pegasus Books cloth edition March 2022

ISBN: 978-1-64313-934-0

10 9 8 7 6 5 4 3 2 1

Printed in the United States of America
Distributed by Simon & Schuster
www.pegasusbooks.com

For my father.

Contents

Introduction   1

1   Emporium of the East   21
2   'Blood will flow'   46
3   The Engineered Society   65
4   The Singapore Dream   84
5   The Model City   104
6   Authoritarianism with Gucci Handbags   125
7   Fighting Disease: From TB to Covid-19   150
8   'No one owes Singapore a living'   165
9   Taming the Internet   182
10   Singapore Inc   196
11   Asian Values   214
12   The Art of Resistance   232
13   Sin City   247
14   The Demographic Challenge   263
15   The Future   279

Epilogue   291
Acknowledgements   297
Endnotes   299
Further reading   315
Index   317

Introduction

In the last weeks of the southwest monsoon season, before the thunderstorms and drenching rain yield to the sticky heat of October, Singapore honours its ghosts.

As dusk falls, families head outside to thrust joss sticks into the grass by the kerbside and set out trays of tangerines and rice cakes with cups of milky tea. From old to young, most are dressed casually in shorts and flip-flops, but the atmosphere is solemn as sheafs of 'spirit money' – sheets of scented paper printed to resemble bank notes – are set alight on the tarmac. In the seventh month of the Chinese lunar calendar, as hungry ghosts wander the earth, the living offer food and money to send them on their way back to the afterlife.

Like Halloween, the Hungry Ghost Festival is a celebration for the living too. In open fields in Singapore's housing estates, pavilions will be set up for elaborate communal banquets under red-and-white striped awnings. On open-air stages there are *getai* shows, where singers perform a mix of energetic electronic dance and syrupy ballads in Chinese dialect, entertaining the living and the dead alike. Superstitious folk will avoid buying or moving into a new home. It's a glimpse of an older Asia, just a few miles from the glass and steel towers of Singapore's financial district. The Taoist and Buddhist custom of honouring the dead in the seventh month is fading into history in China, where communism has frayed ties with tradition. But this combination of feasting and mystical communion with the past still holds sway on a tropical island more than 1200 miles from the southernmost tip of mainland China.

I moved to Singapore from Berlin in late 2015, with my wife and two young children – a nine-year-old boy and a girl aged five. It was a radical contrast: moving from the German capital's graffiti-clad walls and hipster beards to a city of razored cheeks and slick office towers.

The clichés about Singapore were familiar to me: the efficiency of Changi airport, the theme-park style entertainments revolving around shopping and eating, the chewing gum ban, caning for vandalism, hanging for drug traffickers; an iron-fisted wonderland infamously summed up by William Gibson as 'Disneyland with the death penalty'.

But I knew it from the inside too. My father, who had died a few years earlier, had grown up in Singapore and as children we visited regularly. I remembered family outings to the food courts to feast on chicken satay and fried noodles with juicy prawns served in brimming melamine bowls; shopping for jewellery in the air-conditioned chill of the Indian goldsmiths off Serangoon Road; and walking through the baroque gateway of a Hindu temple just as the fierce tropical afternoon gave way to a balmy evening.

I had discovered in my twenties that I was not – as I had assumed for all of my childhood – my father's first-born, the eldest of three children. My father had been married once before, when he lived in Singapore, and I had an elder half-sister from that marriage.

Finding out about Chitra, my half-sister in Singapore, had subtly changed my relationship with my dad. I had always had an inkling that there was more to this respectable patriarch than met the eye. Dad's conservatism had thickened with age but there was evidently an adventurous streak in the man who had crossed the world in the hope of bettering himself. The façade crumbled when I knew that he had been married before. He was vexed when I confessed this knowledge to him. He had spent time constructing an image of himself as a married, hardworking, homeowning father-of-three. But this self-portrait was always a little fuzzy around the edges. Like Singapore itself, there was a darker and sadder history beneath the outward sheen of his material prosperity. In his case, this was a failed marriage across boundaries of caste, a daughter abandoned as a child, and a second marriage, against convention, to my mother.

When I returned to Singapore as a correspondent for the *Financial Times*, I had been away for years. While there were still glimpses of the narrow Chinese shophouses and neo-classical British architecture I recalled from my childhood, the waterfront was now a forest of glass and steel, neon-lit at night with bank logos. Driverless cars were being tested in a zone reserved for tech entrepreneurs. Singapore is on a global circuit of bankers, lawyers and IT contractors, drawing capital and white-collar talent from the US, Europe and Australia. Despite this, it is an exotic and mysterious location for many Westerners, bracketed with Hong Kong and Shanghai as modern centres of the Asian world.

Singapore is different from those other Asian cities. It is an inspiration in many distinct ways to people around the world, and is frequently cited as a role model; for the success of free enterprise if you are an American right-winger, or for the efficiency of authoritarianism if you are an African autocrat. From London to Los Angeles, educators around the world have adopted Singapore-style maths teaching. Singapore is not just a centre of modern Asia, as Hong Kong is, but something bigger – an Asian city state around which the modern world, seeking illumination, revolves.

In the middle of my first year in Singapore, Britain voted to leave the European Union. Brexit was greeted with peals of bemused laughter by Singaporean friends. Then came Trump. Here was further evidence of the unreliable results that an untrammelled democracy could throw up. To observers in Singapore it seemed a vindication of the need for a firm guiding hand tamping down on social divides in case they grew so wide that they ripped a country apart. Democracy, Singapore's deputy prime minister told me in autumn of that year, 'is not having a great run'.

The early decades of the twenty-first century have been a troubling time for liberal democracies, buffeted from outside by confident dictators, seduced from within by strongmen. Capitalism, meanwhile, is the preferred economic model nearly everywhere on the planet. For Singapore, there is nothing new in the strange marriage of consumer choice and political control that has taken hold everywhere from Beijing to Moscow. While the tiny island nation holds regular elections – and these are free and fair – each one has returned an overwhelming majority for the same party. In Singapore, the elections are not tampered with, but stuffing ballot boxes isn't necessary for the ruling party to keep on winning. The country's democracy is built on a framework of tight control, with restrictions on free speech, a free press, freedom of assembly, and the independence of trade unions and human rights activists. The Singapore example has been closely studied by China, and by authoritarian states across the post-Soviet sphere. The temptation is obvious; Singapore has succeeded in narrowing the political space while achieving First World prosperity.

Singapore's ban on the import of chewing gum, which

took effect in 1992, remains the best-known example of its founder Lee Kuan Yew's mania for order. But there are plenty more rules that highlight the intensity with which the country manages the lives of its people. The government has campaigned against spitting and littering too, with fines and public shaming – through photographs published in the media – of people caught in the act. The gum ban was introduced on the grounds that gum residue stuck between train doors could disrupt the smooth running of the mass transit service. This was a genuine problem, with two incidents in 1991 of trains stopping because the doors could not close. Yet Lee Kuan Yew could sometimes give the impression that humanity itself, with all its messy imperfection, was a gum residue that clogged up the smooth running of his system. In a speech delivered a few months after a peaceful popular uprising had ousted the dictator Ferdinand Marcos in the Philippines, Lee declared: 'We decide what is right – never mind what the people think.'

To understand modern Singapore, it is necessary to go back to the year it all began: 1965. Forget the Singapore of mirrored office towers, the city of elevators and air conditioning. Conjure a low-rise city with walls stained grey by cooking fires, bustling with street traders hawking their wares in a babble of Asian languages – a trading settlement with a cluster of colonial buildings surrounded by merchants' shophouses and then a sprawl of shanty towns.

Elsewhere, the 1960s are in full swing. The first American combat troops arrived in Vietnam this year, The Byrds have just had a number one hit with 'Mr Tambourine Man', and *The Sound of Music* is enthralling cinema audiences around the world.

Singapore faces a crisis. Malaysia, the sprawling federation that takes in the Malay peninsula, numerous small islands and a chunk of vast, jungle-clad Borneo, is expelling the tiny island at its southern tip. The cause of the break-up is rooted in the tense racial politics of the region. But it is the consequences that preoccupy Lee Kuan Yew, the Cambridge-educated barrister who is Singapore's first prime minister.

Lee, a member of the island's ethnic Chinese majority, was a brilliant man with a forceful personality. Elected Singapore's leader in 1959, when it was still a British colony, he had taken his country into a federation with Malaysia in 1963. A televised press conference from 1965 captures his distress vividly. 'For me it is a moment of anguish,' Lee says, dressed in a crisp, white shirt and dark tie, hair slicked back from his broad, high forehead. 'Because ... you see, the whole of my adult life' – and here his voice catches, he sits back in his chair and dabs his eyes with a white handkerchief, before going on. 'I had believed in merger and the unity of these two territories.' The union had been an unhappy experience, but its dissolution left Singapore vulnerable. The island lacked natural resources, and was reliant on the neighbouring Malay peninsula even for its water. Its ethnic mix, a Chinese majority with Malay and Indian minorities, made it unique and conspicuous in a region with a history of anti-Chinese xenophobia.

By the time Lee died at the age of ninety-one in 2015, Singapore was one of the richest countries in the world. But at the time, it had a modest industrial base, producing goods such as mosquito coils as well as processing rubber and tin. The severing of ties with Malaysia stripped the island of a substantial domestic market.

Singapore's most powerful advantage was its location. The island lies at the mouth of the Strait of Malacca, the waterway between the Malay peninsula and the island of Sumatra which offers the most direct shipping route between India and China. Because this strait is so narrow – just 1.5 nautical miles across at its narrowest point – and the goods passing through it are so valuable, the power that controls it can enjoy a lucrative share of the world's trade.

Sir Thomas Stamford Raffles recognised the virtues of this location when he established the British settlement in Singapore in 1819, writing in a letter home that year of the commercial and geopolitical advantages of the new base. He described planting the British flag on Singapura, City of the Lion as it was called by the Malays, and described it as 'a great commercial emporium and a fulcrum, whence we may extend our influence politically'. Silks from China, nutmegs, mace and cloves from the Spice Islands in present-day Indonesia, manufactured goods from Europe – all were shipped through Singapore. The city, where nowadays drug traffickers are sentenced to death, was once a linchpin of the British Empire's opium trade, flowing from the poppy fields of Bengal and Bihar to addicts in China. For most of the nineteenth century, the poppy accounted for between 30 per cent and 55 per cent of the colonial administration's revenues. The island had been a fishing settlement in ancient times, and then, by the fourteenth century, a flourishing regional trading centre known as Temasek. But it was Raffles and the drug trade that laid the foundations of modern Singapore.

Trade boomed after the Suez Canal was built, slashing the sailing time between Europe and Asia. In 1869, the year the Suez Canal opened, 99 steamers called at Singapore's wharves. A decade later that figure had risen to 541. Traffic in opium and the subsequent trade in rubber and tin enriched the British rulers and their Asian middlemen, creating a powerful class of ethnic Chinese traders and financiers. Colonial

Singapore, a port city with a transient and largely male population, had a seamy underside of brothels, violent criminal gangs and opium dens.

In 1965, the year of its painful break-up with Malaysia, Singapore was already one of the wealthiest cities in Asia. But it was highly unequal; the vast majority of the population were poorly paid manual labourers. It was also vulnerable – both to military conquest, as Imperial Japan demonstrated brutally in 1942 – and to internal division. Lee, who was forty-two at the time of separation from Malaysia, governed a volatile mix of races and languages; even the ethnic Chinese majority was splintered by dialect, speaking Hokkien, Teochew or Cantonese. 'We don't have the ingredients of a nation, the elementary factors,' Lee told the *International Herald Tribune* years later. 'A homogenous population, common language, common culture and common destiny.' The mixture had already proved highly combustible; in 1964 two outbreaks of communal rioting had resulted in more than thirty deaths.

By 1965, unemployment was running at about 9 per cent. A few years later, the British landed a further blow, announcing the closure of their military bases, which employed around 40,000 people. Singapore faced soaring unemployment *and* the prospect of being left defenceless.

Singapore's fortunes were transformed by an extraordinary burst of political energy. Lee's government turned to export-led industrialisation and invited multinationals to base themselves in the country. Left-wing trade unions were brought to heel, to ensure good labour relations while the government invested in housing, education and world-class infrastructure. Officials acquired a reputation for honesty which reassured investors. This blend of clean and efficient rule combined with a hard-working population and economic liberalism made Singapore an outlier in the region. It was a recipe for success: the Lion City roared, with growth averaging 9 per cent a year over the subsequent decades. In fifty years, this steamy and malarial colonial entrepôt city transformed itself first into a hub for the manufacture of semiconductors, from the late 1960s, a global financial centre from the 1970s on and a centre for petrochemicals from the 1980s.

Good timing played its part too. When Singapore launched its export industries, much of the rest of Asia was closed for business, pursuing economic doctrines of self-reliance rather than export, or sealed off under Communist rule. Singapore, along with the other tiger nations, Hong Kong, South Korea and Taiwan, were trailblazers for globalisation. From the 1960s to the 1990s, the four tigers achieved spectacular economic growth year after year. In all four, this economic success brought change at dizzying speed. The grandchildren of illiterate labourers became university graduates who take foreign holidays. The relationship between the state and citizens changed, as an educated and affluent population clamoured for a much bigger say in politics. Women achieved a much greater measure of equality and, increasingly, went to work outside the home. As traditional bonds of village and clan became looser, new forces such as radical politics and religion took their place. By the time growth began to slow, the four were among the most prosperous societies on the planet. Singapore, an island of just 5.7 million people, is now home to twelve billionaires, according to the 2020 *Forbes* list. By comparison, there are twenty-four billionaires in the UK and fifteen in Italy.

Singapore today is a comfortable city that presents a cosmopolitan face to the world; most first-time visitors are dazzled by the city's glitzy skyline, rooftop swimming pools and stylish cocktail bars. In 1965 its GDP per capita – a measure of its citizens' standard of living – was on a par with Jordan. Now it has outstripped Japan. The upside of the Singapore model is not limited to the super-rich. The welfare safety net is narrow in scope but robust. There is no dole for unemployment, but the government ensures there is a state-built home for everyone. There is very little homelessness – a count in 2017 found just 180 people, mostly male, sleeping rough in Singapore. The state-funded education system is one of the best in the world, regularly topping global league tables for the teaching of maths and science.

The whole system bears the deep imprint of one man's personality. There are no statues of Lee in the city he built, and only one institution named after him – a school of public policy – but anyone who wants to see his monument has only to look around them. Lee held power as prime minister from 1959, when Singapore was granted internal self-government under British rule, to 1990, when he stepped down. After quitting as premier, he remained in cabinet, first as senior minister then with the title of minister mentor, until 2011.

Lee had a love of the absolute ban that is often found in people who fear betrayal by their own appetites. A heavy smoker in his youth, he quit and became a fanatical anti-smoker, ordering cabinet colleagues to leave the room when they wanted a cigarette. He exercised religiously on a stationary bicycle, and was fastidious about healthy eating, favouring clear soups, tiny pieces of steak and plenty of fruit. Just once in a while, every four months or so, he would give way to temptation and send out for a *murtabak*, the oily, meat-stuffed pancakes that are an immensely popular snack on the island. He lived modestly, sharing a spartan bungalow with his wife and three children. His marriage to Kwa Geok Choo, another Cambridge-educated lawyer, was long, faithful and happy. In later years, when she was bedridden after a series of strokes, he would end the day by reading her favourite poems aloud.

By contrast with this domestic tranquillity, his public demeanour was often aggressively scornful, combining a barrister's courtroom swagger with the skilled politician's acid turn of phrase. 'Human rights? Are they bankable?' he sneered in a 1984 speech. While showing no propensity for violence in his personal life, his fondness for brutal imagery spoke of a deeply pessimistic view of human nature. 'Anyone who decides to take me on needs to put on knuckle-dusters,' he warned opponents, adding that 'There is no other way you can govern a Chinese society.'

Among the four Asian tigers, South Korea and Taiwan transitioned from dictatorships to democracies in the late 1980s. In both countries, parties compete for power. Hong Kong became an increasingly imperilled liberal island, with freedom of speech, independent courts and a free press, in one of the world's most autocratic states.

Singapore took its own path. Lee's People's Action Party brooks no challengers. The ruling party has close ties with all the alternative centres of power, from the media to trade unions. Newspapers deemed subversive or threatening to the national interest have faced closure or the detention of senior executives. Opposition voices, from rival politicians to bloggers who criticise the government, have been silenced through defamation actions.

Outsiders quickly discover just how little freedom there is in Singapore. Draconian laws allow activists to be prosecuted for holding peaceful gatherings unless they have a police permit. A teenage blogger who would have been dismissed as a minor irritant in most other countries has been sent to prison twice for his provocations. Sex between men remains a criminal offence. The last time Singapore had a legal strike was in 1986, when workers picketed a small American oilfield equipment company called Hydril. Authorities have reacted brusquely to strikes that are not officially sanctioned. When Singapore Airlines pilots took illegal industrial action in 1980, Lee told them: 'You play this game, there are going to be broken heads.'

The guiding value of Singapore's ruling elite is meritocracy. There is a fierce struggle for the top positions in the country's government. Its ministers hold degrees from some of the world's finest universities, including Cambridge, Harvard and Yale. Their qualifications range across hard science and social science – when the finance minister collapsed during a cabinet meeting in 2016, three colleagues who had trained as doctors rushed to assist him.

Singapore has no time for nostalgia. Dishevelled colonial-era workers' cottages, with their incense-laden shrines and shady verandahs, are swiftly ripped down to make way for air-conditioned high-rises, maximising property values on the crowded island. The hawker handcarts that once prowled the streets serving up sizzling strips of fried rice cake and sloppy bowls of prawn noodles have been corralled into hygienic open-air food courts. Even the language – in so many countries a cherished symbol of national unity – is not immune to this impatience with the past; the southern Chinese dialects that were once a mother tongue for the majority were pragmatically junked to make way for Mandarin. Singapore's success is underpinned by a determination to take difficult decisions in the national interest.

*

My father lived in Singapore as a young man, in the early 1960s, before emigrating to Britain, but when I went in search of his old lodgings, in 2016, I found the building had been obliterated to make way for a station on the public transit network.

A few months after I arrived in Singapore as a foreign correspondent, sipping a cup of thick black coffee in one of the government's imposing neo-classical buildings, I found myself telling my father's story to a senior official. I had arranged the meeting hoping for some insight on matters of public policy, but instead found the official prompting me to reveal more of my personal entanglement with his country.

Dad, born in the dusty far north of Ceylon, had stowed away on a ship steaming east across the Bay of Bengal. Once ashore in Singapore, he had found work as a policeman; I found a picture of a smiling, mustachioed young man in a khaki uniform when I looked through family albums after he died. A few years before Singapore's independence from Britain, he took another ship – buying a ticket this time – and sailed west, via Djibouti and the Suez Canal to Marseilles, and from there, a new life in London.

'Ah, you see,' said the official, leaning forward on the dowdy government-issue sofa. 'Your father's journey reminds us of the importance of the Suez Canal to Singapore.' He raised a light brown hand, sketching maritime trade routes in the air between us. 'Before the Suez Canal was constructed, much of the shipping passed further south.' The building of the canal transformed a swampy island into the commercial nerve centre of Southeast Asia. Another shift in the world's trading networks – the melting of the Arctic ice enabling polar navigation, for example – could alter Singapore's fortunes again, and for the worse.

City states are vulnerable places. Their early history can be glorious; Athens and Sparta left an enduring imprint on our societies. Venice had a good run, holding sway over much of the Mediterranean for centuries. But ultimately they fall victim to shifts in broader global currents – Venice lost out when the spice trade shifted to the transatlantic route – or are swallowed by bigger powers. Singapore's planners have always been conscious that their island's fate turns on forces beyond their control, the official told me. If Singapore has seemed restless in its pursuit of advantage, ruthless in its elimination of any excess baggage – from traditional languages to free speech – that paranoia at the top might explain it.

For those who do not question the system, life in Singapore can be very good. Unemployment is low, incomes are high, crime – especially the threats to personal safety that can make daily life miserable in many developing countries – is a rarity. In 2017 violent crime hit an all-time low with just seventy-one robberies that year, according to police figures. The material benefits of Singapore's progress are visible everywhere from the Prada and Hermès stores on Orchard Road to the families feasting on roast duck and noodles, paired with a fragrant Château d'Yquem, at restaurants on the upper floors of office towers. The consumption of the city state's elite is extravagant enough to have earned a Hollywood homage; the 2018 Singapore-set romantic comedy *Crazy Rich Asians* featured a bachelor party on a container ship, with one of the party-goers firing a military rocket launcher as part of the celebrations. But daily life in Singapore can sometimes feel like a gilded cage. Unlike Westerners, Singaporeans cannot read an unmuzzled press. They cannot join a trade union that is independent of government or easily add their voice to a pressure group that challenges government policy.

The few activists that exist in Singapore often find themselves hounded by the legal system.

Even those who accept the political constraints complain about the intense pressures at work and at home. Singaporean children spend long hours studying under tutors after their formal school day ends. Their mothers and – especially – their fathers spend so long in the office that an Eat With Your Family Day was launched in 2003. Employers are encouraged to let staff go home at 5 p.m. to enjoy a meal with their children. But the culture of long hours is so ingrained that Eat With Your Family Day is scheduled just four times a year.

Open to global flows of capital but largely closed to political change, Singapore is a reform-minded dictator's dream, suggesting that a country can enjoy the prosperity that comes with being open to foreign trade and investment without giving its people democratic freedoms. Deng Xiaoping, architect of China's market reforms, had this epiphany after the fall of the Soviet Union, when he remarked that Singapore enjoyed 'good social order' and said that China should learn from the tropical island state. 'Clean and beautiful,' was North Korean leader Kim Jong-un's verdict after posing for a selfie with Singapore's foreign minister in 2018. The country's dictatorial fans tend to be selective in their learning. They concentrate on dealing ruthlessly with their political opponents, as Lee Kuan Yew did, while ignoring the way that Singapore's rulers won legitimacy by improving their people's lives and rooting out official corruption. Post-Soviet leaders who claim to admire Singapore are often case studies in mismanagement of their countries' resources.

In the West, policymakers are more likely to cast an admiring glance at selected aspects of the system, such as its superb state schools. 'Make America Singapore' ran the headline on a *New York Times* piece describing Singapore's healthcare as the 'marvel of the wealthy world', with excellent health outcomes despite modest spending compared to the US and Western Europe. Singapore has emerged as a puzzling exception to the rule that industrialisation inevitably brings greater political freedom. At a time when China opens up its economy while its politics takes an increasingly illiberal turn, the planet's most successful city state offers a glimpse of another future for humanity. Authoritarianism, but with Gucci handbags.

From the 1950s onwards, Western theorists proposed that prosperity is the midwife of liberty. As a country becomes well-to-do, the growth of an urban working class and the expansion of education systems to meet new economic needs brings with it political change, they argued. That has certainly been the case elsewhere in Asia. In South Korea and Taiwan, traditional elites yielded in the face of pressure from trade unions and student movements. But while Singapore's economic success has brought with it potentially disruptive social change, its ruling elite has largely succeeded in assimilating or quashing threats to its dominance. A case in point is the challenge of absorbing a surge in immigration in the 1990s and the first decade of the twenty-first century.

By the 1970s, Singapore was attracting investment at a pace that outstripped the capacity of the local workforce. Migrant workers were imported to fill the gap, manning production lines and construction sites. The level of immigration soared in the 1990s. The migrant surge laid bare the flaw in Singapore's economic miracle. Productivity is usually boosted through technological advances or improved management practices – think of Henry Ford introducing the moving assembly line, and slashing the length of time it takes to build a car. But Singapore was growing, as Lee Kuan Yew later acknowledged, largely by importing labour. There were other factors too: more of Singapore's people were going to school and on to higher education, both to universities in Singapore and abroad, and the country was attracting higher levels of investment. But the Singapore economy's reliance on an expanding supply of migrant labour made its growth hard to sustain.

The 2011 general elections took place against a backdrop of public displeasure over immigration, with widely voiced complaints about competition for jobs and crowded public transport. The PAP, Lee Kuan Yew's party, still won, but it gained its lowest ever share of the vote. Singapore's system may restrict free speech and stifle the press, but the voice of the people had broken through nonetheless. A clampdown on migration duly followed, with the government lowering the cap on the number of foreign workers companies could hire. In the next elections the PAP scored a decisive victory, increasing its vote share to nearly 70 per cent.

The result of this compromise is a toxic mix. Singapore faces a future in which its labour force will shrink rapidly, squeezed by some of the world's lowest birth rates and reduced immigration. The likely prospect – without a significant ramping up of productivity or some technological breakthrough – is of years of feeble economic growth. As growth slows, couples become even less likely to have children, in a vicious cycle which has taken hold in Japan and is likely to become increasingly prevalent across Asia as the populations of many countries rapidly go grey, which makes them even less inclined to welcome young foreign workers. Despite family-friendly policies, there is little sign that young Singaporeans are choosing to procreate in the face of highly pressured workplaces and a demanding education system which requires heavy parental investment.

Increased healthcare spending is not the only financial

implication of this shift. The new generation of pensioners is more likely to live alone – staying on in their own housing rather than maintaining the Asian tradition of living under the same roof as their children – and that means more construction will be needed to provide homes for the young. Already, a third of the domestic workforce is aged fifty and over. This demographic time-bomb, which has been building for years, will reverberate throughout the economy and society, putting strain on public and individual finances. As the need for health and welfare spending rises, there will be fewer workers to pay for it all.

It's a familiar story, but in Singapore this comes with a twist; its model of benevolent authoritarian capitalism is built on low taxes – the top rate of personal income tax is 22 per cent, while companies have been lured there with staggeringly advantageous corporate tax deals. If Singapore is to pay its bills in future, taxes must rise. Singapore introduced a new tax on consumption, the goods and services tax, in 1994. The rate was set at 3 per cent and has since risen to 7 per cent. Ruling party politicians have warned of the need to raise taxes further to balance the books. But in 2020, a planned increase in the rate of the consumption tax was postponed amid the Covid-19 pandemic.

Demography is not the only challenge. The rise of China is an opportunity – and a threat. China's growing strength has bolstered the position of Singapore's ethnic Chinese, who make up around three-quarters of the population; their grasp of Mandarin and business networks mean they are ideally placed to exploit growing commercial opportunities. The economic connection is vital but the political relationship is often prickly. Singapore's close military ties with the US and Taiwan are a source of irritation to Beijing, while China's assertiveness in the South China Sea has made Singapore bristle. China has added missile shelters, runways and radar domes to islands in the South China Sea, militarising a waterway that is an essential conduit for global trade, and Chinese ships have harassed other countries' shipping in these disputed waters.

Singapore has watched these developments with anxiety. Like all small nations, it fears great powers that flout global rules, and its prosperity depends on shipping of all nations being allowed to peacefully navigate Asia's seas. The city state faces a delicate balancing act, needing to maintain economic links with Asia's superpower while asserting its own independence and neutrality.

The coming years are likely to be tough for Singapore. A slowing economy and stagnant wages will chip away at a prime justification for Singapore's repressive one-party rule: its claim to have transformed the island from a 'mud-flat swamp', in Lee Kuan Yew's words, to a sparkling metropolis. If Singaporeans are no longer being rewarded for their acquiescence with material gains, demands for a greater say in government are likely to grow. There are already signs that Singaporeans are chafing at the limits of personal freedom. The clampdown on migration after the 2011 elections showed Singapore's rulers could listen to their people. It also showed that they are now willing to sacrifice economic advantage for political expediency. But this did not mean they were willing to let up on their vigorous policing of the boundaries of free speech. Activists who question Singapore's politicians or judges continue to face harsh penalties.

The greatest challenge now facing Singapore is whether its system has the flexibility to survive an era in which technological change moves at an increasingly rapid tempo. The country has shown a remarkable ability to reinvent itself, from the creation of a hi-tech manufacturing sector in the 1960s and 1970s to the shift into financial services in recent decades.

Singapore's rulers approach globalisation as though it were a buffet dinner. They have helped themselves to the economic benefits of world trade while shunning the idea that liberal values such as free speech or gay rights can be universal. The nation forged by Lee Kuan Yew is still thumbing its nose at the idea that economic freedom goes hand in hand with wider freedom. Whether the system endures or cracks in the years ahead, the story of Singapore holds lessons for us all.

1

Emporium of the East

Raffles and the founding of Singapore

Geography shapes history, and there are few places where the force of geography on people's lives is clearer than in Singapore, a diamond-shaped island one degree north of the equator. From the eastern point of the diamond, where Changi airport occupies land claimed from the sea, to the industrial zone of Tuas in the west is a distance of thirty miles. From north to south it measures just fifteen and a half miles. Singapore is tiny and surrounded by giant neighbours; Malaysia lies on its northern border and the archipelago of Indonesia sprawls to its south.

The Singapore River bisects the heart of the city, flowing from the west and spilling out into the sea at Marina Bay. On the south bank of the river is Raffles Place, the commercial heart of the city, named after the imperial adventurer who founded the modern city more than two centuries ago. At Raffles Place, office workers spill from the MRT, Singapore's subway, and head through air-conditioned underpasses to their desks at banks, insurance companies and real-estate developers. As a woman hurries

up the escalator, you catch the flash of a red sole. Her heels
are Louboutin.

There has been tumultuous change in Singapore. Its population has risen from as few as 1000 people two centuries
ago to more than 5 million now. Mangrove swamps have
been cleared for industrial estates. Jungles where tigers once
roamed have made way for high-rise housing. When you
understand how fast this change happened, the notion of
appeasing the ancestors at the Hungry Ghost Festival makes
sense. The transition has happened at such speed that it feels
entirely plausible to believe that restless ghosts linger in the
shadow of expressways and shopping malls.

The old and new worlds of Singapore have remained con-
nected. The office worker in Louboutin heels will pick up
her lunch from the hippest ramen place in town, but once
home she will ignite a stick of incense and spend a moment
in contemplation for her ancestors. But a great deal of its past
has been obliterated too. What Singapore remembers about
its past, and what it has forgotten, sometimes deliberately, is
crucial to explaining its extraordinary rise.

The official version of the Singapore story is inscribed
on a plinth beneath the gleaming white statue of Thomas
Stamford Raffles, moulded from a glossy artificial material
resembling marble, that stands on the north bank of the
Singapore River. Unveiled 150 years after Raffles landed
and seven years after Singapore became an independent
republic, the inscription on the plinth begins with exactness
about a place and time, and then unspools a narrative thread
that links the British coloniser to contemporary Singapore.
Written in Singapore's four official languages, English,
Chinese, Malay and Tamil, it reads: 'On this historic site,
Sir Thomas Stamford Raffles first landed in Singapore on
28th January 1819, and with genius and perception changed

the destiny of Singapore from an obscure fishing village to a great seaport and modern metropolis.'

Around the globe, the impact of the West is recalled in many countries as a collective disaster. China invokes the memory of a 'century of humiliation' at the hands of Western powers. Across Africa, imperialists brought ruthless economic exploitation in diamond mines and rubber plantations, alongside a cruel system of racial dominance. In Singapore, the name of its European founder is a mark of prestige.

Raffles Place lies at the heart of the business district. Boys destined to rule the country attend the Raffles Institution. When Singapore Airlines first took to the skies, its business travellers were greeted in Raffles Class (this was the case until 2006, when the name was changed to Business Class). The neo-classical civic buildings at the colonial heart of the city have been carefully preserved while other historic buildings were ripped down to make way for hotels and offices. The proclamation on the plinth identified Singapore with a colonial project and declared the country open for business with the West at a time when many other Asian nations were taking a different path. When the statue of Raffles went up in 1972, the Vietnam War was in its final phase, China was staunchly communist, and India under Indira Gandhi had largely closed itself off to foreign investment and trade.

Like all histories, Singapore's story is more tangled than the tidy narrative on the Raffles plinth suggests. Its history of human settlement and trade stretches back hundreds of years. Merchants and warriors visited its shores before Raffles. Singaporeans are fond of saying that theirs is a young country, and it is true that it only achieved independence from Britain in 1963. But it is only a little younger than modern India, which came into being in 1947, or modern Germany, founded in 1949 – both of which regard themselves as the heirs of much older traditions.

In the fourteenth century, Singapore was already a mercantile centre known as Temasek, with a thriving trade in aromatic laka wood and hornbill casques, the horny growths above the bird's beak, which are carved like ivory. The island is said to have acquired its modern name when a seafaring prince from a neighbouring island spotted a mysterious beast which he decided was a lion. That is unlikely, as the Asiatic lion never ranged that far east, but the name stuck. He founded a settlement named Singapura: 'Lion City' in Sanskrit.

Since the 1980s, the archaeologist John Miksic has led excavations which have unearthed Chinese ceramics and coins, Chinese and Indian glass, and gold jewellery, evidence that even in medieval times the island lay at the confluence of an international trading network. Beneath Fort Canning Hill, where the first British colonial governors resided, is the remains of an ancient royal palace. The island's fortunes rose and fell in the centuries that followed, but far from being the 'young country' of popular imagination, Singapore had a 700-year history of settlement and civilisation.

Singapore is a nation created by migration and still shaped by it today. It has 4 million citizens and 'permanent residents', the official phrase for foreigners allowed to stay indefinitely, perhaps because they have a Singaporean husband or wife, or because they are investing in the country. Around three-quarters of this population are of Chinese heritage, many of whom trace their descent from Fujian province in southeastern China. Another 13 per cent are ethnic Malays from Singapore's Southeast Asian hinterland, while 9 per cent are Indians, mainly Tamil-speakers from southern India and Sri Lanka. Alongside this core population, there are another 1.7 million foreign workers and students, making up 30 per cent of the total population. The island is a stew of cultural influences. Sometimes these blend together, as in the distinctive street language of Singlish, in which English is cut through with loan-words from Hokkien, Malay and Tamil. Sometimes the cultures remain distinct; each ethnicity tends to keep to its own faith. Malays are largely Muslim, Indians mainly Hindu, while the Chinese practise Buddhism, Christianity or Taoism.

Several modern-day nations owe their existence to colonialism, but Singapore is the only non-white nation composed entirely of the descendants of settlers (except for the island nations of the Caribbean, where the native people were wiped out and replaced by enslaved Africans). Unlike the US, Canada and Australia, Singapore's migrants were not associated with the colonial power and did not conquer or exterminate an indigenous people. But like many migrant nations, it is more socially fluid than societies where wealth and privilege has been transmitted over many generations.

The story of modern Singapore begins in the early nineteenth century, when the Dutch were the dominant European power in Southeast Asia, controlling the trade routes between China and India. Nutmeg and cloves came from the Spice Islands, now known as the Moluccas and a province of present-day Indonesia. Porcelain was shipped from Japan and China, and chintz from India. Silk, silver, copper, coffee and tea were all traded between Europe and Asia. The Netherlands' maritime might allowed them to seize ports and govern tracts of land, and their most treasured possession was Java, a vast and fertile island in the Indonesian archipelago, where the peasantry were forced to grow export crops such as coffee, pepper, rice and indigo, bought by their European overlords at a set price. Raffles was driven by rivalry with the Dutch, and inspired by an idealistic vision of empire as a force for good. While the core of all imperial projects remained violent and exploitative, liberal imperialists like Raffles believed that benevolent British rule could bring benefits to its subjects. He was opposed to slavery and opium trafficking, a supporter of free trade, and took an interest in the language and history of the Malay people who lived across the Southeast Asian archipelago. His personal ambition and desire to expand British trade were fuelled, according to the historian Mary Turnbull, by a sense of 'messianic mission', a belief that Britain would revive the ancient cultures of Southeast Asia under the influence of the European enlightenment.

Thomas Raffles was fourteen when he entered the service of the East India Company. His father was a captain of merchant ships, plying between England and the West Indies. The family struggled for money, forcing him to cut short his education and find work to support his mother and sisters. He was industrious, hiding determination behind a diffident nature. In his own words, he was 'insatiable in ambition though meek as a maiden'. His life was one of spectacular success which never proved durable, followed by dramatic reversals which never quite crushed him.

Aged twenty-three, he earned an appointment to Penang, an island at the north of the Strait of Malacca which was Britain's toehold in the region. A crucial test of Raffles' views came in 1811, when Java was seized by the British and, at the age of thirty, Raffles was made its lieutenant governor. On the positive side of the balance sheet, Raffles attempted to reform Java's agricultural system, and ended the practice of using forced labour for public works. But British rule was nonetheless backed up by violence. In June 1812 British troops sacked the royal palace at Yogyakarta, an act still remembered as a calamity in Indonesia.

The financial performance of the colony was poor and Raffles was removed from his post. In 1816, Java was returned to the Dutch, part of the European settlement that followed the Napoleonic wars. He returned to England, where he defended his reputation so successfully that the Prince Regent awarded him a knighthood in 1817. Around this time, Raffles sat for the portrait painter George Francis Joseph, and the image of him now in the collection of Britain's National Portrait Gallery is every inch the confident imperial administrator. He wears the black coat and white cravat that he is likely to have worn to court for the ceremony. The sheet of paper he clutches is the official confirmation of his knighthood. Behind his right shoulder is a glimpse of Asia, a stone carving of an eastern deity.

In 1818, Sir Stamford returned to Southeast Asia, this time to a posting as lieutenant governor of Bencoolen, now the Indonesian city of Bengkulu, on the island of Sumatra. Then as now, there are two main passageways for ships sailing between India and China, and both of them pass by Sumatra. One route is the Sunda Strait, between Sumatra and Java. The other is the Strait of Malacca, which lies further north, between the east coast of Sumatra and the Malay peninsula. When Raffles arrived in Bencoolen, he found both under the control of the Dutch. 'The British have now not an inch of ground to stand upon between the Cape of Good Hope and China, nor a single friendly port at which they can water and obtain refreshment,' he wrote to London. Raffles was authorised by the British governor-general of India to establish a base at the southern end of the Strait of Malacca. His task was to find a suitable spot that was free of Dutch control.

After scouting the Carimon Islands, Raffles arrived at Singapore at the head of a flotilla of sailing ships, the red and white ensign of the East India Company fluttering from their masts and 120 soldiers from the Company's Bengal Army on board. His ships dropped anchor off Singapore in January 1819. He knew of it already, referring in a letter home to 'the ancient city of Singapura'.

When Raffles arrived, two half-brothers, Hussein and Abdul Rahman, were struggling for control of the Malay sultanate, which claimed Singapore along with a swath of surrounding territory. Raffles exploited the feud, siding with the elder half-brother and signing a treaty which allowed the British East India Company to establish an outpost in Singapore. Under the terms of the treaty, Hussein, the sultan, and one of his senior officials were paid annual stipends by the British, and retained their title to the land. Singapore had about 1000 inhabitants at the time, mostly members of the seafaring people known as the Orang Laut. On 6 February 1819, the union flag was raised over Singapore. Raffles left the next day, placing William Farquhar in charge.

Farquhar's fate has been the opposite of Raffles'. A Scottish soldier in the service of the East India Company, Colonel Farquhar was instrumental in the creation of modern Singapore, but his name has largely disappeared. Singapore used to have a Farquhar Street, which ceased to exist during redevelopment works in 1994, although a Farquhar Garden, opened in 2019 for the bicentennial of Singapore's founding, offered modest amends for this erasure.

Farquhar had been chief engineer in the East India Company expeditionary force that seized the port of Malacca from the Dutch in 1795. Ruling the port as resident and commandant, the chief civilian and military authority, he was a respected figure known as the 'Rajah of Malacca'. He learned to speak Malay and lived with a local woman named Antoinette 'Nonio' Clement, of Malaccan-French descent. The couple had six children (a great-grandson migrated to

Canada, and is the ancestor of prime minister Justin Trudeau). Farquhar kept a menagerie that included a leopard, a porcupine and a cassowary. He was the first European to identify the Malayan tapir, adding one to his household bestiary; the pet tapir was, he noted in a letter to Britain's Royal Asiatic Society, 'very fond of attending at table to receive bread, cakes or the like'. Once he was given charge of Singapore, Farquhar's reputation attracted settlers from Malacca, while traders were drawn by the profits to be made in supplying a new colony. Raffles returned in June 1819, bringing supplies of timber and tools, but then left again for over three years, leaving Farquhar to govern Singapore.

Singapore thrived, attracting trading ships and settlers. Its location was convenient, just as Raffles had predicted, while British military strength provided a guarantee of security in a region where pirates were a persistent menace, and Raffles' commitment to free trade meant that merchant ships were not charged duties on their goods. But Singapore's early prosperity owed as much to Asian enterprise as it did to British power.

Among the earliest entrepreneurs to settle in Singapore was Tan Che Sang, who left China at fifteen to seek his fortune in Southeast Asia. When Tan moved to Singapore from Malacca, he was in his fifties, wealthy and well-connected. He has been the agent in Malacca for ships bringing tea and silk from China, iron and cotton goods from India and Europe, and when he moved, this business moved with him.

The Indian merchant Naraina Pillai came to Singapore with Raffles. Spotting an opportunity in the speed at which the settlement was growing, he set up a brick kiln, brought in bricklayers and carpenters, and became Singapore's first building contractor. Asian muscle built Singapore. Convict labourers from India cleared swamps and built some of the earliest roads, as well as public buildings and bridges.

Raffles had left clear instructions for Farquhar about the running of the new settlement, but his vision ran into conflict with reality. Required to run Singapore at minimal expense, Farquhar defied Raffles, a staunch opponent of gambling who frowned on drugs, by tolerating slavery and auctioning monopoly rights to run gambling dens, and to sell opium and arrack, the fiery spirit popular across India and Southeast Asia. He strayed from Raffles' vision of town planning too. When merchants protested that Raffles' original demarcation of the settlement had left them with a coastal strip where the water was too shallow to bring goods ashore, Farquhar permitted them to move to a new location. On Raffles' return to the island in 1822, the two men clashed, and Farquhar was ousted. Raffles prohibited gambling and abolished slavery, though hidden forms of slavery persisted. The open sale of human beings could be banned, but bondage in exchange for working off debt was harder to uncover and eradicate.

One of Raffles' final acts in Singapore was to make a donation to create a new school to educate the sons of the regional elite. He laid its foundation stone a few days before sailing home to Britain. 'It should be our care that while with one hand we carry to their shores the capital of our merchants, the other should be stretched forth to offer them the means of intellectual improvement,' he wrote. The school, which welcomed its first pupils in 1834, was the Raffles Institution, the cradle of Singapore's postcolonial elite.

Raffles' time in Singapore was brief, but he left an indelible stamp. His vision for Singapore as a centre of trade, his strict town planning, passion for education and puritanical disdain for gambling found a parallel over a century later in the personality of Singapore's founding prime minister. But the pragmatic drive of Farquhar endures too. Modern Singapore may have scruples, but they are often sacrificed when the need to make money arises.

The original 1819 treaty between Britain and the traditional Malay rulers of the region had simply given the East India Company the right to set up a trading post in Singapore. The terms of the treaty meant the British shared power with the Malay nobility, and this quickly led to friction. The Malay chiefs' supporters frequently brawled with incoming settlers from Malacca. A Malay chronicler of Singapore memorably described their attitude towards the newcomers as 'like that of tigers towards goats'.

It was traditional for the captains of ships calling at Singapore to give gifts to the Malay chiefs, swelling their wealth and allowing them to exercise patronage, but Raffles believed these privileges were incompatible with running a free port. Putting pressure on the chiefs by withholding their stipends for three months, the British forced them to sign a new treaty in 1824 ceding Singapore in its entirety to the East India Company. In a display of power, the British sailed the East India Company warship *Malabar* around the island.

Singapore was now firmly under British control. But it was also, unmistakably, an Asian city. The English navigator George Windsor Earl wrote in the 1830s: 'The wharfs were absolutely crowded with natives from all parts of India; vast numbers of Chinese labourers were pulling bales and boxes out of the merchants' warehouses and putting them into boats, where they were received by [South Indian] boatmen from the Coromandel coast.' Earl described scenes of industry, with craftsmen building boats and furniture, sailors twisting rope, washermen hanging out laundry and dairy farmers milking cows. The houses in the city's main streets were brick-built, but were surrounded by humble dwellings of wood and palm frond thatch. Then as now, the island was surrounded by shipping. Brightly painted Chinese junks, with eyes marked on their bows to guide their path, arrived on the northeast monsoon wind. There was silk, tea and Chinese manufactures in the holds, but on the decks were crowds of settlers eager for a glimpse of their new home. Over the next few decades the island would be transformed by immigration on a huge scale. Migrants to Singapore were commonly young, uneducated men who had come in search of work. By the 1860s there were more than 80,000 people in Singapore and the Chinese were the ethnic majority. Among the Chinese and Indian migrants, the sex ratio was severely skewed. For much of this era, there were around eleven Chinese men for every woman. A high proportion of the women had been trafficked to Singapore to work in brothels.

Singapore was a destination in its own right, but also an entry point to Southeast Asia for migrants from across China. It was a hub for the produce of Southeast Asia – rice, pepper, and gambier, a herbal extract used as a dye, as well as tin and gold from mines in Malaya. But most important of all, in the government's eyes, was the opium poppy. For most of the nineteenth century, opium accounted for between 30 per cent and 55 per cent of the colonial administration's revenues. For the exhausted labourers unloading sacks on Singapore's docks, the drug blunted the contours of a harsh life. The trade was legal, with the British granting franchises to Chinese businessmen. The opium trade filled the coffers of the colonial government but enriched Asian entrepreneurs too.

The Asian migrants to Singapore lived in separate neighbourhoods. Indians settled first in Chulia Street, now at the downtown heart of Singapore, and then Little India. Geylang, now on the eastern fringe of the city centre, was a Malay village. The Chinese lived in clusters according to the dialect they spoke. The Hokkien Chinese, who made their living trading spices and other goods, lived around the mouth of the Singapore River, on the island's south coast. The Teochew Chinese, the second biggest group after the Hokkien, lived on the north coast and made their living as fishermen and boatmen. The interior of the island was jungle, settled by Chinese migrants who carved out patches of farmland to grow gambier. A British naval officer, James Brooke, wrote: 'Their habitations may be distinguished like clear specks amidst the woods, and from each a wreath of smoke arises, the inmates being constantly engaged in the boiling of gambier.' These farmers 'may be said to live beyond the reach of all law'.

New immigrants were recruited into secret societies such as the Tan Tae Hoe, the 'Heaven and Earth Society' which was reputed to have up to 20,000 men in its ranks. These sworn brotherhoods granted protection and provided a sense of belonging to men far from home. The secret societies soon acquired an economic function, controlling the supply of labour to plantations and tin mines and extracting protection money from brothels and opium dens. Violence flared up between them over these lucrative fiefdoms. The British sought to work with the societies at first, dealing with their leaders as intermediaries with the Chinese community, but eventually resorted to suppressing them after mounting violence in the colony. The final straw came when a civil servant, William Pickering, was attacked by a gang member wielding an axe. The Societies Ordinance, which came into effect in January 1890, made groups with more than ten members illegal unless they had been granted official approval.

Singapore's location at a maritime crossroads had always been fortuitous, but advances in technology during the

Victorian age were to underline this advantage. The opening
of the Suez Canal in 1869 and the arrival of the steamship
transformed the journey, slashing the time and cost of the
voyage between distant corners of the Eurasian landmass.
As elsewhere in Asia, Singapore experienced modernity at
the hands of a dominating Western power. The lessons of
Western might were clear. The capitalist system generated
both the technology and finance to equip and deploy powerful armies and navies, overwhelming the rest of the world.
Japan, alone among Asian empires, thoroughly absorbed
and adopted these lessons, becoming a colonial power in its
own right.

Singapore's growth was driven by three commodities: tin,
rubber and oil.

Rubber was introduced to Singapore in 1877, when
the British dispatched a shipment of seedlings from Kew
Gardens. The crop was grown commercially on the island
but it was cultivated on a far greater scale in Malaya, where
large swaths of tropical rainforest could be cleared for plantations. Tin was mined in the western provinces of the Malay
peninsula. Demand for both tin and rubber boomed in the
late nineteenth century, serving the new global industries of
canned goods and car manufacture.

Singapore was the port through which these products
flowed out to the world. Men from China and India who
came through Singapore provided the labour that dug for tin
ore and tapped rubber trees for latex. Singapore's merchants,
both European and Asian, took advantage of the investment
opportunities. Tan Kah Kee, a Hokkien-speaking migrant
from Fujian province in China, bought 500 acres of jungle
in Singapore in 1904, clearing it for a pineapple and rubber

plantation. Tan diversified his business interests across pineapple canneries, a rice mill later converted into a rubber mill and then a factory producing rubber goods.

When, back in China, a revolution in 1912 swept away the inefficient and corrupt Qing dynasty, which had suffered a series of military defeats at the hands of foreign powers, Tan and many of his fellow Singapore Chinese were supporters of the new Chinese republic, rejoicing in the revolution and raising money to send home. Tan and other Chinese businessmen financed education for their community in Singapore, setting up schools including the Chinese High School, the island's first Chinese-language secondary. Tan also founded *Nanyang Siang Pau*, a Chinese-language daily newspaper. This pairing of patriotism for the motherland and Chinese-language education was to have enduring consequences. Singapore's Chinese schools created a group of highly educated young people who were keenly aware of China's fortunes and would become increasingly politically active.

The most affluent in Singapore's society, of all races, attended English-language schools. A 'Chinese-educated' student was likely to be a patriot who regarded the British as colonial interlopers, while the 'English-educated' student might aspire to study at Oxford or Cambridge and seek a position in the colonial civil service. The language in which they were schooled became a dividing line that cut through Singapore's Asian middle class.

Tin smelting was Singapore's first industry. In 1890, the Straits Trading Company, a partnership between German entrepreneur Herman Muhlinghaus and Scottish businessman James Sword, built a tin smelter on the island of Pulau Brani, just off the south coast (Pulau means 'island' in Malay; Pulau Brani translates as 'island of the brave'). The furnace was a modern kind that used coal, and Singapore's location on major shipping lanes meant the fuel could easily be brought in by sea. By 1912 the ore smelted by the company generated two-thirds of Malaya's tin output.

Oil and petroleum products from the Dutch East Indies were stored and shipped through Singapore. From 1897, Shell used the island of Pulau Bukom to store petroleum, and this developed into its hub for the region. The processing and trade of the three commodities showed it did not matter whether Singapore itself possessed valuable raw materials. The city could profit from its deepwater port, its strategic location, and the ingenuity of its European and Asian businessmen to sell its services to the surrounding region.

Out of the rubber trade, Singapore began to establish itself as a financial centre. Like all agricultural commodities, rubber fluctuates in price according to swings in supply and demand. Pests or poor rainfall may blight a harvest, while the outbreak of war may stimulate a boom. Rubber prices set at auction in Singapore became a benchmark for buyers and sellers, even if they were not conducting their transactions in the city. To this day, Singapore sets a pricing standard for the global rubber trade.

Both producers and buyers of rubber needed a way to shield themselves from swings in price, and so rubber 'futures' contracts were created – agreements to buy rubber at a fixed price on a future date. These were some of the first financial products traded in Singapore.

Two of the world's biggest tyre manufacturers, the US companies Goodyear and Firestone, both created Singapore subsidiaries, in 1917 and 1919, to handle their rubber purchases, an indication that the city was acquiring global importance as a commercial centre.

By the start of the twentieth century, there was a growing

Asian middle class in Singapore, of which merchants and industrialists like Tan Kah Kee, as well as lawyers and doctors, were members. While much of the population still lived in overcrowded 'shophouses', a Chinese and Southeast Asian style of property with a business opening onto the street and living quarters on upper floors, or in wooden huts, there were also signs of prosperity and modern technology, with cars in the streets and telephone connections to the world.

A causeway between Singapore and Malaya was completed in 1924, providing an alternative to the ferries that brought passengers and goods back and forth. The creation of a terrestrial link further stimulated trade between the island and the Malayan peninsula, allowing Malayan planters to send their produce directly by lorry or train to Singapore's merchants without incurring the costs of transshipment. The causeway enhanced Singapore's position as the chief port of the region. By the time of the 1931 census, over half a million people lived in Singapore. By 1941, the city had its first skyscraper, the sixteen-storey Cathay Building. The cinema inside, opened in 1939, was the first air-conditioned theatre in Singapore, while the restaurant on the second floor – serving European food – was one of the most fashionable in the city.

Colonialism had divided the world into countries that produced raw materials but saw little of the profit, and countries that processed these goods, set prices and sold financial products on the back of them. Singapore, unusually for a colony, established itself as one of the winners of the imperial system. The concentration of trade and industry in Singapore created a virtuous circle, making it the natural spot for further investment. When Shell was deciding where to open a new refinery in 1959, Pulau Bukom was already the largest oil storage base in Southeast Asia. The refinery opened in 1961 became Shell's biggest in the world, capable of turning out half a million barrels a day.

It is a short and pleasant climb to the top of Bukit Batok, a forested hill in the west of the island. Lush foliage on either side of the pathway offers shade, and a chorus of birdsong keeps you company. The last few metres of the walk take you up a flight of broad concrete steps. At the top, where the red and white pylons of a TV transmission tower now stand, Australian prisoners of war built the 'Syonan Chureito', a twelve-metre-high wooden obelisk topped with a cone of brass, to commemorate the war dead of Singapore's Japanese conquerors. The obelisk is gone now, demolished by the Japanese at the end of the war to prevent it falling into enemy hands, but scars of the three-year occupation remain.

The Japanese occupied Singapore from February 1942 to September 1945, when the British officially resumed control a month after Japan's surrender. Propaganda images showed the conquest as a liberation, part of a broader drive by Japan to present their empire as a force that would turn back the tide of Western colonialism and create a benevolent 'Co-Prosperity Sphere' under Japanese leadership, spanning East Asia. Clocks in Singapore shifted to Tokyo time, one hour ahead, while schools began teaching in Japanese. But the reality of the occupation was fear, scarcity and brutal repression for Singapore's people, especially the ethnic Chinese.

Before the war in the Pacific broke out in December 1941, China and Japan had already been at war for five years. The Sino-Japanese conflict drew sympathy and outrage from Southeast Asia's Chinese diaspora, a sentiment stoked by news of atrocities including widespread rape and the massacre of civilians. Led by Tan Kah Kee, Singapore's Chinese community set up a relief fund that raised millions of dollars from tycoons and ordinary workers alike. Chinese consumers and businesses boycotted Japanese goods. In 1939, responding to an appeal from the Chinese government, Tan recruited thousands of volunteers to aid the Chinese war effort as drivers and mechanics. They drove trucks along the Burma Road, a winding path through mountainous terrain linking Burma and southwest China, which became a vital supply route after Japan took control of China's coastline.

Fearing the rise of imperial Japan, British naval planners had advocated Singapore as a base from which to defend the empire's interests around the Pacific rim. A *New York Times* report on the government's decision noted: 'Today Singapore stands unrivaled as a trading centre in this part of Asia ... it may be readily understood that, considering the awakening of the Far East, the advance of Japan, the slow but not less sure development of China, the great future in store for Australia, the importance of Singapore will increase rather than diminish as the years go by.' Technological advances in naval warfare meant that a larger dock was required for the resupply and repair of battleships. The world's largest dry dock, named after King George VI, was opened in Singapore in 1938. But there was no permanent fleet stationed in the East. Instead, British policy was to advance a fleet to Singapore when a threat was imminent.

A Royal Navy battleship, HMS *Prince of Wales*, and battle-cruiser HMS *Repulse*, were finally dispatched to Singapore in 1941, only to be sunk by Japanese bombers on 10 December, a few days after Pearl Harbor. That month Japanese forces swept through Malaya, arriving at the causeway linking the peninsula to Singapore at the end of January 1942. Chinese leaders in Singapore offered the British their help and the colonial administration agreed to recruit a volunteer force to bolster the city's defence. Thousands of Singapore Chinese joined what became known as 'Dalforce', after its commander Lieutenant Colonel John Dalley, an officer in the Malayan police. The volunteers, given basic training and weapons, fought fiercely alongside Commonwealth troops.

Despite this resistance, the defenders were forced to surrender on 15 February. The capitulation laid bare Britain's inability to defend scattered global possessions while fighting for national survival against European foes. The Japanese victory and the heroism of Dalforce showed, in different ways, where the future lay. The threat to Singapore's security now came from a rising Asian power rather than European colonisers, while its own people had rallied to the city's defence.

Having occupied the city, the Japanese renamed it Syonan-to, meaning 'Light of the South'. They imposed discipline underpinned with terror. Outside the Cathay Building, an emblem of the city's pre-war prosperity and modernity, an awestruck crowd gathered around a pole which displayed the severed head of a Chinese man, executed because he had been caught looting. In the first few weeks of the occupation, every Chinese man between the ages of eighteen and fifty was ordered to report to screening centres across the island. Here they were examined by Japanese military police in an operation known as 'Sook Ching' – in Chinese, 'purge through cleansing' – which took place from mid-February to the beginning of March. Thousands of suspected 'anti-Japanese elements' were transported to remote spots and murdered. At the time, and for years afterwards, their families had no idea whether their missing loved ones were still alive. One unofficial estimate of the death toll places the number of dead between 40,000 and 50,000, though this may include civilian victims of shelling and bombardment during the military campaign.

Tan Kah Kee, a target for the Japanese, managed to evade capture and escape to Java where he hid for the duration of the war. Many of the Dalforce volunteers escaped to the jungles of Malaya, where they joined the Malayan People's Anti-Japanese Army, a guerrilla force under Communist leadership.

Violence against Singapore's people continued throughout the occupation, including the 'Double Tenth' incident in which civilians were tortured and murdered for suspected involvement in sabotage of Japanese shipping. In the streets, civilians would be slapped across the face for minor misde-meanours, such as failing to bow to a Japanese soldier. The historian Gregg Huff notes that people in Malaya bowed to passing cars 'since it was unlikely that anyone except Japanese would be riding in them'. The Kempeitai, Japan's military police, set up its headquarters at the YMCA building on Stamford Road, in the heart of the city, with substations across Singapore. Confession was routinely obtained through torture; the screams of victims were audible to neighbours. The grim catalogue of methods included waterboarding, inflicting cigarette burns, and dislocating limbs. Among the civilian victims of torture was Elizabeth Choy, who ran a hospital canteen with her husband and secretly gave food, medicine and money to British civilians who had been interned. Choy was held by the Kempeitai for 200 days and subjected to repeated torture, including electric shocks.

Compounding the bitterness of the occupation, the Japanese extorted millions of dollars from Chinese commu-nities in Singapore and Malaya in the early months after the conquest. The money was intended as an atonement for their 'anti-Japanese' activities. Japan issued a new currency for use within its occupied territories in Southeast Asia. The notes were illustrated with tropical images, such as banana trees; because the Japanese printed them in large quantities, allowing the value of the currency to fall rapidly, they became known derisively as 'banana money'. It was, effectively, another form of extortion. Singapore's people were forced to trade their goods and labour with the occupiers for notes that were increasingly worthless.

The brutality of occupation was accompanied by food shortages, especially of Singapore's staple crop, rice. Japan expected Malaya and Singapore to be self-sufficient, but in any case the destruction of its merchant fleet, mainly through US submarine warfare, meant that as the war went on, Japan struggled to meet the needs of its own home islands, let alone its scattered empire. Alongside terror, access to food became a means of controlling the population. People employed either by the Japanese military administration or a Japanese business received part of their wages in rice, a significant incentive as paper money lost its value. Vegetable gardens sprang up across the city, even in the Padang, the playing field in front of the Supreme Court which had been used for cricket under the British. Sweet potato and tapioca, a fast-growing plant that flourished in Singapore's climate, became substitutes for rice.

Singapore's people were not only short of food but basic goods like clothes, shoes and shaving razors, as well as medicines. Increasingly, cash became useless and people bartered for goods. For Lee Kuan Yew, eighteen years old when Singapore fell, this was a formative time, giving him an insight into the raw power that comes with total control over a society. The Japanese conquerors, though hated, were able to exact total obedience through fear.

The collapse of European empires during the Pacific war was an inspiration to Asian leaders who wanted to free their countries from colonial rule. The Indian nationalist Subhas Chandra Bose and Burma's independence leader Aung San – father of Aung San Suu Ki – both allied themselves with the Japanese. Bose came to Singapore in 1943, and announced the formation of a provisional government of free India in a ceremony at the Cathay cinema hall. From captured British Indian troops, he recruited a force called the Indian Nationalist Army which fought alongside Japan.

The British returned in September 1945, a few weeks after Japan had accepted defeat following the dropping of atomic bombs on Hiroshima and Nagasaki. Lord Louis Mountbatten, supreme allied commander in Southeast Asia, accepted the formal surrender of the local Japanese forces in the Municipal Building, now known as City Hall. Newsreel footage captures the sound of the crowd booing as the Japanese officers walk up the building's steps.

Elizabeth Choy, who survived the war, represented Singapore at the coronation of Queen Elizabeth II in 1953. She was feted by her fellow Singaporeans as an exemplar of courage and Christian faith in the face of cruelty. A play about her wartime experience, Not Afraid to Remember, was staged at the Singapore Drama Festival in 1986 and her story is told in the history gallery of the National Museum. A lifelong fear of touching electrical switches was a grim after-effect of her wartime suffering.

Choy's life combined idealism with a practical desire to put her moral code into action. A teacher before the war, she became the first Principal of the Singapore School for the Blind in 1956. The conquest of Singapore left her convinced of the vital importance of national security and she joined the Singapore Volunteer Corps, a civilian defence force, encouraging friends to do the same.

In 1962, mass graves holding the remains of victims of the

Sook Ching massacre were unearthed at fourteen sites across the island. The discovery prompted an outburst of public anger, including a rally demanding 50 million Malayan dollars in compensation for 'blood debt'. The rally was held at City Hall, and drew 120,000 people, making it the largest demonstration in Singapore's history. The *Straits Times* described banners hanging from the palm trees outside the building, showing 'the various tortures practised by the Japanese'. The episode was uncomfortable for Lee, who sought Japanese investment in Singapore and was reluctant to stir up the past. In October 1966, Japan agreed to settle the blood debt claim. On a state visit to Singapore a year later, Japanese prime minister Eisaku Sato made no mention of the war, except for a single oblique reference to 'unhappy incidents'.

Diplomatic relations between the two countries are now cordial and Japan has become a major investor in Singapore, but a residue of bitterness remains. As recently as 2017, there was an outcry after a government agency named a wartime exhibition 'Syonan Gallery', using the hated name given by the Japanese. The exhibition was renamed 'Surviving the Japanese Occupation'.

Every year, Singapore marks the date of surrender with Total Defence Day, when school children practise first aid and remember the privations of their forebears by exchanging 'ration coupons' for austere lunches of steamed sweet potatoes and rice porridge. If the past sometimes hangs heavy in Singapore, this freighted history helps explain why. A generation saw a system as robust and seemingly permanent as the British Empire disintegrate overnight.

When I moved to Singapore at the end of 2015 I discovered while flat-hunting that many Singaporean homes had built-in bomb shelters, inner rooms with reinforced walls and heavy blast doors. In a society which has known decades of peace, these have often ended up filled with bric-a-brac, or used as a maid's sleeping quarters. Over lunch with a worldly-wise Singaporean banker I questioned the country's high level of military alertness, seemingly out of proportion with the level of threat in its neighbourhood. He smiled and said: 'We believe that if you can't defend it, it isn't yours.'

2

'Blood will flow'

The split with Malaysia and the birth of modern Singapore

When he was twelve, Yeo Oi Sang's education was cut short by his family's poverty. He dropped out of school and did odd jobs for a while, working everywhere from building sites to bakeries, before a family friend got him an apprenticeship at a Chinese bookstore. Yeo taught himself to read, starting with children's books and moving on to more sophisticated fiction. He began with menial tasks, but even when he was sweeping the floor he would sharpen his mind by memorising the position of each book on the shelves. 'The bookstore business opened a new world of literacy for me,' Yeo said. 'From books I absorbed new ideas and broadened my worldview.'

Yeo became the publicity and education officer for the union that represented booksellers and printing press workers. He wanted to share the new world that had opened up to him through literature. 'I was passionate about exposing our illiterate union members to drama productions and other educational and cultural activities to help them grow into productive members of society,' he said.

The aftermath of the Second World War, when Yeo Oi Sang was a boy, was a bleak time in Singapore. There were office towers in the city centre, with a growing English-speaking middle class of white-collar workers. But around them were the teeming shophouses, two or three storeys high, that combined a narrow shop opening onto the street with residential quarters. The shophouses were often packed with families, and were grimy and run-down. Their original bright colours had faded to façades of grey, with laundry strung on bamboo poles from balconies.

Communism had an especially powerful appeal for Southeast Asia's ethnic Chinese, who witnessed the rebirth of their motherland under the red flag. But the seduction of an egalitarian and anti-colonial creed cut across all ethnicities. On the neighbouring Malayan peninsula, communist guerrillas had won prestige for their resistance to the Japanese during the war, as well as acquiring a fearsome reputation for post-war reprisals against alleged collaborators. From 1948, the Malayan communists – who were predominantly ethnic Chinese – launched a revolt against the resumption of British rule.

You did not need to be a communist to see that Singapore was ripe for change. For those who did not belong to the English-speaking minority, hours were long and pay was meagre. Workers who did not toe the line could easily be replaced from the ranks of the unemployed. Students from Singapore's Chinese high schools became increasingly militant in their opposition to colonial rule. The island's Chinese community funded their own schools, but graduates could not go on to university, which required English, or get a job in public service. This lack of opportunity fuelled resentment.

The fates of Malaya and Singapore were intertwined. On the peninsula, the communists returned to armed struggle against the British. In June 1948, after three European managers of rubber plantations were murdered, Britain declared a state of emergency in Malaya. In July of that year, the Communist Party was banned in Singapore.

The star of Singapore's left was Lim Chin Siong, a charismatic and good-looking young man famous for his oratorical skills in Hokkien, the dialect spoken by many Singapore Chinese. A student activist who had been expelled from high school, Lim became a union leader at the age of twenty-one.

Yeo and Lim were friends. 'His speeches were legendary,' Yeo said. 'He never used flowery language but he deeply understood the struggles of the working class and enthralled them in native Hokkien absolutely anybody could understand. His speeches were compelling, sincere and transparent. To listen to him was to fully understand his story, his rationale and his aims. Many were moved to support him.'

Thousands swelled the ranks of unions, demanding better pay and shorter hours, and Singapore was hit by waves of industrial action. One afternoon in 1952, two years before Yeo got his apprenticeship at a bookstore, four postmen came to the offices of the Singapore law firm Laycock & Ong, seeking an advocate to represent them in a pay claim against the government. In a humid outer office, made noisy by traffic and hawkers' cries from the street outside, they met a young barrister, Lee Kuan Yew, who had just returned from his overseas education. Lee, known to family and friends as 'Harry', made an unlikely ally for the trade unionists. He was from a prosperous, ethnically Chinese family which had been settled in Singapore for generations. Lee's family spoke English at home, and he struggled to express himself in Chinese.

Lee had been educated at an elite English–language school, the Raffles Institution, and from 1947 to 1949 read law at Fitzwilliam College, Cambridge. His intellect was clearly exceptional; at Cambridge he graduated with a First, and his result in the second part of his final undergraduate examination placed him at the top of his cohort. Related by marriage to Tan Chin Tuan, a prominent banker, he belonged to the upper echelons of Singapore society. He was 'Straits Chinese', part of a sliver of Singapore Chinese society that had lost much of its traditional culture, absorbing influences from Southeast Asia, such as using coconut milk in their cooking, as well as aspects of British culture. Lee was the eldest of five children, and four of them had English names – as well as Harry himself there was Dennis, Freddy and Monica. His heritage made him an outsider both in Singapore, where he was born and brought up, and in Britain. This vantage point proved to be a strength, allowing him to be dispassionate about both West and East. His interviews would be a swirl of intellectual references, from Confucius to the British Marxist Harold Laski to the Harvard political scientist Samuel Huntington, famous for the 'clash of civilisations'. What this melange indicated was a man who was a pragmatist, flexibly adopting theories to suit his instincts about what worked.

As if in demonstration, in late 1943 Lee had applied for a job in the Japanese propaganda department, the Hodobu, which had been set up in the Cathay Building. He was to work there for fifteen months. His job required him to piece together reports by Allied news agencies such as Reuters and the Associated Press (AP), which had become garbled during radio transmission. 'I had to decipher them and fill in the missing bits, guided by the context, as in a word puzzle,' Lee recalled. Unlike Bose and Aung San, the Indian and Burmese nationalist leaders, there is no indication that Lee's work with the Japanese was ideologically motivated. Rather, it was a means of survival. He quit working for the Hodobu by the end of 1944, aware from the news reports he was piecing together that Japan was losing the war. Lee turned to black market trading to survive. His mother's circle included many formerly wealthy women with jewellery to trade, so he began bartering jewellery and other valuables on behalf of his mother's friends. On the streets, heirlooms could be traded for medicine, food or cigarettes.

For Lee, a legacy of the wartime occupation was an obsession with strength and order. He was repulsed by the barbarism of the Japanese occupier, but quietly admired the rarity of crime under Japanese rule (true, if you ignore the flourishing black market and the fact that the regime was itself criminal). Lee had little interest in religion. He was agnostic and dismissive of Chinese ancestor worship as a meaningless superstition. Combined with his slender ties to Chinese culture and language, this meant he was well placed to be a neutral arbiter between Singapore's cultures and religions. Instinctively, he did not turn to culture or religion to hold Singapore together. Popular validation came from clean, efficient government and economic growth.

This background enabled him to be a political chameleon too, changing colours according to what best served his view of the national interest. He would employ anti-colonial rhetoric when he needed to drive the British out, but embrace Singapore's colonial heritage when he needed to lure Western investment. While he believed in a hierarchy of races, and thought the Chinese most talented, he had no hesitation in promoting able members of other races – although his appointees tended to be English-educated, and under Lee, Singapore's leadership was uniformly male. Throughout his life, he never swerved from a belief in eugenics. Intelligent parents would produce intelligent offspring. The children of labourers would occasionally out-perform their parents, but this was a rarity, he thought. 'If you have two white horses, the chances are you breed white horses,' he told an interviewer late in life.

Lee's tactics on behalf of the postmen were effective. Working in tandem with a sympathetic journalist, Sinnathamby Rajaratnam, who wrote supportive editorials in his newspaper, the *Singapore Standard*, he was successful in winning public sympathy for the striking postmen. The colonial government backed down and dozens of other unions sought him out as their legal adviser.

Around the same time a political discussion group formed around a core of young Singaporean men educated in Britain, who began meeting on Saturday afternoons in the basement dining room of Lee's home, a bungalow on Oxley Road, a well-to-do area near the Orchard Road shopping district. The men were nationalists, determined to fight for independence from Britain but wary of communism. Among them was Rajaratnam, who had gone into journalism after his education at King's College London was disrupted by war. Another was Goh Keng Swee, the son of a rubber plantation manager, who had studied economics at the LSE.

It was obvious to Lee that his discussion circle, English-educated and from middle-class families, represented a minority in Singapore. To win over the majority, including discontented workers and high-school students, he needed allies from the left. The circle in his basement launched a new political movement, the People's Action Party (PAP), which brought moderate nationalists together with left-wingers. The new party's symbol, crucial at a time when many voters were barely literate, was a red lightning flash

in a blue circle. For their inaugural meeting in the ornate
surroundings of the Victoria Memorial Hall, in November
1954, the founders wore white shirts meant to symbolise
incorruptibility.

In April 1955, tensions between unions and employers
spilled over into a broader confrontation that convulsed the
entire country. The trigger was a dispute over workers at
the Hock Lee bus company who had been sacked for union
membership. The conflict began at the bus depot, which was
picketed by strikers for days. Men sat on the ground outside,
linking arms and legs to block buses from leaving. When
police tried to disperse them by spraying them with water
jets from high-pressure hoses, the dispute escalated. The
use of fire hoses against strikers brought other workers and
students from Chinese-language schools out in sympathy.
Across Singapore, buses came under attack while thousands
converged on the depot. Police firing tear gas battled crowds
who lobbed bottles and stones at them.

In the rioting that night two policemen were killed: a
detective named Yuen Yau Phang burned to death when his
car was set on fire, while volunteer constable Andrew Teo
was beaten by protesters and died in hospital of his injuries.
An American journalist, Gene Symonds, was also caught up
in the violence and killed. Among the protesters a sixteen-
year-old schoolboy named Chong Lon Chong suffered a
fatal gunshot injury, most likely from a police officer who
fired shots over the crowd. The night of violence showed
the depth of anger among workers in Singapore, and the
speed with which a coalition of workers and students could
paralyse the country, bringing its streets to a standstill. To
the colonial authorities it looked like a communist-inspired
plot. A union activist's May Day speech that year warned:
'there is bound to be some bloodshed in the course of a

revolution.' But it was also an illustration of the desperation in 1950s Singapore.

London's grip on Singapore was steadily loosening. Across Asia, after the Japanese surrender, nationalists fought for independence rather than a return to European dominion and dozens of new countries were coming into being. India and Pakistan became new nations in 1947, Burma and Ceylon (later, Sri Lanka) in 1948, while Indonesia's independence was recognised in 1949.

Students at Singapore's Chinese-language schools, founded and financed by businessmen like Tan Kah Kee to preserve and transmit Chinese culture, were particularly active in resisting British colonial rule. Their students felt discriminated against under a system in which government jobs required English. In May 1954, hundreds of Chinese students gathered to protest against the imposition of national service by the colonial authorities, leading to violent clashes with the police. Told to disperse, the teenagers hurled stones at police instead. The riot squad responded with baton charges. An attempt to ban students from getting involved in industrial disputes or party politics led to a protest sit-in at six schools and further riots in 1956.

In 1959, Singapore became self-governing, though the British retained control of defence and internal security. An election was held in May to create a new Legislative Assembly that would run the country. The crucial issue was filling the rice bowls of ordinary families. The ranks of the jobless were predicted to swell: the population was growing rapidly, while the traditional import and export trade that had sustained Singapore was unlikely to provide enough jobs to feed all the hungry mouths. In any case, while storing, processing and exporting rubber, tin and oil were profitable businesses for Singapore, it meant the fortunes of the country were tied to the volatile prices of commodities. Handling raw materials – especially oil – would remain a crucial part of Singapore's economy, but Lee and his circle grasped the need to diversify, and they promised to industrialise the economy.

The PAP offered social change too, promising to build a new nation that drew together Singapore's disparate racial and linguistic elements. At the time, they believed the Malay language would provide a unifying force. (English has since taken the place of Malay as the country's lingua franca, but Singapore's national anthem, 'Majulah Singapura', is still sung in Malay.)

The campaign showed that Lee, when it suited him, could be a firebrand. A Reuters report from 1959 quotes him saying he would restore the dignity of Singapore's Asian population and 'fight the white man'. Electoral politics took him to a world that the English-educated middle class would not normally visit. He felt distaste at the smells of waste water, the rats, and drains filled with garbage and leftover food from hawkers' stalls. In his memoirs, he recalled 'retching' from election visits to run-down housing. When he got home, washing his hands was insufficient. He bathed and changed his clothes.

Left-wingers in the party fired up ordinary voters, combining a vision of a more equitable society with a patriotic appeal to preserve Chinese culture. They addressed voters in their own dialects. 'They spoke with a passion that filled their listeners with emotion and exhilaration at the prospect of Chinese greatness held out to them,' Lee wrote in his memoirs, remembering rallies staged from the backs of lorries by orators wielding megaphones.

The PAP won a landslide victory and Lee Kuan Yew

became Singapore's prime minister in June 1959. He was thirty-five, and had no experience of administration. Even managing his law firm, Lee & Lee, founded in 1955, had largely been left to his wife Kwa Geok Choo and his younger brother Dennis. Goh Keng Swee was appointed finance minister and Rajaratnam was minister for culture. Toh Chin Chye, a lecturer in physiology who was another member of Lee's Oxley Road discussion circle, became deputy prime minister. But the triumph laid bare the uneasy alliance between the right and left of the party.

The right, led by Lee, favoured a merger with neighbouring Malaya, creating a common market and providing additional resources to help drive economic growth. Malaya had become independent in 1957, led by a conservative elite; the country's first prime minister, Prince Abdul Rahman, was the son of one of the sultans, the country's traditional rulers. Malaya's communist insurgency was in retreat and would finally be declared over in 1960. The victory, a rare reversal for communism in Asia, was achieved in part through a massive resettlement programme that split rebel fighters from sympathetic civilians.

Singapore's left-wingers preferred the idea of an independent socialist state. The PAP split in 1961. Lim and other left-wingers formed the Barisan Sosialis – in Malay, the Socialist Front. Many of the PAP's activists defected to the new organisation. The union movement split too, most trade unions siding with the new socialist party.

In the early hours of 2 February 1963, more than a hundred people were arrested by police and Special Branch officers in Operation Coldstore. The detainees included Lim and other leaders of Barisan Sosialis, trade unionists and student activists. Described by the authorities at the time as an essential move to counter the threat of armed insurrection by a communist conspiracy who wanted to turn Singapore into the Cuba of Southeast Asia, Operation Coldstore remains an acutely sensitive topic in Singapore. Former left-wingers and some historians argue there was no evidence of a plot and that the security sweep was used to suppress the left for reasons of political expediency. The government describes this as 'revisionism' and insists the threat of communist insurrection was genuine.

The bookseller Yeo was held for fifteen months. 'I felt this to be unreasonable as I had done nothing wrong and was in fact doing my part to contribute to society,' he said. 'Our educational and cultural activities were well-received and union relations were good and peaceful. They just stuck a communist label on me to detain me. I felt these were their dirty tactics to consolidate political power.'

Yeo, now in his eighties, still lives in Singapore, where he runs Xinhua Cultural Enterprises, a bookstore occupying one of the corner spaces in the old and relatively shabby Bras Basah retail complex in the city centre. The store is well-lit, clean and comfortable, if a little cluttered. Neat stacks of Chinese-language books rise from the floor in blocks, towering over you. There are narrow pathways just wide enough for a single body to weave through amid the book stacks, some of which end in a dead-end of even more books. The musty smell of old paper pervades the air-conditioned space. 'The fifteen months of detention were a true test,' Yeo says. 'I spent four months in solitary confinement, in a tiny room with just one bed and one [chamber] pot. They wanted to break me. But the bigger the force, the stronger the resistance. I knew I had done nothing wrong, and I held on to that.

'I spent my time planning what I'd do once I got out. I had a goal and I had hope – I knew I was passionate about

Chinese societal and cultural education and I could continue this through the bookstore business. Do you know, detention was never scary for me? I knew what I'd done and what I hadn't. I'd never betrayed myself, my fellow citizens, or my country.' The months of detention changed him for life. 'I'm more open-minded now. I let go more easily. Problems barely worry me. I survived four months of solitary confinement. What compares with that?'

In contrast, Lim, the charismatic orator, was broken by his years in detention. The *Straits Times* reported that he was treated in prison for depression. Lim wrote to the prime minister in 1969 announcing that he would quit politics and go overseas. In a separate letter addressed to fellow social-ists, he declared: 'I have completely lost confidence in the international communist movement.' His letter to Lee is an insight into the once-amicable relationship between the two men. Lim addresses the prime minister by his intimate name, 'Dear Kuan Yew', and reveals with heartbreaking candour that he had contemplated suicide rather than confess that he had lost faith in communism. He was freed from detention that year, and left for the UK with his fiancée Wong Chui Wan, who had also been detained. He returned in 1979, but never recovered his place in Singapore politics, and died of a heart attack in 1996.

With the left-wing leaders out of the way, the island's gov-ernment pursued a merger with Malaya to form a new state, Malaysia. The union was due to come into being at the end of August 1963. When this was delayed by the government in Malaya's capital, Kuala Lumpur, to allow time for a United Nations team who were investigating whether people in two states on the neighbouring island of Borneo wished to join the new country, Lee went ahead and declared Singapore's independence from Britain on 31 August. In a speech on the steps of City Hall, he announced the end of colonial rule and looked forward to joining the union with Malaya. 'This proclamation today is an assertion of our right to freedom,' he said. The unilateral declaration met with disapproval from both the Malayan and British governments, who believed Lee had grabbed the right to control Singapore's foreign and defence affairs without being granted them constitutionally. It was an inauspicious start to the union of the two countries, which came into being in September 1963.

The union of Malaya and Singapore between 1963 and 1965 was always an uneasy one. The two countries are like siblings. And like siblings, their likeness is often a cause for bitter argument. While both countries are made up of the same ethnic mix – Malay, Chinese and Tamil – their politics is very different. Malaya was dominated by Malays, the traditional inhabitants of an archipelago stretching across Southeast Asia, and in 1963 the country was predominantly rural. Singapore had a Chinese majority, many of them recently arrived in the region, and was largely urban. Under colonial rule, Malaya's occupations had been roughly divided on ethnic lines; Indian immigrants and their descendants worked on rubber plantations and in government offices, the Malays worked the land. The Chinese worked in tin mines and factories, while some prospered in commerce.

Like other ethnic minorities whose wealth catches the eye, the Chinese attracted the resentment of Malay nationalists. The Malay peasantry were some of the poorest people in the country, while some of the wealthiest in Malaya were Chinese tycoons. As the communist movement was also identified with ethnic Chinese, they drew additional suspicion – they represented both the capitalist exploiters and the

Red menace. The Malay majority was favoured through a programme of affirmative action, detailed in the constitution drawn up when the country won independence from Britain in 1957. This conferred benefits in business and education to the people known as *bumiputra* – the sons of the soil – under a system that endures to this day.

In Singapore, Lee's government was unwilling to concede special racial privileges. 'Resisting Malay hegemony,' he wrote in his memoirs years later, was the 'root cause' of the dispute. This attitude angered Malay politicians, who felt that Lee and men like him were arrogant and selfishly lacking in concern for the poor. A leading Malay newspaper accused Lee and his party of mistreating Malays in Singapore. Hardliners on the Malay side warned that 'blood will flow', according to Lee, if their wishes were not respected.

In 1964, blood did flow, as lethal rioting broke out between Malays and Chinese in Singapore following a celebration of the birthday of the Prophet Muhammad in July. The unrest took days to bring under control. A second wave of rioting broke out in September. A Malay schoolboy, Zainul Abidin Rasheed, caught up in the second wave of riots, saw young Chinese workers attacking Malays with 'acid bulbs, bicycle chains and iron rods' gathered up from ironmongers and other workshops. Escaping to a Malay neighbourhood, he saw the same scenes in reverse with Malays attacking Chinese. 'In peacetime they were all friends, they lived together – fruit sellers, market stall holders, Malays, Indians, Chinese, we were at best of relations,' said Zainul, who went on to become a Singaporean diplomat.

Singaporeans were appalled. Theirs had been an island in which every race rubbed along together. A total of thirty-six people died in the two bouts of violence, but the spectre of communal bloodshed has left a scar on Singapore's memory out of proportion with the death toll.

For Lee, and leaders of the Chinese community in Singapore, there was an added source of anxiety; the police force in Singapore was dominated by ethnic Malays and under the control of the central government. If push came to shove, there was some uncertainty about whether they would intervene to defend Chinese neighbourhoods. Privately, Lee was preparing for a separate future, noting in a memo that year that splitting with the Malaysian federation would provide Singapore with 'an escape, if there is to be trouble in Malaya with communal clashes'.

In May 1965, Lee rallied opponents of affirmative action, emphasising the need for economic development that would lift all races. 'They say they are worried about the Malays?' he asked. 'I say, so are we. We want to raise their standard of living and we will, and faster than they can.' To his supporters he was arguing for a Malaysia based on a shared national identity rather than racial categories. To Malay nationalists, it seemed that he was plotting a Chinese takeover of the country.

The political arrangement holding the two territories together had been severely damaged by the riots. Now it was unravelling fast. The two sides clashed sharply over how much Singapore was expected to contribute in taxes to the central government. In July 1965, Singapore's finance minister Goh negotiated in secret with the Malaysian leadership. These talks, only revealed in 1996, suggest both sides agreed that a complete secession was the only way out for Singapore. In August of that year, Malaysia expelled Singapore from the federation. At a televised press conference, Lee's eyes brimmed with tears as he spoke of a 'moment of anguish'.

Lee later wrote that he felt guilty at abandoning those

across Malaysia who had rallied to his idea of a multiracial nation. But firecrackers went off in Singapore's Chinatown that night, a sign that many were relieved at the prospect. If Singapore and Malaysia remained one country, but kept quarrelling over affirmative action, the threat of ethnic violence loomed permanently on the horizon. Separation meant this fear had receded. At the time, though, Singapore's future looked fragile. The island became a port without a hinterland, cut off from the country that supplied about half of its drinking water. From a combined population of 11 million in Malaysia, Singapore had shrunk to a statelet of 2 million.

An abandoned railway track runs through the heart of Singapore, from the docks on its southern coast across the forested hill of Bukit Timah to the northern coast where a narrow stretch of water separates the country from Malaysia. Thick green foliage overhangs the parallel lines and the contrast between man-made symmetry and riotous nature makes this a perfect Instagram spot; most days you will find at least one bride posing in white silk by the black steel of a gantry with her entourage.

Disused since 2011, the line has become a public park, the only park in the world that runs across the entire span of a country. Just after sunrise, while it's still cool, curious monkeys watch joggers pound past, while nature lovers kneel to catch a mobile phone shot of butterflies in gorgeous hues of metallic red and blue. Yet the line is a reminder of the distance between two countries, Malaysia and Singapore, that share a common ethnic and cultural inheritance.

For years, the two neighbours wrangled over the line, which ran through Singapore along parcels of land owned by Malaysia. The dispute only reached a final settlement in

2010, with a swap of land that gave Singapore ownership
of the line. Aside from the railway, the two nations have
found plenty to squabble about, including the price of the
water that Singapore imports from southern Malaysia, and
the sovereignty of Pedra Branca, a granite outcrop in the sea
east of Singapore. Relations between the two countries since
separation have warmed and cooled with changes of leadership, though they have never tipped over into open conflict.
Even when political relations were at their frostiest, the two
countries were bound in kinship.

My father grew up in Singapore, my mother in Malaysia,
just across the border in the coastal city of Johor Bahru.
When they crossed back and forth, and when they went back
from the UK to visit family on either side in the decades that
followed, there was little to distinguish the everyday life of
the two places; the same dishes of rice and noodles were set
out on plastic tables in the streets of Chinatown, the same
Tamil tunes spilled from shop doorways in Little India, the
languages you heard on the street were all the same.

The post-war decades were decisive years for Singapore,
shaping the country's present-day outlook on some of the
biggest questions it faces, from politics to economics to
race relations. Under Lee, Singapore would be vigorously
anti-communist. The Lion City embraced private enterprise, welcoming investment from Western multinationals,
while providing the social housing, education and healthcare needed to keep its workforce content and productive.
But while rejecting their economic creed, Lee and his allies
adopted an element of the left-wingers' style. The communists were admired for their dedication to their cause, and
their austerity. Lee decided that living a relatively simple and
Spartan life would help shield him from criticism.

The state would be vigilant about maintaining racial

harmony. Its National Pledge, written in 1966, declares that Singaporeans are 'one united people, regardless of race, language or religion'. It is recited in school assemblies, with a fist clenched above the heart. Singapore championed the ideal of meritocracy, in contrast with Malaysia's approach to levelling up through affirmative action. In theory, though it did not always work out this way in practice, political and economic advancement in Singapore would be open to anyone, regardless of their class or racial background.

These early years revealed the first glimpse of a state that would rule through a mix of coercion and cajoling, caring for the welfare and living standards of its people but capable of using an iron fist against perceived opponents. Coercion in Singapore would always stop short of the arbitrary execution wielded against internal foes in the world's worst dictatorships. But the fear of being locked away for years, without hope of release through trial, was a potent terror. Above all, Singapore under Lee bristled with suspicion. Fear of communism would become an enduring motif, a catch-all accusation that swept up a range of internal opponents. Anxiety about hostile neighbouring powers would become the reason to build up military might and a way to unify and galvanise Singapore's people.

Singapore marks its National Day with a public holiday on 9 August. The day features school bands, light entertainment and plenty of military pomp including a twenty-one-gun salute and a giant flag flown from the tail of a Chinook helicopter. The day does not mark 1959, when Singapore became self-governing, or 1963 when the country declared independence from Britain, but 1965, Lee's 'moment of anguish' when it split with the Malaysian federation. It is a combative choice of date, as if the country frames its identity in opposition to its neighbour.

When Singapore separated from Malaysia in 1965, the country lost the margin for error that bigger nations enjoy. A larger country with a reputation for corruption or instability might still attract investment because of the sheer size of its market. If Singapore failed to win over foreign investors in its early years, there was a risk that it would spiral into long-term decline. In a speech made in October of that year, Lee was blunt about this. 'This is an exercise in survival,' he said. 'And it calls for some very savage and brutal methods sometimes.'

If Singapore genuinely had no second chances, no opportunity to recover from a serious mistake, then it had to avoid making mistakes in the first place. The result was a determination to tightly manage the daily lives of its population. In the decades after independence, Singapore's rulers would make clear their belief that their country was not ready for a Western-style democracy, where political ideals clashed at the ballot box. They had snuffed out communism and seen off the prospect of Malaysian-style affirmative action. When political ideals clashed in Singapore, the losing ideal usually ended up behind bars or in exile.

3

The Engineered Society

How Singapore's ruling elite
created a nation

Moments before the bomb went off, a witness saw smoke pouring from a canvas bag near the lift entrance on a mezzanine floor of MacDonald House, a ten-storey red-brick building that housed the Singapore office of the Hongkong and Shanghai Banking Corporation. Set with a timing device, it went off at 3.07 p.m., seven minutes after the bank closed for the day, when the offices were still crowded with employees. The explosion, powerful enough to rip out the lift doors, shatter windows and destroy the staircase linking the first and mezzanine floors, killed three people: Suzie Choo and Juliet Goh, both secretaries at HSBC, and Mohammed Yasin, a driver.

The perpetrators of the attack were discovered, quite by chance, three days later when a boatman found two men clinging to a plank in the open sea. The pair, identified by a bus conductor who spotted them before the explosion, were convicted of murder and hanged. The men were Indonesian

marine commandos, and the attack in March 1965 was the
deadliest in a wave of bombings on Singapore in the 1960s.
The violence was part of a simmering confrontation between
Indonesia and Malaysia that spilled over into a campaign of
sabotage against targets in Singapore.

Fear can sometimes appear to pervade the Singaporean
psyche, and the early years of its independence go a long
way to explaining why. Within a few decades, Singapore
had been conquered by imperial Japan and harassed by
Indonesian saboteurs. Racial riots threatened the island's
tranquillity. Then, in 1965, a vexed relationship with
Malaysia ended in an acrimonious split. The flipside of fear
is often a craving for security, order and strength, and this
has been the pattern of Singapore's politics ever since. Fear
of external threats led Singapore to build up its defences.
Fear of internal rivals led to crackdowns on left-wing politicians and trade unionists. The imperative to build up the
new nation's strength prompted a single-minded focus on
economic growth. The craving for order places social harmony above individual liberty.

Defence is the most obvious disadvantage of a tiny country. It not only faces being overrun in wartime, but also
risks being an accidental victim of conflicts between bigger
powers. When Singapore split from Malaysia, its defence
force was minute and untested; two infantry battalions, a
navy consisting of two wooden vessels, and no aircraft. Lee
Kuan Yew's government turned to Israel for help.

Both were new nations with small populations, limited
space and large, hostile neighbours. Israel had earned military prestige with its victory in the 1948 war against its
Arab neighbours. At the time, the Singapore government
referred to their new advisers as 'the Mexicans' to keep the
contact discreet. The Israeli advisers trained a cadre of local

commanders and instructors who would form the spine of the fledgling army.

They taught the Singaporeans combat doctrine, studying the Japanese invasion of Malaya for insight into how this doctrine should be adapted to local conditions: one conclusion was to acquire small boats that would allow infantry to sneak up the shore or along jungle rivers to outflank an enemy. Singapore built an army on Israeli lines, with compulsory national service and a reserve force of men who could be called back to the frontline for years afterwards.

Modern Singapore is one of a handful of advanced and wealthy nations in a belt of countries around the equator. From Colombia to Congo, other nations in the tropics are far less developed than their counterparts in temperate zones. Some economists, such as Jeffrey Sachs, attribute this gap between global north and south to geography. Tropical soils are more vulnerable to erosion and harbour more pests and parasites, the argument goes, which means temperate countries like Canada and Argentina produce higher yields of staple crops than tropical regions, while tropical diseases like malaria have proved harder to bring under control than infectious diseases in Western countries.

A differing explanation suggests that institutions are crucial. As the MIT professor Daron Acemoglu argues, a country will prosper in the long run if its institutions allow investors and innovators to prosper without fear their gains will be looted by a predatory elite. According to this argument, many tropical countries ended up with systems in which a ruling elite dominated and exploited the majority. The Mughal empire in India or the Incas in South America were examples of systems devoted to extracting resources for the benefit of a powerful minority. As modern prosperity depends on entrepreneurship and embracing technology, countries like these have become poorer over time.

From 1959 onwards, when Lee Kuan Yew won power, Singapore was steered by a small and gifted group of men. Aside from Lee himself, the most important of them was Goh Keng Swee, the country's first finance minister. But the network that runs Singapore extends beyond its government, linking together politicians, civil servants, business leaders in companies with government connections and military officers.

The initial connection between politicians and civil servants was established with the creation of the Political Study Centre, which operated for a decade from 1959 to 1969. Senior officials were sent on courses at the centre, which operated from a grand colonial-era villa secluded on a wooded estate in central Singapore. The sessions encouraged civil servants to accept and support the political leadership's goals for the country. In language that sounded an unconscious echo of communist rhetoric, Goh explained in 1960 that the intention of the sessions was for civil servants to understand 'what the masses think about political affairs', so that bureaucrats could be more effective in implementing their political masters' wishes.

Lee took a harsh view of corruption, which had been rife in colonial Singapore. Early on, his government brought in legislation that strengthened the powers of anti-corruption investigators, authorising them to make arrests, and to search suspects' bank accounts and premises. Reducing temptation, Singapore's civil servants and politicians are given very high salaries compared to their counterparts internationally. (Its prime minister currently earns an annual salary of S$2.2 million, making him the highest paid head of government in the world.)

Singapore's founding fathers pioneered policies that

improved the lives of the population and made them fit to work in an industrial society, transforming public health, housing and education.

The second decisive factor in Singapore's early years was its shift towards export-oriented industry. When the Dutch economist Albert Winsemius arrived at the head of a UN mission in 1960 to survey the country's prospects for industrial growth, his initial impressions were of a destructive confrontation between labour and capital. The island seemed plagued by strikes and riots, and business confidence was low. Winsemius soon recovered from his initial gloom, admiring the deft mechanical skills of ordinary Singaporeans after watching men working at the roadside making new bicycles out of parts of old ones.

Winsemius, a chain smoker who spoke English with a gravelly accent, presented his report to Lee in June 1961. When the prime minister asked him for a summary, the economist's response was bold and nakedly political. Winsemius laid down two preconditions for Singapore's success. First, to 'eliminate the communists' who made any economic development impossible, and second, not to remove the statue of Sir Stamford Raffles. The advice was so simple, Lee wrote years later, that he burst out laughing when he received it, though it seems the laughter was more from shock than because he found it funny. He nevertheless acted on both recommendations, which were aimed at making Singapore an inviting place for Western multinationals.

The report itself offered detailed recommendations for the country's economic development. Winsemius noted that Singapore had no shortage of entrepreneurs, but they were largely in commerce and not manufacturing. If Singapore wanted industry, and could not attract foreign or local investment, the government might need to step in directly to start businesses. The economist suggested creating a government agency to implement a programme of industrialisation. Singapore's leaders acted on this immediately, establishing an Economic Development Board in August 1961 with the goal of promoting investment and developing industry.

From that time on, Winsemius became Singapore's unofficial economic adviser, forming a close bond with Lee, his finance minister Goh, and Hon Sui Sen, the civil servant appointed the first chairman of the EDB. He never settled in Singapore but visited from Amsterdam twice a year, staying for about three weeks each time. When he returned to the Netherlands, the government sent him copies of the *Straits Times* by airmail to keep him updated. The relationship endured for over two decades, until the early 1980s, when Winsemius was in his seventies. Lee particularly admired his ability to cut through the detail of a complex situation and grasp the basic point.

Winsemius was sceptical of the union with Malaya and the economic focus on import substitution – producing goods to replace foreign imports, rather than goods which could be sold to the world. He was delighted when Singapore was expelled from the Malaysian federation, calling it 'the best day in Singapore we ever had'. Instead of restricting imports in order to shelter domestic manufacturers, Singapore brought in foreign capital and focused on export-led industrialisation. The separation from Malaysia helped Singapore lure more Western investors. The Malaysian central government had meddled in Singapore's attempts to offer tax incentives to investors and now the island state was free to steer its own course. In an echo of the 'free port' status that had drawn nineteenth-century merchants to Raffles' colony, generous tax breaks were offered to exporters. Legislation introduced in 1967 cut taxes on the profits from exports from the headline rate of 40 per cent to 4 per cent.

Alongside tax concessions, Singapore created the infrastructure that businesses needed. Jungle and swamp were levelled to make way for roads and the shells of factories, ready for new businesses to occupy. Singapore's first industrial estate, at Jurong in the west of the island, opened in 1963. The timing was fortuitous: Western companies were looking to move semiconductor assembly to lower-cost countries. While designing semiconductors is a highly skilled task, the task of assembling the components can be done by unskilled workers.

Trade emissaries were dispatched to Hong Kong and New York. Singapore's man in Hong Kong once described part of his mission as hanging around the airport to intercept US company representatives heading to Japan or Taiwan, and persuading them to make 'a little side trip' to Singapore.

In 1969, Texas Instruments, the world's biggest manufacturer of semiconductors at the time, opened its first plant in Singapore. Along with Hong Kong, Taiwan and South Korea, the island became part of a global network that wove together Asian labour with Western capital and expertise. For three heady months in the 1960s, a new factory opened in Singapore every day.

A further catalyst to Singapore's military and economic buildup came from the UK. In January 1968, the UK announced a total withdrawal of its military 'east of Suez' by 1971. The speed of the British pull-out came as a shock to Singapore, still in the early stages of building its own armed forces and reliant on Britain not only for security but as a major employer at the naval base. Singapore therefore tripled defence spending, and drew closer to the US. When Singapore's prime minister visited the US in December of that year, his coverage in the press was adulatory: columnists described him as blunt and brilliant in equal measure. Lee is 'by far the ablest leader in Southeast Asia', a columnist in the *Chicago Daily News* wrote, adding: 'his problem is that his country isn't big enough for his talents.' Setting a pattern for future years, Lee was seen as an oracle, interpreting Asia for a Western audience. He told the US they had fumbled, so preoccupied with the reconstruction of Europe that they had allowed China's Reds to win. Bombing Vietnam would not lead to victory, he said, but he urged America to stay the course long enough to bring the Viet Cong to the negotiating table.

The Vietnam War brought profit to Singapore as the country became a supplier of goods to US forces, hosted GIs on R&R breaks and gained contracts to repair military aircraft for Lockheed. On the streets, anti-American graffiti was painted on bus shelters and left-wing protesters marched, but the war did not stir wider public opinion. The left had been smothered in the security crackdown of 1963, and further arrests stamped on the embers.

Minimal taxes were one part of the deal that brought foreign corporations to Singapore. The other draws were the English language, a favourable political climate and an obedient workforce after Lee's government pacified the unions. The left-wing Singapore Association of Trade Unions was banned in 1963, and the labour movement represented by an organisation affiliated to the ruling party. After its decisive election victory in 1968, the government brought in legislation stripping away powers from the unions, such as the right to protest against a dismissal, and restricting workers' entitlement to benefits such as overtime. Strikes went from being a routine tactic to a rarity. In 1986, when workers at an oilfield equipment company went on strike, it was the first industrial action that Singapore had seen in nine years. Union leaders, employers and government came together on the National

Wages Council, which aimed to build consensus on pay. In those early years, its citizens swallowed the medicine with remarkably little protest, accepting the fact that their wages were held down, their rights at work were restricted and their degree of political choice limited.

The Barisan Sosialis had refused to take up their seats in parliament in 1965, claiming that Singapore's independence was 'phoney'. In reality, the left-wingers claimed, the Singapore government was a front for British and US interests. They planned to fight back through street protests and industrial action. At elections in April 1968, boycotted by the Barisan Sosialis, the People's Action Party won every seat in parliament. Singapore was visibly being transformed in a way that brought benefits to all. Squatter settlements made way for modern tower blocks, while new schools and clinics were built.

The rapidly growing economy, increasing in size by around 9 per cent a year, brought well-paid jobs in factories. When Singapore became self-governing in 1959, around one in ten of the population had been unemployed. By the early 1970s, the country had achieved full employment. The government was staunchly opposed to welfare redistribution through taxes. But jobs, housing, and the improvement of education and healthcare were proof of its commitment to bettering people's lives. The emphasis was on personal responsibility, with citizens required to save to pay for housing and retirement.

In the programme for reform outlined before the 1959 election, the PAP had committed itself to improving women's rights, both for moral and practical reasons. Women were needed for the task of nation-building, and Lee's circle thought the historic second-class status of women was shameful. In Singapore, taking concubines was a common practice among wealthy Chinese men, as it was in mainland China and Hong Kong. A Women's Charter enacted in 1961 banned polygamy for all except Muslims, who were granted an exception as multiple marriages are permitted by the Qur'an. The charter included broader rights, such as allowing married women to keep their own surnames and own property. The government also encouraged women to seek economic independence. In 1957, 18 per cent of Singapore's labour force was female; by 1978 that figure had reached 33 per cent.

The container trade has revolutionised the global shipment of goods, allowing the seamless movement of cargo from ships to trains and minimising the time ships spend in port. In the late 1960s, Singapore's government took a gamble on the future of shipping by building the first container terminal in Southeast Asia. It replaced the labour-intensive unloading of ships by dockworkers with a mechanised process involving men operating towering gantry cranes and forklift trucks. Building port facilities to handle containers is expensive, and at the time there was no certainty that container shipping would be widely adopted on the shipping routes between Europe and East Asia. But Winsemius advised the government that even if the terminal were to lie idle for half a year, with interest to be paid on a loan and no revenues coming in, Singapore needed to adopt the new technology first. When the container terminal opened in 1972, it beat Hong Kong's first container port by a few months. By the early 1980s it had become, alongside Rotterdam and Yokohama, one of the three busiest ports in the world. As the economic rise of China has reshaped the flow of trade, Shanghai has become the busiest hub on the world's shipping network, but Singapore remains in second place and this early investment in a new trend was crucial. Location mattered, but another nation in Southeast Asia could have seized this lead if it had the same degree of boldness and foresight.

Singapore Airlines, established in 1972, and Changi airport, which opened in the early 1980s, strengthened these international connections. Singapore's cityscape was changing too, as skyscrapers went up in the business district to meet the growing demand for office space. The 63-storey OUB centre, built for a local bank and now known as One Raffles Place, was the tallest building in the world outside North America when it was completed in 1986. Fast modernising, there were still glimpses everywhere of a traditional Asian metropolis. In the streets, food hawkers sold bowls of noodles from handcarts, while other vendors touted consumer goods like sandals and towels. There were still roadside barbers, cycle rickshaws on the streets, and flat-bottomed sampan boats among the container vessels in the harbour.

During the 1970s, the Singapore government's focus shifted to industries that demanded higher skills than semiconductor assembly. The country's leaders identified the manufacture of personal computers and their accompanying disk drives as growth industries and focused on attracting these companies; Apple started making PCs in Singapore in 1981. Seagate, the world's biggest maker of disk drives, opened a Singapore factory in 1982, its first investment outside the US. By the 1980s, the US was the biggest foreign investor in Singapore, a position it still holds today.

Singapore had been a regional banking centre since the nineteenth century. Banks based on the island provided finance for companies that operated across Southeast Asia, especially the rubber and tin industries of the Malayan peninsula. After independence, it began to establish itself as a global financial centre. Again, it was Winsemius who spotted the opportunity, pointing out that Singapore's location meant that it was open for trading between the close of business in the US and the opening of London and Zurich. It was an

English-speaking city at the heart of non-communist Asia, and rapid industrialisation in the surrounding countries meant there were attractive investment opportunities for international banks. The government therefore encouraged the creation of an 'Asian dollar market' – allowing banks based in Singapore to hold and lend out deposits in US dollars. Funds flowed in from wealthy investors around the globe, and were loaned to companies in the region. Bank of America was the first to enter the Asian dollar market in Singapore, but it grew rapidly with more than eighty banks authorised to trade in it by the late 1970s. To facilitate this market, Singapore eliminated the 'withholding tax', the amount that banks were expected to withhold before paying out interest on deposits. The government relaxed controls on buying and selling foreign currencies and finally, in 1978, abolished these controls altogether.

The flow of capital was binding Singapore closely to the West, but the government was determined to resist another Western import: individualism and the youth revolt of the 1960s.

From US campuses to the streets of Paris, student movements were challenging an older generation across the West. Singapore shut down the University Socialist Club, where a number of left-wing leaders had cut their teeth in politics, and created a new students' union that was under the control of the administration.

The drive to establish conformity was relentless and occasionally absurd. Long hair on men, associated with hippies, was the target of a government campaign in the 1970s. Called Operation Snip Snip, the crackdown meant that men with shaggy hair were served last in government offices.

Employers were discouraged from hiring long-haired men. In 1975, at least sixteen men were sacked and around 1600 received warnings for refusing to get a trim. Clubs playing rock'n'roll, often performed live by local bands, had been increasingly popular in Singapore, but in the early 1970s, anxious about young people listening to 'soul-moving music in a hallucinatory atmosphere', the government shut down several discos. The rest were subject to increasingly tight restrictions: men had to wear formal attire, and several had their licences to serve alcohol withdrawn.

Such restrictions, including the demand that male patrons should wear a tie, were eased a few years later, after hotels appealed. But cracking down on nightclubs playing rock was an easy way to win approval, offending only a handful of young people, musicians and club promoters. Puritanism was good politics. Particularly among Singapore's Chinese-educated population, there was a revival of conservatism in the twentieth century. Vices like opium-smoking were associated with China's nineteenth-century decline, which had left it at the mercy of the Western powers and Japan. A return of moral rectitude was associated with China's national revival. These attitudes spread to Singapore through teachers in its Chinese-language schools.

By presenting themselves as moral guardians, cracking down on vices ranging from drugs to prostitution and gambling, the PAP could legitimise their political power and reassure conservative voters at a time when much else was changing. It could even be presented as an anti-colonial gesture; early on the government gave cinemas instructions not to show cowboy films which presented Native Americans as 'barbaric and backward'.

Maintaining Singapore's traditional Asian culture – in particular, encouraging the use of their mother tongues – would

provide young people with 'ballast', ministers argued, allowing them to resist the tide of the permissive West. But there
was a risk it could go too far. Lee restrained his home affairs
minister from clamping down too hard on prostitution.
Arresting Triad pimps was one thing, but closing the red
light district would deprive visiting sailors of their 'crea-
ture comforts', Lee argued. And it could backfire. As their
opponents would occasionally point out, Lee's circle were
themselves highly Westernised. Lee's preferred recreation was
golf, which he played in the evenings as well as on holiday.
Ministers quoted Shakespeare during parliamentary debates.
Piroska, the wife of Lee's foreign minister Rajaratnam, was
Hungarian, and the couple had met in London. Singapore's
elite wanted to create a new kind of society which would
absorb technical knowledge and skills from the West while
remaining culturally Eastern. But many of the leaders were
themselves products of English-language schools and elite
overseas universities, and were most comfortable speaking
in English. They could prophesy about a promised land
that combined East and West, but could never be part of it
themselves.

While they chivvied the people to be obedient, Singapore's
leaders were also scrupulous to avoid ostentation, both in
their personal lives and by keeping their names off roads,
public buildings and the airport. When, in 1986, Teh Cheang
Wan, a minister under investigation for accepting bribes
from property developers, committed suicide by taking
an overdose of sleeping pills, he insisted in a note to the
prime minister that it was the right thing to 'pay the highest
penalty' for his actions. It was striking that corruption had
become so shameful that a government minister had chosen
suicide rather than face trial.

The elite kept in touch with public opinion through

regular 'meet-the-people' sessions. Lee learned to speak Mandarin, so he could communicate more effectively with ordinary people from the Chinese majority. An arm of the ruling party created a network of kindergartens, establishing an intimate connection with family life.

Singapore's economic transformation had brought jobs and prosperity for many, but the new wealth was unevenly distributed. Thousands of families had been resettled in new public housing, but when construction slowed in the early 1980s the waiting list for housing suddenly grew much longer. At a 1981 by-election, this discontent found an outlet when voters backed the opposition candidate, a lawyer named Joshua Jeyaretnam. The constituency was Anson, a blue-collar district bordering Singapore's financial centre, where tenants were being evicted to make way for the expansion of the container terminal. Most of the tenants were dock workers and their families, whose landlord was also their employer, the port authority. Resentment at being forced out of their homes was coupled with dismay when they were refused priority for new public housing.

Jeyaretnam, whose sombre expression, mutton-chop whiskers and booming voice gave him the look of a statesman from a bygone age, called attention to the human suffering that lay behind the façade of clean streets and gleaming high-rises. He accused Lee's Singapore of focusing solely on economic progress. Popularly known by his initials, 'JBJ' never succeeded in being more than an irritant to the ruling elite. He lost his seat in parliament in 1986 and faced a succession of libel suits from Lee Kuan Yew, as well as from Lee's son Lee Hsien Loong. He estimated that he paid out more than S$1.6 million in damages and costs. Unable to pay his creditors, he was declared bankrupt, which disqualified him from running for parliament.

Libel suits against opposition leaders became a feature of Singapore politics, often for rhetoric which would have been dismissed as a standard element of combative electioneering in other countries. In particular, any hint that members of the Lee family had gained some undue advantage through nepotism became an especially sensitive point.

Singapore's electoral system is tilted in favour of the ruling party. In 1988, Singapore introduced 'group representation constituencies', where a team of candidates stands for election together. The official reason for introducing GRCs was to increase ethnic minority representation. But by forcing smaller parties to produce teams of candidates rather than individual challengers, the change makes it harder for the opposition to achieve a breakthrough. Candidates returned from GRCs now make up the majority of seats in Singapore's parliament.

Lee was strongly influenced by the British historian Arnold Toynbee, and was fond of quoting his ideas in cabinet meetings. Toynbee, famous for a sweeping comparative survey of history, focused on how civilisations responded to challenges. Facing unprecedented challenges, either from their physical environment or a political rival, civilisations successfully adapted or collapsed. Those that survived did so because they were led in their heroic response to this challenge by a 'creative minority'.

It is easy to see how postcolonial Singapore could be framed as a heroic struggle, first against communism and then against the forces of ethnic chauvinism. This framing took on racial overtones. Lee saw the native people of Southeast Asia as essentially placid and happy-go-lucky, contrasting this with the materialism and drive of immigrants from China. There was a widespread stereotype among European colonisers of the 'lazy native', applied to indigenous people such as Malays or Filipinos who appeared reluctant to trade their labour for wages. Lee's preferred explanation for this was environmental, believing the fertile soil and teeming waters of Malaya had fostered a leisurely way of life. Lee's view of his own ethnic community could be equally disparaging, though for different reasons. He believed the stability of Chinese-majority countries like Singapore rested on firm leadership, backed up by the threat of force. 'There is no other way to govern a Chinese society,' he declared.

British government files on the Tiananmen Square crackdown, declassified in 2016, revealed that Lee expected a drastic response after the students directly challenged Deng Xiaoping, a challenge he considered an 'act of folly'. He told the British ambassador that this was something he 'felt in his bones as a Chinese'.

The outlook of Singapore is one of a society prepared for permanent struggle. Lee's vision, showing the influence of Toynbee, was of a ruling elite who needed to constantly sharpen their edge through prevailing against repeated challenges. This struggle is often expressed as an economic or political one, as the pursuit of industrial development or the need to face down internal or external foes. In a 1966 speech on the first anniversary of Singapore's separation from Malaysia, Lee contrasted a 'fun-loving' society with a 'rugged, robust, disciplined, effective' society. The latter society, he told his citizens, was led by a dedicated group thinking about and analysing the country's problems. 'And all the time we are two, three steps ahead of the problems.'

This sense of a rugged society can be hard for outsiders to spot in Singapore. Life in the city state often feels a cosseted and risk-averse progression from days of intense study to long hours working for a bank or a government office, leavened by the sanctioned leisure activities of eating out and going to gym classes. But a sense of national vulnerability, and a concomitant need to be tough and resilient, is drilled deep into its people through citizenship lessons at school and the national service that is compulsory for all young men.

Lee governed Singapore for more than three decades, stepping down in 1990 but staying on in cabinet until 2011. His death in 2015 prompted a national outpouring of grief. His body lay in state at Parliament House, a slate-grey neo-classical block in the city centre, while Singaporeans queued for hours in bright tropical sunshine to file past and pay their respects. The country he left behind was wealthy, secure and disciplined; an engineered society in which everyone knew what was expected of them. The system he created remains in place.

Like an overprotective parent, Singapore's rulers have constantly fussed over their people, alternately cajoling or threatening in order to tip them in the desired direction. At times, Singaporeans have been urged to focus on study-ing English for practical reasons, while at other moments they have been admonished to remember their Asian roots as a defence against corrupting Western influences. A vivid Chinese cultural heritage has been largely stifled, because many Chinese-language artists were regarded as suspiciously left-wing.

Elsewhere in Asia, there are lively democracies such as South Korea, Taiwan and India, where political incum-bents risk losing office and there is open criticism of leaders. Singapore has traded an equally lively political climate for the air-conditioned rule of the PAP, breezes stilled, windows sealed, the dial turned down to a uniform chill.

Lee did not anticipate that this level of control would last forever. In interviews given in his later years, after stepping down as prime minister, he acknowledged that a more educated population would demand greater participation in politics. He framed it as a byproduct of the economic need for education, rather than a romantic aspiration for liberty, but saw it coming nonetheless. 'One simply cannot ask a highly educated workforce to stop thinking when it leaves the factory,' he said in an interview published in the journal *New Perspectives Quarterly* in 2009.

The rise of a more globally integrated economy has weakened the traditional nation-state. Despite the temporary hardening of borders triggered by the Covid-19 pandemic, the world is becoming more fluid, with record flows of capital and people between countries in recent decades. These global connections have made Singapore's size less of a disadvantage. Cut off from its natural hinterland by the separation from Malaysia, Singapore made the world its hinterland in the 1960s. Its small pool of domestic labour matters less when it can draw on the resources of migrants. Increasing global flows of information have brought added economic benefits, with companies like Google and Facebook choosing Singapore as the location for regional data centres to meet the rapid growth in users of their services in Asia. But, as Lee predicted, a more educated and sophisticated population – which has grown up accustomed to the benefits of a prosperous society – is proving less willing to accept the kind of sacrifice their parents and grandparents made.

4

The Singapore Dream

Wealth, faith and society

Gathered in a vast marquee in the grounds of the family mansion, employees of one of Singapore's biggest banks were invited to toast the Chinese New Year. Alongside traditional Southeast Asian delicacies, a chef carved slices of sashimi. Many of the women wore Chinese cheongsam dresses, and quite a few wore sparkling diamond jewellery, choosing rocks that were a little more showy than the ones they would normally wear to the office. The bank, UOB, had been run by the same Singapore Chinese family for decades. The annual party at the Wee family mansion was an act of generosity intended to bind employees close, the equivalent of an office Christmas party, but it was typically Singaporean to welcome your employees into your home. Or at least, into your grounds.

The Wee family made their fortune in banking, but had since diversified into property and luxury hotels. Waiters from the family's hotel chains moved among the guests that day, topping up glasses of champagne and wine. The Wee family is 'old money', with a mansion, swimming pool and tennis court in Bukit Timah, one of Singapore's wealthiest neighbourhoods. Their world is beyond the reach of most ordinary Singaporeans, but it is the pinnacle of a system to which many aspire.

This is one of the wealthiest cities in the world, with a modern economy ranging from hi-tech manufacturing to finance and other professional services. To a visitor from another Asian country, it remains tangibly familiar, with public address announcements in Malay, Chinese and Tamil, and the same mix of convenience stores, jewellers, temples and mosques that are found dotted all over similar Asian cities.

The ideal version of the Singapore dream runs like this: clean, green, modern and affluent, it remains a nation in contact with its Asian heritage. It is free of graft, both the large-scale corruption of ministers stuffing pockets and the petty version of police officers demanding bribes. For women as well as men, it is a safe place to walk after sunset. It is a society with a substantial middle class, who enjoy a comfortable lifestyle of restaurant meals, nights out at the theatre and cinema and the occasional lavish foreign holiday. It is common for middle-class families to have a maid, usually from a neighbouring country such as Indonesia or the Philippines, who helps with childcare as well as cooking and cleaning.

From a vantage point high above the city, Singapore's panorama combines a seemingly endless array of moving machinery and vehicles. There are cars, trains, bustling escalators, cranes at work and ships out to sea. Interspersed with this activity is greenery, usually in the form of well-tended lawns and strips of shrubbery flanking both public and private housing. The city is designed to resist rather than accommodate its sultry equatorial climate. White-collar workers occupy air-conditioned tower blocks, and climate-controlled pedestrian tunnels connect many city centre offices and malls. The combined effect of this architecture is to give an impression of human mastery over nature. It's the opposite of Hong Kong, where untamed wilderness is visible from the upper floors of skyscrapers.

Singapore's elite has successfully instilled a powerful sense of material aspiration in its people. This stemmed from the need to make a living and invigorate the economy of a newly independent nation, but it carries an ideological purpose too. A nation seduced by material goods is more likely to be quiescent in the face of tight political control. 'You take a poll of any people. What is it they want?' Lee Kuan Yew argued in an interview for a 1997 biography. 'The right to write an editorial as you like? They want homes, medicine, jobs, schools.' In the decades after independence, as Singapore's basic needs were met, these desires shifted up a gear into aspirations that set the super-rich apart from the herd.

These days, Singapore's affluence is obvious; from the high-pitched shriek of sports cars on its streets to the cavernous designer stores on Orchard Road, a degree of naked materialism is on public display. There's a shorthand for this kind of aspiration – the 5Cs: career, car, credit card, condominium and country club. It's not entirely clear where the expression 5Cs came from, but every Singaporean knows it. Each of the Cs represents a successive level of aspiration. A career and not just a job, a car in a country where car ownership is tightly regulated, access to credit as well as cash, a private apartment rather than a government-built flat and a country club membership for the highest level of exclusivity.

The cost of car ownership in Singapore is kept artificially high to keep traffic flowing on an island with limited space for roads. To own a car, you need a 'certificate of entitlement', which permits you to drive a car for a decade and can be transferred when you sell the vehicle. The CoE price is determined through a public bidding exercise, and therefore fluctuates, but at the end of 2020 it was nearly S$50,000 for a car above 1600cc.

Yet in spite of its people's wealth, their long and healthy lives and a lack of corruption, all of which are factors which tend to make societies happier, Singapore is one of the world's gloomiest rich countries. Since 2013, the UN has published a World Happiness Report, an annual ranking of countries which tracks how satisfied people are with their lives. The Nordic countries tend to claim the top spots, while Singapore languishes outside the top thirty. Academics suggest that high levels of status anxiety and limited personal autonomy may be factors that contribute to this unhappiness.

'Wealth is the sole criterion of success in Singapore,' said K. C. Chew, a businessman who was detained without charge for thirteen months in the late 1980s for his interest in left-wing politics. 'Society tells you who it values in monetary terms. That's true everywhere, but there's another part of society that says we admire the struggling artist. I think that admiration is quite real in the US and in Europe, but in a place like Singapore, we pity the poor struggling artist. That's why Lee Kuan Yew felt it was necessary to pay his ministers millions of dollars.'

Dreams of escaping the rat race and accompanying fears of being dragged down into penury are persistent themes in Singapore cinema, from *Singapore Dreaming*, a low-budget movie in which the central character wins the lottery only to find that the wealth he has dreamed of does not automatically bring happiness, to *Ilo Ilo*, where a boy is raised by his family's Filipina maid as the 1997 Asian financial crisis disrupts his parents' lives. The family at the centre of *Singapore Dreaming* struggles with debt and dead-end jobs, but its patriarch clips pictures of the cars and apartments he desires out of the newspaper. When he wins the lottery, his feckless son borrows money meant to start a business and squanders it on a sports car. The symbols of success are everything. 'If you want to make it, you've got to look like you've already made it,' the spendthrift son tells his fiancée.

Singapore's National Day Rally is an occasion for the prime minister to review the year and exhort his people to strive harder. This televised speech, the equivalent of the State of the Union address in the US, is scrutinised by Singaporeans for details of the government's planning in sensitive areas of public policy like tax, migration and housing. In 2003, a weak economy and the advent of the Sars epidemic prompted the prime minister, Goh Chok Tong – who succeeded Lee Kuan Yew in 1990 – to quote a downbeat citizen who feared her hopes of a more prosperous future had evaporated. The citizen had complained of 'lousy' pay and felt she would have to slog twice as hard just to keep her job. Quoting her, the prime minister went on: 'Now, we may never be able to make long-term plans such as buying a car or a bigger home. This is tantamount to the shattering of the Singapore Dream.' Goh did not use this opportunity to offer a different vision of Singapore. Instead, he told his audience that after the grey clouds, sunshine and growth would return, but only if they kept their side of the bargain by accepting the need to keep Singapore's wages globally competitive.

From an early age, Singapore's culture divides winners from losers and encourages winners to feel their achievements have been earned purely through merit. Their merit is signalled through financial rewards, and the high salaries of Singapore's political leaders are justified on this basis. The imprint of the process begins in childhood with an intensely competitive education system, funnelling the highest achievers into elite universities.

The fierce competition imbues, in some, a disdain for their perceived inferiors. In 2006, an eighteen-year-old pupil on a government scholarship at one of Singapore's most renowned schools wrote a blog dismissing an older Singaporean's anxieties about losing his job. 'We are a tyranny of the capable and the clever,' the pupil wrote, closing with the words: 'please, get out of my elite, uncaring face.' An uproar ensued, and the schoolgirl's father, an MP, offered an apology that rubbed salt into the wounds. 'I think if you cut through the insensitivity of the language, her basic point is reasonable,' he suggested. In her father's view, the pupil's point was that Singaporeans should not complain but 'get on with the challenges of life.'

The anger over the MP and his daughter was fuelled by a sense that the Singapore dream was increasingly hard to attain. An analysis in the *Straits Times* suggested that a high proportion of government scholarships went to some of the country's wealthiest families. Rather than driving social mobility, public money was entrenching privilege. The highest achievers in the Singapore system just happened to be the children of the most affluent. Singapore's system idealises meritocracy, but very few of those who rise to the top are genuine outsiders.

Goh was himself a product of the Singapore dream. The son of a single mother who went to an elite school, then studied at university on a government bursary, he distinguished himself by turning around a loss-making state-owned shipping line before being invited to enter politics. But his tenure in politics marked the last time that a man from such a humble background made it to the apex of Singapore politics.

A society that changes as rapidly as Singapore's, without

much of a social safety net to compensate, will inevitably lead to greater inequality. Those who prosper in the system are better able to help their children to get ahead, and those who lose out find the gaps grow wider as the winners pile up advantages. Teo You Yenn, a sociologist and author of *This is What Inequality Looks Like*, a 2018 collection of essays that became an unexpected bestseller in Singapore, argues that the claim of meritocracy is more pernicious, however, dressing up an unfair system as the result of personal striving or failure. 'Meritocracy is a system that legitimises those who end up its victors,' she suggests.

The country's tiny size raises the stakes in this competition. Singapore, at 728 square kilometres, is a little smaller than New York City. Unlike New York or any comparable metropolis, there is nowhere else for Singaporeans to move without leaving the country. Space is a perk of wealth, and there is no equivalent of down-at-heel bohemian neighbourhoods like Hongdae in Seoul or Shoreditch in London which offer cheaper spaces to incubate careers as artists or entrepreneurs. Instead, any young Singaporean with a riskier vision of the future must either live with their parents or hope for state support, such as government-subsidised studio space for artists or grants for entrepreneurs.

The elite live in 'landed houses', usually sprawling bungalows surrounded by private gardens. For nearly everyone else, there is some variety of high-rise living, either a privately built apartment or a state-built one, the latter known as 'HDB flats' after the acronym for the government's Housing and Development Board. Height matters. Singaporeans prefer to live on the upper storeys, above the sounds and smells of the street and the usual range of mosquitoes and other winged pests. These coveted altitudes have higher prices or rents to match.

Older Singaporeans recall a time when ostentation was frowned on. A Hong Kong tycoon might have a chauffeur-driven Rolls-Royce, but a Singapore oligarch would keep a lower profile. Old money in Singapore is identified with a more discreet style of living; an old house with a garden, patrolled by dogs. New money knocks down the colonial structure and builds right to the edge of the plot. Compared with Europe or the US, there are few of the subtle gradations that distinguish traditional wealth from the nouveau riche. After all, for the most part even Singapore's 'old money' elite only goes back a few generations to penniless migrants.

'There were only a handful of places that were exclusive,' a Singaporean executive told me. 'The Tanglin Club, the American Club. They used to be all-male and closed-list. You couldn't get in if you weren't inherited wealth. The government did their best to break that up by imposing quotas.'

Religion fits into a hierarchy too. Anglican and Methodist worship are associated with an Anglophile establishment. 'Prosperity gospel' churches, a more flamboyant style of Christian worship that blends spirituality and materialism, attract the up-and-coming. The prosperity gospel, a form of Christian belief pioneered in the US, teaches that God grants good health and material success to the faithful. It has won thousands of adherents in Singapore, often first-generation Christian believers whose parents were Buddhists or Taoists. Figures from the 2010 census showed Christianity was growing rapidly, the number of adherents rising from 15 per cent of the population in 2000 to 18 per cent a decade later. Buddhism and Taoism predominate among older and less well-educated Singaporeans, but among university graduates, Christianity is the most popular faith.

The prosperity gospel offers a brand of Christianity that suits life in Singapore. It is politically inconspicuous, offering no challenge to the state, unlike more socially conscious forms of Christianity. Its presentation is slick, with gospel-tinged rock performances and a pastor preaching a sermon in front of a giant video screen. It encourages worshippers to strive for career progression, and it provides bonds of community that offer reassurance and stability. One of the main prosperity gospel churches, City Harvest, attracted crowds of up to 16,000 to a convention centre auditorium before services were suspended during the Covid-19 pandemic. 'It doesn't contradict with what most people want to do with their lives,' says Andrew Koay Lim, who attended City Harvest as a teenager. 'It allies itself with the ambitions of most people.'

Its vast scale was made more intimate by clustering the congregation into 'cell groups' of around twenty people, usually organised according to age. 'You would spend your whole Sunday with people at church,' Lim explained. 'If you're with a cell group you might spend an evening as well. If it's your birthday, people from your cell group will come to your house, make you a cake.' Over time, Lim came to feel there was a gap between the church's outlook and the Christian teachings he had absorbed as a child. 'I'd grown up in a church environment where I was taught that's not necessarily the case,' he said. 'God isn't necessarily concerned with how prosperous you are in the workplace.'

In 2015, the co-founder of the church, Kong Hee, was sentenced to eight years in prison for diverting millions of dollars of church funds to support his wife's music career. His wife, Sun Ho, who sings Mandarin pop, is also a Christian pastor and co-founder of City Harvest, but she was not charged.

The case fuelled Lim's disillusionment. 'When Kong Hee

got arrested, I began to feel people were blindly following church leaders, adamantly defending the church leaders. Someone had printed T-shirts saying they still supported the church – by that time I started to isolate myself from church.' Supporters of the pastor justified their view by arguing that his wife's pop career was a fulfilment of the church's Christian mission. 'It builds into this idea that God wants you to be prosperous,' Lim said. 'If Sun Ho could be a big star that would be a good witness. God is blessing you as a Christian. That was the thinking.'

Singapore's poverty is less obvious than its wealth. In a city where begging is illegal, the old men and women selling packets of tissues in the street attract sympathy purchases from passers-by. Where there is little by way of a social safety net, driving a taxi or making fast-food deliveries is the easiest way to eke out a living in a crisis.

Yusuf Abdol Hamid set up Vamos Photography, a commercial photographic agency, in 2010 with a fellow student at Nanyang Technological University, Foo Chee Chang. Hamid, who is thirty-five and a father of two young children, is from a middle-class background; his father a retired Singapore Airlines pilot and his mother a housewife who worked as an air stewardess before she had children. When Covid-19 hit, Hamid imagined a life under lockdown of baking and HIIT sessions, like other middle-class Singaporeans. But when, two months in, all of his clients cancelled their shoots, he took a job as a takeaway delivery cyclist for the start-up Grab and discovered another face of his home city. The cyclist's-eye view highlighted the absurdities of wealth: the delivery order of a single scoop of ice cream or seemingly weightless packets of acai berries and ready-sliced fruit.

In Singapore, public housing is often glossy, spacious and

built to compare favourably with private apartments. New government developments have terraced roof gardens and covered walkways linking residents' car parks to lift lobbies. Singapore has no shanty towns and its extremes are narrower than elsewhere in Asia, where slums and luxury residential towers are a common juxtaposition.

On his delivery bike, Hamid glimpsed a more run-down face of the city. After delivering pizza along a street with four red Ferraris parked outside one house, he would drop off an order of fried rice on a down-at-heel estate. 'It was jarring to go to older and much less well cared for public housing, with peeling paint and odd smells,' he told me.

Hamid documented with photographs both wealth and poverty, showing bargain-store clothes on drying racks in concrete corridors of poorer housing blocks. In luxury apartments, his eye was drawn to the florid and occasionally surreal marketing language which turned the forty-fifth floor into the 'Cloud9 Banquet Penthouse Suite' and a yoga space into a 'Zen Fitness Garden'. Hand-written notes pinned up by doorways showed residents scolding each other for smoking in the corridor or piling up rubbish bags on the ground. Hamid wondered at their lack of neighbourliness.

The heart of the city offers a physical representation of Singapore's guiding spirit: orderly, hierarchical and driven by the pursuit of economic success. A steel structure fashioned in Glasgow and shipped to Southeast Asia, Singapore's Cavenagh Bridge is a testament to Victorian engineering that spans the Singapore River. The suspension bridge links a cluster of civic buildings with Singapore's central business district. North of the bridge is Parliament House, a grey rectangular slab of a building, and the pale gothic bulk of St Andrew's Cathedral. Here too is the old Supreme Court building, a neo-classical structure with Corinthian columns and decorative statuary which now houses the country's National Gallery, and before it is the Padang, the playing field where a victory parade was held to celebrate Japan's surrender in 1945. South of the bridge a dense grid of streets contains the headquarters of numerous local businesses, as well as the stock exchange. Reclaimed from the sea in the 1970s, Marina Bay extends south of the commercial district. Here are more banks, and the Asia–Pacific headquarters of multinationals. The northern border of the business district is marked by Chinatown.

Christian places of worship, belonging to multiple denominations from Armenian to Anglican, are dotted about the city centre. A shoe rack indicates the presence of a mosque. The fragrance of incense carries the scent of a Taoist temple. This diversity is carefully managed. My Singaporean elder sister lives in an HDB flat on an estate in the west of the city. During celebrations for a Hindu festival one year, a selection of family friends dropped by for snacks. The ethnicity of the visitors – Chinese, Malay, Tamil – was as heterogeneous as the buffet meal.

By law, Singapore seeks to prevent the emergence of racial enclaves either in public housing blocks or neighbourhoods. A buyer of a government-built property must be within the ethnic quota for their block and neighbourhood. Singapore classifies all citizens as 'Chinese, Malay, Indian or Other'. A mixed-race household can choose their ethnicity when they buy – opting for either the husband or wife's race – but must keep the same one when they sell.

Bonds based on language and kinship once had a tangible impact on people's lives. Chinese clan associations brought together communities who claimed a shared lineage and spoke the same dialect. These associations founded schools, managed temples and provided financial support for the

vulnerable members of their community. The Hokkien Huay
Kuan, with around 5000 members from Singapore's Hokkien
community, remains a large and wealthy organisation.

Language functions as a marker of status. Singapore's elite
tend to be Anglophone, educated at English-language schools
and often speaking English in the home.

In 1979, the government launched a campaign to persuade
the Chinese community to speak Mandarin instead of dialect,
to create a common spoken language. As a result, speakers
of Chinese dialects tend to be older and less well-educated.

There are still neighbourhoods where ethnic minority
traders cluster. Kampong Glam is a Malay and Muslim quarter, centred on the golden onion dome and minarets of the
Sultan Mosque. The grid of streets around the mosque is,
incongruously, a popular spot for cocktails as well as being
home to traders in caftans and central Asian carpets. Little
India, with its busy flower stands, meat and fish markets,
ornately carved temples and budget restaurants, remains the
heart of community life for Singaporean Indians and South
Asian migrant workers.

At independence, there was little sense of a 'Singaporean'
identity. If they thought in terms of national identity at all,
people felt ties to ancestral homelands in China or India, or
regarded themselves as 'Malayans', part of a broader community that included the Malayan peninsula.

The racial profile of migration to Singapore is managed
by the government to maintain an ethnic balance in which
Chinese make up the majority. Chinese Singaporeans tend
to dominate the upper echelons of government and the military. Since independence, Singapore's ethnic communities
have coexisted peacefully, and individuals from the country's
minorities have risen to senior positions. But there is widespread low-level racism. In 1992, the ruling party MP Choo

Wee Khiang said in parliament that he found Little India dark, 'not because there was no light, but because there were too many Indians around there'. Choo apologised for the comment, claiming his remarks were a joke.

While citizens from all racial groups benefited from Singapore's post-independence economic growth, the Malay community has lagged some distance behind. According to the 2010 census, Malay households' monthly income from work was S$4575, compared with S$7326 for Chinese and S$7664 for Indian households. In part, this is rooted in Singapore's separation from Malaysia. After the split, Malays were less likely to be called up for national service and less likely to be accepted into the military, a traditional employer of Malay men. When there was a prospect of Singapore going to war with Malaysia or Indonesia, the state feared Malay servicemen might have divided loyalties. Of the small numbers who were called up, 'some were shunted to the cook house, others diverted to the transport section and became drivers, while a handful were deployed as physical instructors,' noted Ismail Kassim, a Singapore Malay and a former political correspondent for the *Straits Times*. But though fewer Malay men were called up for the military, they were not exempted from conscription. As a result, employers were reluctant to hire or train workers who had the threat of being drafted hanging over them. The unwritten policy of not recruiting Malays to the army faded by the 1970s, but many Malay Singaporeans believe they are still excluded from sensitive positions in the military, such as intelligence roles.

Concerns about the appeal of militant Islamism among Malays may be a factor in official thinking here. Singapore bans the wearing of the Muslim headscarf in schools and in some professions, such as the police. Muslim women, including nurses in government hospitals, claim they have been explicitly told by managers not to wear headscarves to work. Many Singaporeans, of all races, feel these prejudices highlight the fraying of the social fabric. Perhaps because there have been no flare-ups of violence since independence, Singaporeans have managed to avoid serious confrontation with their society's racial attitudes.

At its apex, Singapore remains a largely male-dominated society. At the end of 2019, women held 16 per cent of board positions in major listed companies (the comparable figure for the UK is one in three), and for most of its history its political leadership has been entirely male. This masculine network is forged partly through education; elite boys' schools are still the recruiting grounds for the senior ranks of business, politics and the civil service. The practice of drafting military personnel into civilian leadership also favours men.

While the streets are safe for women, including those travelling alone, harassment remains deep-rooted in a culture which tends to bury rather than confront sexual misconduct. When Monica Baey, a student at the National University of Singapore, caught a fellow student filming her in the hostel showers and posted about it on social media, the reactions illustrated the fluid attitudes towards victims and perpetrators. The student who filmed her was given a twelve-month conditional warning by police and suspended for one semester. Following an outcry over the leniency of his punishment, the perpetrator faced such harsh criticism that some began describing him as a victim.

Prosperity is the goal that drives Singaporean society. There are few viable alternatives. Singapore has an excellent publicly funded education system and an insurance-based health system. But welfare provision for the unemployed is narrowly focused on getting people back to work. There are state-backed programmes to help workers who have lost their jobs acquire new skills and a 'workfare' scheme through which the government provides cash top-ups to the lowest paid 20 per cent of workers. But the ruling party has repeatedly rebuffed proposals for unemployment insurance, fearing this will erode the dignity of self-reliance and lead to higher long-term unemployment.

Elements of the Singapore dream, such as its compulsory retirement savings scheme, might yet be copied by policymakers in the West. Singaporeans are forced to contribute a fifth of their salaries to pay for retirement, as well as healthcare and housing purchases. The savings, along with contributions from their employer, go into a personal fund, known as the Central Provident Fund (CPF). Unlike other defined contribution pensions worldwide, which are typically invested in the stock market and a range of other assets including bonds and commercial property, the funds are invested in government bonds which have been specially issued for that purpose. As with the welfare system, enforced savings emphasise self-reliance. Allowing withdrawals from the CPF to assist with property purchases, combined with a widespread public housing scheme, has led to a high level of home ownership, reinforcing Singapore's social stability – the country's home ownership rate of 90 per cent is one of the highest in the world.

The most crucial thing money buys is advantage. From private health insurance to tuition, wealth gives Singaporeans the ability to ease passage through the system for themselves and their children. Singapore households spent an average of S$112 a month on private tuition in 2018, rising to over S$300 a month in the wealthiest families.

Singaporeans, from top to bottom, are concerned that

they lack fellow-feeling. The country's identity is broad, encompassing differences of race and religion, but its roots sometimes feel shallow. From the reverence for queuing in British shops to the preference for quiet on Japanese public transport, the agreed social codes that govern minor inter-actions are important in all societies. But breakdowns in this etiquette usually inspire little more than mild disapproval. In Singapore, breaches of unspoken rules have the potential to spark nasty confrontations. One evening in 2017, a middle-aged Singaporean couple had settled down for dinner at a hawker centre when an elderly man approached their table carrying his tray. The couple were filmed verbally abusing and shoving the old man. The case, which led to the pair being convicted and fined, turned the spotlight on a per-ceived lack of civility and tolerance in Singapore society. As press reports noted, the table could have seated five.

Government rhetoric occasionally identifies this absence of civility, urging the creation of a more 'gracious' society. In 2002, a ministerial committee was even set up to investigate the question. The Remaking Singapore committee had five subcommittees, each of which alluded in the title to one of the 5Cs: from 'Beyond Career' to 'Beyond Club'. The committee drew on a range of ideas to encourage more identification with a common Singaporean project, from encouraging more widespread use of national symbols like the flag and lion, to loosening the rigidity of the education system and creating more public space for self-expression. Remarkably for a state which is often so touchy about criticism, the committee's report spoke of urging young Singaporeans to play a more 'active and constructive role in public affairs'. In a turbulent region where other countries have swung between popular revolution and military dictatorship, to have built a society that is wealthy and secure is no small feat, but there is clearly a deep-seated fear that Singapore has sacrificed an essential element of mutual goodwill along the way.

Another way to escape the rat-race is to leave Singapore altogether. Emigrants have been derided by the government as 'quitters' and 'fair-weather Singaporeans', but it's often a decision that makes sense for practical rather than emotional reasons.

Migrating allows Singaporeans to escape the country's restrictions on space. Outside Singapore, owning a car and living in a house with a garden are no longer privileges reserved for the very wealthy. It expands the scope of personal freedom too, allowing gay Singaporean men to live in a country where their sex lives are not criminalised. On average, about 1200 Singaporeans give up their citizenship every year (Singapore does not recognise dual citizenship after the age of twenty-one). Australia, now home to around 55,000 Singaporeans, is one of the principal destination countries.

In a 1994 *Straits Times* article, Catherine Lim, a bestselling author of romantic novels, suggested that while Singapore's rulers had achieved tremendous material success, there was a gap in matters of the 'heart, soul and spirit' between government and people. The ruling party was seen to govern in a style that lacked sensitivity, she suggested, and while Singaporeans were reluctant to speak out, their resistance was often expressed passively, such as in a refusal to put out the national flag for fear of being seen as sycophantic. She termed this gap the 'great affective divide' between the PAP and the people. The column, and a companion piece, provoked a belligerent official reaction, which helped make her point for her. 'If you land a blow on our jaw, you must expect a counter-blow on your solar plexus,' prime minister Goh Chok Tong growled in response. This aggressive language was the limit of the official reaction, however. On that occasion, the government's bark proved worse than its bite, perhaps because Lim presented no real threat to their hold on power.

Lim's criticism has endured and reverberated over the years, as an increasingly sophisticated electorate has chafed at a high-handed style of government. Two recent elections, in 2011 and 2020, saw sharply reduced majorities for the PAP – though they held onto power and their share of the vote, at around 60 per cent in both these elections, would be an endorsement in most other democracies.

Catherine Lim, now in her late seventies, is still writing. A petite, bright-eyed woman with black hair in a pixie cut, Lim is a late riser who wakes in the afternoon and goes to bed at 5 a.m. She suggests 10 p.m. for an interview and is filled with energy and enthusiasm at this hour. In her three-bedroom apartment in Sixth Avenue, a prosperous residential neighbourhood, the walls are decorated with paintings of flowers and Chinese calligraphy. One of her walls is covered with framed newspaper stories, magazine covers and articles featuring her – she calls it 'the vanity wall'.

'I had seen, and everybody knew, nobody cared for the PAP,' Lim says. 'People were quite happy to benefit from the efficiency but I don't think they cared one jot. I could see the antagonism and I tried to understand that.' Lim speaks in a quick and animated tone, gesturing to draw you in as she tells her stories, at times clasping her hands and closing her eyes dramatically, and then narrowing her eyes and pointing an index finger indignantly.

She remained calm through the backlash against her. Lim had been a project director for the Ministry of Education and then worked as a lecturer, but by the time she published her critical columns she had quit to be a full-time writer. That insulated her from pressure, she says. 'If I had been working, the bosses would not have taken kindly because they would be scared of the government coming in.'

Lim was buoyed up by the public's reaction. 'I was telling the truth, and that can hurt. It was just amazing how people rallied around me. Somebody said, "We have the same thoughts but we cannot express it as well as you. You have spoken for us." And I said, "Oh, that is wonderful. That is what I want."' The 'affective divide' she described in her columns may have narrowed as a younger leadership seeks a more consensual style of government, Lim reckons. 'They are more consultative. But they have no choice. Because the whole world is moving in that direction of opening up.'

5

The Model City

Urban design, housing and the architecture of climate change

Turning down a wide and leafy suburban street, you arrive at a wire-fenced compound with a row of single-storey warehouse-style buildings. Inside one of these buildings, there are rooms with trays of micro-greens a few centimetres high stacked on shelves, under artificial lighting in a temperature-controlled environment. Opposite are clumps of banana trees with glossy green leaves, sprawling sweet potato vines, and bags of compost sprouting little bushes of herbs. The only sound is the quiet hum of insects. As she weaves her way through the farm, Kimberly Hoong stops every few minutes to pluck something and hand it over to taste, from an edible flower to a sprig of spearmint with such a fresh and fierce taste that it numbs the mouth. She offers explanations of each plant's uses in cooking and medicine, pointing out food crops that flourished so abundantly in the wild they were thought to be weeds.

A few kilometres away, there is bustling traffic and the

familiar city of malls and high-rise housing. But at Edible Garden City, an urban farm in the suburb of Queenstown, Singapore is experimenting with a more sustainable future.

In the space of a few decades, Singapore's city planners swept away the slums and sprawling squatter villages of the colonial port, creating a modern metropolis of office towers and apartment blocks. It became a model for development across Asia. Now, as Singapore faces increasing environmental constraints, it offers a glimpse into the future of the world's megacities. Richard Hassell, co-founder of the WOHA architectural practice in Singapore, describes the city as 'a canary in the coalmine', as humanity brushes up against the safe operating limits of the planet. 'It has come up against all kinds of limits much earlier than other places,' says Hassell. 'So it is a laboratory for what's happening elsewhere in the world.'

Land is Singapore's most obvious constraint. Indonesia plans to build a new capital to replace Jakarta, a congested megacity built on a swamp, while Malaysia's capital Kuala Lumpur can sprawl into the surrounding countryside. For Singapore, the options are limited to building up, excavating, or the increasingly expensive business of claiming land from the sea.

The creation of new land from the sea has been extraordinary; between 1965 and 2019, Singapore grew from 581.5 square kilometres to 728 square kilometres. Lacking its own supply of sand for this construction work, Singapore has become the world's biggest sand importer. Marina Bay Sands, the landmark hotel shaped like a wicket, is built on reclaimed land, but so is much else in modern Singapore. Beach Road now runs through the city centre, but as its name implies, it began life on the coast.

Climate change poses a further challenge. The Southeast

Asian city is effectively on the front line of the increasingly uncomfortable and unpredictable environment that many of the world's tropical megacities will confront in the next few decades.

As a city state without a rural hinterland, Singapore has always been preoccupied with achieving self-sufficiency in water and food. The country has abundant rainfall but limited space to build reservoirs, and prolonged dry spells frequently lead to water shortages. For over half a century Singapore has relied on importing water from southern Malaysia to meet around half of its freshwater needs. During severe droughts in 1961 and 1963, which affected both Singapore and southern Malaysia, water levels fell so low that the government introduced rationing, cutting off the supply to households several times a week. In 2003 Singapore began recycling waste water, returning it to the system as purified drinking water. This treated water now supplies up to 40 per cent of the country's needs, and is expected to provide more than half of Singapore's water by 2060.

Nearly all of Singapore's food, around 90 per cent, is imported from around 170 countries. Hong Kongers are similarly reliant on imports for everything they eat, though most of their food comes from mainland China, while Singapore's supply chain is diverse, a deliberate policy that creates a buffer in times of crisis. On supermarket shelves, the greens are shipped in from China and Malaysia, the steak and wine from Australia and the apples from Hokkaido in northern Japan. The pandemic and its accompanying disruption to global supply chains put the system to the test, but Singapore was able to find new food sources, including flying in eggs from Poland and frozen Red Sea shrimp from Saudi Arabia.

The globalisation of Singapore's food is a recent shift. The island commercialised its agriculture to become self-sufficient in poultry, eggs and pork in the 1970s, but as the city grew, the waste and smells from industrial farming – especially of pork, the meat of preference for Chinese Singaporeans – became hard to tolerate. Instead, Singapore has outsourced its meat production, importing live pigs for slaughter from the nearby Indonesian island of Pulau Bulan, which is home to one of the world's biggest pig farms with over a quarter of a million animals, while frozen and chilled pork was shipped from Brazil and the Netherlands. A Singapore developer has established an agricultural project in Jilin, in northeast China, to grow rice and rear pigs for the Singapore market. The venture occupies an area of 1450 square kilometres, twice the size of Singapore itself. Even the country's signature dish of chilli crab, the famously messy delicacy that diners wear a bib to eat, is typically made with crab imported from Sri Lanka.

As well as diversifying its foreign suppliers of food, the government has encouraged more domestic production. That includes hi-tech urban farming, from multi-storey aquaculture in which fish are reared in stacked seawater tanks to growing greens in warehouses under artificial lighting, as well as vat-grown meat and manufacturing plant-based alternatives to animal protein. Urban farmers have been granted permits to turn car parks on the rooftops of apartment blocks into vegetable farms. In October 2020 Singapore became the first country in the world to approve the consumption of lab-grown chicken. Eat Just, the US start-up that cultured the chicken cells, said it planned to start manufacturing the meat in Singapore. The technology requires far less land, energy and water than rearing animals for slaughter. According to one study, cultured meat can be produced with 96 per cent less water use than conventional meat farming.

By 2030, Singapore aims to produce 30 per cent of its food needs locally. The government's economic planners believe the agricultural technology systems being developed for the island's needs could become a valuable export, as other countries grapple with a scarcity of farmland and overfished oceans. A Singapore start-up, Sustenir, has succeeded in cultivating strawberries, which usually do better in temperate climates, on shelves in an industrial building in the north of the city. Its success suggests that technological solutions can rear the most exotic crops in the midst of densely populated cities.

The state has also set up a stockpile of rice, to safeguard against ever running out of the staple carbohydrate. Rice suppliers are required to keep two months' worth of imports in a government-designated warehouse. The rice placed in the stockpile continues to belong to the importer, but the government has the right to acquire it in an emergency.

From water scarcity to food security, many of Singapore's constraints have been overcome through technological advances. But the challenge of building a greener and more resilient city has also taken Singapore back to elements of its past. At Edible Garden City, Hoong encourages people to rediscover food crops growing wild in the city's streets and remaining forests, from wild pepper to 'wartime' foods like tapioca that fed people during the Japanese occupation, restoring lost ties to its landscape and natural flora. 'Growing food is about connecting people to their food,' Hoong says. 'It's about the human-nature connection.'

Hoong sees urban farming as part of revitalising the city's ecosystem. 'The way I try to design gardens is to try to make it as biodiverse as possible,' she explains. 'Not just planting food for us, but also for the animals. Planting pollinator-attracting flowers, plants that can be pruned for use in green manuring and mulching.'

Singapore has gone through one of the fastest urban transformations in history. In 1960, more than two-thirds of its estimated 1.89 million people were squatters or slum dwellers. By 1985 there were no squatters and all of the slums had been cleared. But the pace of change pulled traditional communities apart and cut Singaporeans off from a style of living that was closer to the land.

In squatter colonies known as 'kampongs' – the Malay word for village which gave rise to the English word 'compound' – families had supplemented work in factories or warehouses by growing vegetables and rearing pigs and chickens. There were makeshift backyard workshops crowded in alongside dwellings. Illumination at night came from kerosene lamps, and water was fetched from standpipes or wells. 'We never locked our doors,' recalls Tan Cheng Eam, who grew up on a kampong in the 1960s. 'There was no need to because everyone knew everyone. There were coconut trees all around and we raised chickens, ducks and pigs, and grew vegetables and fruit trees like guava and jackfruit.' The Tan family lived on a plot of land that belonged to the businessman Tan Lark Sye, but in the 1960s Tan was forced to sell his land to the government for redevelopment.

Singapore used methods more commonly associated with left-wing governments to serve conservative ends. The government nationalised huge chunks of land – by the mid-1980s more than three-quarters of the island were state-owned – and launched a massive programme to build public housing. The scale of the transformation in Singapore's early years outstripped the capacity of the private sector. The government responded by setting up state-owned companies to produce building supplies, from sand to bricks. As thousands of graves were exhumed to make way for development, and the bodies cremated, the government even set up its own crematorium to handle the volume of remains.

The reason that Singapore has the highest home ownership rate of any rich country is that from early on, housing was available to buy rather than rent, creating a property-owning middle class with a lifelong commitment to the stability of the system. But as the government began selling the public housing known as HDB flats, the Tan family's neighbours began to move away and houses were left vacant. 'We used to be so close we would go to each other's houses to chit-chat and celebrate festivals together,' Tan recalls. 'All that was scattered to the four winds. Neighbourliness dissipated and crime flourished instead.' The family moved to a twelfth-floor apartment that was much smaller than their palm-thatch kampong house. Her mother was so afraid of the elevator that she cried every time she got in. The family missed their coconut trees, vegetable patches and livestock.

'Moving to a HDB flat didn't just mean a change in living conditions,' Tan said. 'It meant the end of freedom and self-sufficiency in many ways. You don't grow and make things yourself anymore, you pay for them. Everything is about money now. You even have to pay to throw your garbage away. Each morning you open your eyes and it's immediately about the money, money, money.'

In the 1960s, high-rises were already attracting criticism in the West. The collapse of Ronan Point, a tower block in east London which was ravaged by a gas explosion, shook public confidence in high-rise living. But Singapore's planners were determined that building upwards was the only solution on a land-hungry island. They decided that mixing the population in housing estates would help them avoid the trap that Western cities had fallen into, where tower blocks had become ghettoes for the most desperate in society. In the new public housing blocks, former slum-dwellers lived alongside better-off residents, with a mix of apartment sizes and the very poorest squeezed into one-bed apartments. Assisted by the withdrawal of savings from the Central Provident Fund, flats were sold with a ninety-nine-year lease, after which the property reverted to the state. Some of the former slum-dwellers could still not afford even the lowest rents, despite steep rent rebates aimed at the poorest tenants, and they quit their apartments to return to living in shacks.

Unused to high-rise living, meanwhile, many residents tossed bulky waste such as broken TV sets from upper floors, a phenomenon known as 'killer litter'. There are stiff penalties – throwing 'killer litter' can be punished with a five-year jail term – but high-rise littering remains a common phenomenon, with up to 2800 reported offences a year. The items most frequently tossed from balconies, cigarette butts and used tissues, are unlikely to cause injury but are frequently a spur for angry confrontations between neighbours. The scale of the offences means the authorities pursue only the most egregious cases. As recently as 2019, a seventy-three-year-old man died after he was struck on the head by a wine bottle dropped from an upper floor. In that case, an Australian IT worker was charged with causing death through a negligent act.

The entire city was being remade. The low-rise shophouses in the city centre were ripped down to make way for offices and hotels. Outside the urban centre, land was cleared for industrial use. Foreign companies were drawn to industrial estates by tax incentives and the promise of cheap labour, quiescent unions and slick bureaucracy.

It was harder to persuade overseas developers to build in run-down areas of the city centre, where the government planned for office blocks and shopping complexes. So domestic developers were incentivised to build in the city centre by allowing them to pay for land in instalments. Property tax rates were cut for new developments, and to encourage developers to build upwards, there were additional tax refunds for every storey they added.

Singapore is one of the most hygienic cities in the tropics, with streets swept clean of litter and public litter bins emptied regularly. From the outset, Singapore's leaders were fastidious about public cleanliness, expecting spotless streets to boost morale, reduce sickness and lead to higher economic growth. Launching the first 'Keep Singapore Clean' campaign in 1968, Lee Kuan Yew declared: 'We have built, we have progressed. But no other hallmark of success will be more distinctive than that of achieving our position as the cleanest and greenest city in South Asia.' Admonishing the public not to drop litter was backed up with the threat of fines and public shaming. The names of adult litterbugs were published in the press, while errant children were reported to their schools. People caught dropping litter could be made to clean the streets under 'Corrective Work Orders', a punishment which remains in force. Offenders can be seen sweeping up while wearing luminous pink and yellow vests as a badge of their shame. The vest used to be entirely yellow, but the upper half was made pink in 2019 to deliberately distinguish offenders' clothing from the safety vests worn by public works staff. The government agency responsible said the design change was meant to increase the 'deterrence effect'. Yet despite this combination of exhortation and punishment, littering is a persistent problem. While a paternal state tidies up after them, it seems a significant minority of citizens are incorrigibly untidy.

Coupled with the drive to keep the streets clean was a plan to make Singapore a green 'garden city', with a campaign that planted thousands of trees and set aside spaces in housing developments for greenery. This has become a distinctive feature of the city, with well-manicured stretches of grass alongside roads and an abundance of city parks and nature reserves, including the MacRitchie Reservoir, where runners and hikers encounter long-tailed macaques and monitor lizards. The last of Singapore's virgin rainforest survives in Bukit Timah, home to a rare native orchid and pangolins, a species of scaly mammal that is critically endangered.

With space on the island at a premium, a smaller offshore island has been turned into a rubbish dump. Refuse is dispatched by barge to Pulau Semakau, 8 kilometres offshore, which is now the country's only landfill after Lorong Halus, the last dumping ground on the main island, closed in 1999. Lined with a plastic membrane and a layer of clay to prevent waste leaching into the sea, Pulau Semakau is itself running out of space and is projected to be full by 2035. Singapore has set a goal of becoming a 'zero waste' society, but this is an unlikely prospect with very low rates of recycling and widespread use of single-use plastics including disposable plates and cutlery at hawker centres. The country recycles a tiny fraction of its plastic waste, just 4 per cent in 2019, and instead burns the waste to generate energy.

The style of public housing designs has become more distinctive over time, as the emphasis shifted from swiftly resettling a squatter population to developing buildings that inspired civic pride. From rectangular slabs with flats sharing a single common corridor, HDB architects turned to 'point blocks' with four apartments arranged around a common landing. The new design was more private, as windows along the common corridor meant passers-by could glance into a flat. Apartment towers have been created in the shape of a letter Y and a clover leaf, while the 'butterfly block', officially known as 168a Queensway, has two curved wings of apartments fanning out from the central tower where the lift shaft runs.

Singapore created planned communities, called the new towns, with shops, schools and sports facilities laid out around the housing. The apartment blocks were designed to encourage communal interaction, with empty zones known as 'void decks' on the ground floor where children played in the mornings and chess players sat at dusk. It was an attempt, in large part successful, to recreate the communal bonds of the kampong.

The policy of integrating races in each neighbourhood and public housing block ensures that Singapore does not have racial ghettos, but it also curtails individual choice of where to live. Tharman Shanmugaratnam, Singapore's deputy prime minister for eight years from 2011, described this as 'the most intrusive social policy in Singapore'. It is also – in his view – the most important.

The emphasis of the public housing programme is on providing homes for married couples. Until 1991, single people were not permitted to buy a public housing flat, and even now a single buyer must wait until they are thirty-five to be eligible. A variety of schemes and subsidies encouraged members of extended families to live near each other. Buying an HDB flat has become a rite of passage for Singaporean couples, a marker of entry into adulthood and a financial commitment that lasts the rest of their working lives.

For most Singaporeans, their state-built flat is their biggest asset. But as the stock of housing gets older and the fixed leases run down, people worry that the value of their property will begin to depreciate sharply, leaving them with little to pass on to their children. Irvin Seah, an economist at Singapore's DBS bank, said: 'Their lifelong savings, everything is in that apartment. There is always this belief that this is an asset that they can pass on, but its value is depreciating by the year.' It is a problem that will manifest itself in a few decades, as residents look to sell the oldest public housing flats towards the end of their lease, and the solution is not straightforward. In some cases, older estates can be rebuilt to make optimal use of land – building higher or adding housing over car parks – creating additional value that can be used to compensate residents. But not every redevelopment scheme will pay for itself in this way. As leases reach the end of their lifetime, the problem is likely to become a political headache.

Singapore had advantages over other developing cities. Because it is a city state, and was able to control migration from surrounding countries, there were no new settlers leaving villages and crowding hopefully into the city in search of opportunity. And its size meant that a single authority could take charge of planning the renewal of the entire country, eliminating conflicts between rival layers of government. Singapore planned for the long term, working towards the city's future needs rather than within the limitations of its present-day capacity. The city's subway system, the Mass Rapid Transit or MRT, was first proposed in the 1960s and included in planning from the 1970s, though it was only in 1981 that the government could afford to finance its construction.

For this reason, the transformation of Singapore has

attracted attention from planners across the world. Housing
the poor was an emblem of the government's effectiveness, a
literal act of nation-building that turned slum-dwellers into
property-owning citizens. But attempts to copy this feat in
other countries have run into a variety of challenges. In São
Paulo, Brazil's biggest city, a conservative administration
launched 'Projeto Cingapura' in the 1990s, a plan to build
high-rises to rehouse families from the favelas. Colourful
Singapore-style high-rise blocks were built in prominent
locations, aimed at former slum-dwellers who would buy
them in instalments. But the apartments were too expensive
for the poor families they were intended to help and many
struggled to keep up with payments.

As millions of people across the world migrate from rural
to urban areas, and cities – especially in East Asia – grow
larger and denser, politicians have sought to replicate other
aspects of Singapore's urban model. In 1994, the governments of China and Singapore signed an agreement to build
an industrial township at Suzhou, a historic city about sixty
miles west of Shanghai. Lee Kuan Yew signed on Singapore's
behalf, an indication of the high hopes placed in the project.
The development combined industry, commerce, residential
neighbourhoods, schools and universities, and was intended
to showcase Singapore's skill at urban planning and attracting foreign investment. The deal followed personal lobbying
from Suzhou's mayor Zhang Xinsheng, who told Lee, 'People
in Suzhou want what they have seen of Singapore on television and in the newspapers – jobs, housing, and a garden city.'

The driving force behind the project was a Singapore
consortium which included the Jurong Town Corporation,
which oversees the development of the city state's industrial
estates, and the EDB, the government agency in charge of
promoting Singapore as a global business hub, while Surbana

Jurong, a consultancy owned by the Singapore government, was the master planner. The 'Jurong' name was a reminder of the 1963 industrial estate that had been the launch pad for Singapore's post-war industrialisation. Both Surbana Jurong and the Jurong Town Corporation traced their roots to that first industrial park. Surbana Jurong, now one of the biggest urban consultancies in Asia with offices across forty countries, grew out of the merger of a government-owned firm which provided planning for industrial developments and an offshoot of the HDB.

It was a moment of justifiable pride for Singapore's planners, who watched a Chinese township take shape on Singaporean lines, including the provision of affordable public housing for workers and a savings scheme known as the 'Suzhou Provident Fund', modelled on Singapore's Central Provident Fund, which could be tapped for retirement or housing purchases. The development took the two countries beyond normal economic ties of trade and investment 'into a new area of cooperation', Lee said. But the pride quickly soured into disappointment. While the project had the blessing of China's central government, it encountered fierce competition from a rival business hub supported by local Chinese officials. Lee complained that these officials had exploited the Singapore connection to get investors interested, and then urged them to settle in the rival business park instead, at a cheaper rate. The park lost millions of dollars in its early years, and was only turned around after the Singapore government transferred majority ownership of the project to China in 2000, to encourage Chinese officials to market the park more actively. The venture has since turned a profit and recouped its losses.

Perhaps the most ambitious attempt to clone Singapore was in southern India, when the state of Andhra Pradesh launched a plan to build a new state capital, Amaravati. Singaporean experts drew up a master plan, and construction began on a fertile swath of land on the banks of the River Krishna, where banana groves and flower farms were cleared to make way for new roads and the concrete skeletons of residential towers. Amaravati was to be a sustainable city with more than half of its area devoted to greenery or water, and its people ferried to work in electric vehicles, water taxis, or pedalling along dedicated cycle routes. Surveillance drones were to be deployed to prevent slums developing on the city's outskirts. But the project ran into opposition from farmers unwilling to give up land for development, and the partnership was scrapped following a change of government in a regional election. Following the struggles of the Suzhou project, Singapore has developed several industrial parks in India and Vietnam, though these have been led by private sector developers rather than the government. The attempt to create mini-Singapores in India and China underlines the difficulties of transferring the city state's model to bigger countries, where conflicting layers of government, stubborn farmers or election defeats can all throw a spanner in the works, in ways unheard of in streamlined Singapore.

Along with the Gulf princedoms, Singapore is one of a handful of wealthy nations that will be in the front line of climate change. Singapore is now heating at approximately 0.25 degrees a decade, about double the trend in global temperatures since the 1950s, according to government scientists. The rapid rise is a combination of global warming and the heat island effect, where human activity and the trapping of heat by roads and buildings makes cities hotter than the surrounding countryside. At night, concrete buildings radiate the solar heat absorbed during the day, meaning there is little respite even after the sun sets.

Lee Kuan Yew was insistent on the virtues of air conditioning, which he regarded as the invention that made development possible in the tropics, allowing office workers to keep going through the baking heat of the afternoon. As well as raising productivity, air conditioning mitigates the health effect of heat and reduces the risk of insect-borne diseases such as malaria. Filtering dust and decreasing humidity as well as heat, cooling systems are also essential for the smooth functioning of office machinery. But climate control has reshaped the city's architecture, making it a less human place. Instead of arranging rooms around the natural ventilation of a courtyard, air conditioning has encouraged tightly stacked flats and offices. By blasting heated air out of buildings, it intensifies the heat on the streets, driving people to seek shelter indoors. Cooling systems disfigure the public face of the city too. Back alleys in Singapore are frequently lined with external condenser units, rows of bulky grey or white boxes fixed to the outside walls of buildings. The need to grapple with the consequences of climate change has become central to urban planning in Singapore.

Buildings like Singapore's School of Design, completed in 2019, offer a template for a new style of design that combines Asia's past and future. A large overhanging roof provides shade, just like the verandahs that gave shelter from the sun in traditional tropical architecture, while harvesting energy through an array of photovoltaic panels. The air is cooled, but is delivered to rooms with more warmth and humidity than it would be under a conventional system. Instead, windows can be opened to let in the breeze and ceiling fans stir the air. But this change in building design needs to fit into a broader reshaping of the city, including a shift towards less consumption and more recycling. 'For Singapore to be self-sufficient it is not enough that buildings are performing better, they need to be operating as components of a self-sufficient city,' says Hassell. 'Where are we going to produce energy, produce food?'

Soon after I arrived in 2015, trials of driverless cars began in a district that was reserved for research and entrepreneurship: One North, named after Singapore's latitude one degree north of the equator, is a mix of biomedical research centres and office space for media and IT businesses. Companies are housed in low-rise glass-and-steel blocks, arranged on a narrow grid of tree-lined streets, with a thin strip of parkland winding through the centre of the development. Passengers were eager to try out the fleet of converted Renault and Mitsubishi electric cars, which scooted down quiet roads as the AI's ghostly hands tugged the steering wheel.

It was the first time anywhere in the world that driverless taxis were made available to the public. Singapore's urban planners hope that more automation will allow further curbing of car ownership, which is already limited by the steep government levies on car purchases which, they envisaged, would free more road space for pedestrians and cyclists. The embrace of driverless cars is part of the 'Smart Nation' project, under which Singapore has encouraged the adoption of technology to transform the way its citizens live and work. This ranges from urging consumers and government agencies to switch to cashless payments to the use of surveillance drones to spot puddles in roof gutters where mosquitoes may breed.

Under the Smart Nation drive, the country is adding surveillance equipment to its lamp posts, fitting sensors to detect environmental changes such as increased pollution and cameras that can track and analyse the build-up of crowds. This intensely localised environmental data will be fed into urban planning, accounting for factors such as wind direction and typical rainfall patterns in future housing and office design. The data on crowd movements could be used to shape the design of infrastructure such as pedestrian crossings and improve public transport, officials say.

Alongside this technological innovation is a growing commitment to sustainability. Every new building in a central location is now required to replace greenery at a '100 per cent' level; that is, the developer must use a combination of grounds, terraces and other green features to provide the same amount of plant life as if there was no building on the site. Khoo Teng Chye, executive director of the Centre for Liveable Cities, set up by the Singapore government to share knowledge on urban sustainability, said: 'We are blessed in the tropics, things grow fast. We have to learn to exploit this to make the city softer and more liveable. We have to learn to live with less air conditioning, to design buildings that take advantage of the wind. That's the next big area that we have to work on if we want to be sustainable.' The challenge is being tackled in a 'multi-pronged' way, Khoo added. Many HDB flats now have solar panels on their rooftops. 'We're using computational fluid dynamics to place buildings in new towns where they catch the wind, cooling the temperature down.'

The shift to a more sustainable style of architecture is likely to be accelerated by the impact of Covid-19. The outbreak of contagion does not appear to have damaged confidence in high-density housing, but it is expected to encourage more outdoor living, which appears to have a lower risk of transmission compared to being in close proximity indoors.

At Kampung Admiralty, a complex which combines housing for the elderly and a medical centre, the main public space has a lofty ceiling and is open to the elements on three sides, creating a covered square with natural ventilation. Since

opening in 2012, Gardens by the Bay, Singapore's waterfront nature park built on land claimed from the sea, has
become a statement of the city's ambitions for urban design.
The gardens are a 101-hectare expanse of greenery at the
centre of Singapore, open to the public and tourists. They
feature conservatories showcasing plants from the environ-
ments most likely to be affected by global warming and act
as a sponge, absorbing and slowly releasing rainwater. Their
best-known attraction, the Supertrees, are vertical sculptures
up to 50 metres high and festooned with orchids, ferns and
other climbing plants. The core of each 'tree' is concrete
wrapped in steel and overlaid with a living skin of vegetation.
At the top, a funnel-shaped array of steel 'branches' reaches
into the sky. Singapore, the gardens seem to say, is scientific
and rational, a city in which the human will has triumphed
over wild nature. Yet it is also a society in which the human
connection with plant life and the natural world is valued.
This aesthetic, emphasising sustainability and using technology to mimic elements of nature, is sometimes described as
'solarpunk'.

The city has reshaped functional waterways, such as canals
used to drain storm floods, into streams. In the Bishan neighbourhood, a canal that once ran straight along the edge of a
strip of parkland now twists through the middle of it. Fish
thrive in the new waterway and other aquatic wildlife has
been spotted in the park, from dragonflies to otters.

Singapore's emphasis on sustainability is drawing interest
from other Asian nations grappling with the need to balance
economic development against quality of life. In Tianjin,
a coastal municipality in China, Singapore is collaborating
with the Chinese government on a new urban development
intended to house 350,000 people, which has been described
as an 'eco-city'. Grant Associates, the Singapore landscape

architects firm that planned Gardens by the Bay, is also designing the 'Friendship Park' in Tianjin, which is inspired by the Singapore park development. In both cases, the green spaces were created before the expansion of the city's buildings. Stefaan Lambreghts, associate director at the firm, says: 'Building the green infrastructure first is very Singaporean, very Chinese. I can't imagine that happening in Europe, where you would have to build houses before the park, or build them together.' The political system in Singapore lends itself to longer-term thinking, the architect says. 'Because of the politics in Europe, if a prime minister lasts for eight years, that's a long time. The difference in Singapore, in Asia, is that things get done faster. In Europe it is sometimes difficult to implement something new. The attraction of China for us, as designers, is that things can happen fast, once you get political support.'

Climate change is expected to bring higher temperatures and sharper contrasts between wet and dry seasons. The risk of torrential rain and sea level rise is being factored into design. Terminal 5 at Changi airport, scheduled for completion in the 2030s, will be built 5.5 metres above mean sea level as a precaution against the melting of polar ice, while flood mitigation measures are being added to Singapore's subway system.

A more extreme climate is likely to emphasise the need for resilient architecture. At SkyVille@Dawson, a new public housing development, all the corridors are lit by daylight and naturally ventilated. 'Buildings that rely on complicated kit make me anxious,' says Richard Hassell of WOHA. 'Buildings where everything is being powered by machines. As climate changes and conditions change, buildings like that are going to feel very rigid.'

Singapore is tiny, and its impact on global phenomena like

climate change is minuscule. But the safe and affluent life-styles of its citizens mean it is also a role model for countries across the developing world. How it overcomes the constraints of land, food and water will set a template for the vast swath of humanity living in the megacities of Asia and Africa.

The Singapore approach is, in essence, one of optimism that technological solutions can mitigate the worst consequences of the coming crisis. This runs counter to the broadly pessimistic view among many experts that a combination of intense heat and rising sea levels will shrink the habitable portion of the earth. Some scientists advocate a strategic retreat from shorelines that cannot be defended and research suggests cities in the Middle East may become inhospitably hot within a few decades. For Singapore, however, retreat is not an option. It must adapt to survive.

6

Authoritarianism with Gucci Handbags

Dissidents, campaign groups and censorship

On a Sunday morning in July 1966, a Singapore politician was arrested while taking part in a demonstration to protest against America's escalating military intervention in the Vietnam War.

Chia Thye Poh, a rake-thin twenty-five-year-old with severe black-framed glasses, had been a university physics lecturer before he ran for election in 1963 under the banner of Barisan Sosialis, the left-wing opposition party. In parliament, Chia became a persistent and thoughtful critic of the ruling party. His probing questions examined the human cost of the transformation of Singapore under the PAP, asking about the compensation paid to squatters who were moved to new state-built housing, and whether they were able to pursue their old livelihoods in new homes.

Authorities had turned down the demonstrators' application to hold a march, meaning the protest was officially illegal. Police dispersed the marchers with tear gas, and arrested more than forty of them, including Chia. In October of that year, Chia and the seven other Barisan Sosialis MPs quit parliament. Chia told the *Straits Times*: 'We cannot remain in Parliament because parliamentary democracy is dead. You can say we are now taking our struggle to the streets.' The struggle would take various forms, he said, from street protests and demonstrations to strikes.

For his part in the Vietnam demonstration, Chia was convicted of unlawful assembly, and chose to go to prison rather than pay a fine. He was released less than a fortnight later after his party paid the fine for him. A few days after he came out of prison, he was detained again, this time under the Internal Security Act, a piece of legislation inherited from the British which allows a person deemed a threat to national security to be detained for up to two years without being brought to trial. Detention is renewable, which means a detainee can be held indefinitely. Chia was to become one of the world's longest serving political prisoners. The government did not explain the reason for his detention until 1985, when a minister said that he was a member of the Communist Party and had engaged in activities intended to destabilise the government. Chia insisted that his activities had always been legal, that he had never been a Communist Party member and that he had never advocated violence.

Though his case was never as well-known globally as those of Nelson Mandela or Aung San Suu Kyi, it attracted international attention. According to Amnesty International, he had been detained because of his role in the opposition.

While he was in detention, Chia says he was driven around the island by government officials, who wanted to show him how rapidly Singapore was developing. He was unimpressed, acknowledging the change but suggesting the government men let him out of the car to talk to people about their lives before he drew conclusions. Indeed, he had been imprisoned according to a surreal logic. When he insisted that he posed no threat and was a peaceful and constitutional opponent of the government, he was considered to be stubbornly concealing his guilt. If he agreed to renounce the violent overthrow of the government, he could be freed. But the cost of his freedom would be accepting that the official version of his life's story was the truth.

That renunciation never came. But in 1987, Canada offered him asylum, and by 1989, it seemed, any threat he appeared to pose had waned sufficiently for him to be released. He was freed from prison in May that year, six months before the Berlin Wall came down. Aged forty-eight, he had served twenty-two years behind bars without ever being charged with an offence. After his release, he was restricted to living on Sentosa, an island off the Singapore coast which is devoted to recreation. Then as now, Sentosa featured theme parks, golf courses, elegant gardens, and a coastal fort which has been converted into a military museum. A monorail whizzes tourists across the short stretch of water separating the smaller island from Singapore. When I lived in Singapore, I regularly visited the island at the weekend. The beaches, filled with imported white sand, were an ideal place for my young children to dip their feet in the sea while my wife and I watched, splitting a pizza and a beer.

Sentosa bustled with tourists. Coaches carrying mainland Chinese visitors would pull up outside the Resorts World Sentosa casino, and middle-aged men and women in baggy trousers and polo shirts would spill out with a visible flutter of excitement. European and Australian families on stopovers queued for the rides at the Universal Studios theme park, children and adults alike slathered in sunscreen. Along the shoreline, young Singaporean men played beach volleyball while women in bikinis took selfies, ankle-deep in the water. The island was once covered in tropical rainforest, and a few patches of this dense foliage remain amid the resort hotels, golfing greens and rollercoasters. It sounds like a pleasant place to be secluded, until you clock that keeping someone prisoner on a holiday island is a deliberate humiliation. Chia spent three and a half years there, living in a sparsely furnished one-room building that had been a guard house.

In 1992, he was permitted to move to the main island, where he lived with his elderly parents, though he remained subject to restrictions on making public statements, attending public meetings or joining any association. It was not until November 1998, thirty-two years after his detention, that all restrictions were finally lifted.

In Singapore, the Cold War contest of ideology between capitalism and the left had become a battle of wills between two men. Lee Kuan Yew paid Chia a compliment of sorts, describing him in 2000 as 'a believer who refused to give up even after communism collapsed worldwide', a 'determined man with stubborn if misguided convictions'. Among politically conscious Singaporeans, Chia's story lived on, instilling a fear that opposing the state could mean sacrificing your youth in prison. What you think of him depends on your political colouring. Conservatives like Lee granted him a grudging degree of respect as a foe with a steely spine. For liberals, he was a martyr; a genteel, softly spoken intellectual subjected to extraordinary punishment. Among the wider population though, he has largely faded into obscurity.

The treatment of Chia became a template for the treatment of any dissenting voice in Singapore. In the eyes of Lee and his circle, the communist enemy was a shape-shifter, able to penetrate society and foment revolution in the guise of anyone who questioned the prevailing order, from an independent-minded trade unionist to a left-wing MP. In reality, the threat of a violent communist insurrection in Singapore had been extinguished with the end of the Malayan Emergency in 1960. Fear of communism remained potent, however, in an era of global superpower confrontation; at home, Lee believed constant vigilance was required to prevent a communist resurgence while, abroad, he championed US intervention in Vietnam, seeing it as the only way to hold back the Red tide in Southeast Asia. Quashing communism was convenient, too, for a secondary reason. Eliminating other centres of power consolidated the strength of Lee and his coterie. In Singapore, there was no alternative movement that could lay claim to power, and no alternative story to the one the ruling party told.

Chew Kheng Chuan, known to friends as 'KC', is an unlikely enemy of the state. The first Singaporean to study at Harvard, he had returned to set up his own design business. One of the triggers for his arrest in 1987 may have been an intercepted letter from a friend, who joked: 'For a Marxist, you make a very good businessman.' Chew was one of twenty-two people arrested that year for their involvement in an alleged 'Marxist conspiracy' to topple the government. The group were a mix of Roman Catholic lay workers, social workers and professionals. The arrests, in a sweep known as Operation Spectrum, stunned Singaporeans. The men and women were largely youthful idealists from Singapore's English-educated elite; rather than seeking violent revolution, their social activism was focused on modest change. If this group could be detained without charge, no one who stepped out of line was safe, no matter how minor their infraction.

From the perspective of Singapore's rulers, things looked very different. In 1986, the year before the Operation Spectrum arrests, a wave of popular protest in the Philippines had deposed Ferdinand Marcos. The Catholic church had played a central role in the resistance to Marcos. In Latin America, the liberation theology movement taught that social activism on behalf of the poor was an essential part of Christian ministry. Lee believed the shape-shifted communist threat had now infiltrated Roman Catholicism.

During an undergraduate degree at the London School of Economics, Chew had joined a discussion circle of Singaporean and Malaysian students. They met, he says, at the home of a former student activist named Tan Wah Piow, who had left Singapore in the 1970s. The government would later identify Tan as the mastermind of the 'Marxist conspiracy'.

'The orientation [of the discussion circle] was left wing,' Chew told me. 'We were trying to understand Marxism better.' The group considered how Marxism might apply to the economy of Singapore. 'The conclusion was clear,' he adds. 'It was very far from applicable.' Chew believes that one of the students in the circle was an agent of Singapore's Internal Security Department, the government agency which counters terrorism, political subversion and foreign espionage. He later spotted the man in a Singapore government building, accompanied by ISD officers and wearing an official lanyard.

Back home, Chew was one of a number of politically engaged Singaporeans. There was, he stresses, no formal group. But people involved in radical theatre, church activism and student politics were all aware of each other. 'What was the mutual interest of all these people? They were critical of the government in some way, that the government could be doing better in terms of certain social policies affecting marginalised groups in Singapore society,' Chew explained. 'It was a natural network but not a formal organisation.' The focus of protest had shifted from the material demands of the 1950s, when striking workers demanded better conditions, and the radical left criticism of the 1960s, when Chia marched against American imperialism. The activists arrested in the 1980s were raising more modest questions about Singapore's direction. 'This was obviously a serious earnest government trying to build the nation, trying to build Singapore as a young nation and doing good in many fields, public housing, healthcare, and that sort of thing,' Chew said. 'But I was keenly aware of this history of political repression in Singapore and was very disturbed by that, because I did not believe that the opponents of LKY deserved the kind of political detention they faced.'

Teo Soh Lung, a lawyer who was another of the detainees in 1987, said their attempts to change Singapore were incremental. 'We did small things, like helping the [opposition] Workers' Party write their newsletter, and "do-gooders work" like setting up the criminal legal aid scheme.' The government claimed the detainees were part of a clandestine network, infiltrating legitimate organisations to further their goal of bringing a Marxist regime to Singapore. While Tan was said to be the mastermind of the plot, a Catholic lay worker named Vincent Cheng was fingered as the local ringleader.

Teo was accused of infiltrating the Law Society. She scoffs at the claim. 'I thought the government was passing too many laws too fast and the Law Society wasn't fast enough in making recommendations. I thought we could improve the laws. But the government wasn't interested in listening to the Law Society.'

The treatment of the detainees was brutal. 'They hit me very hard with an open palm on my face, maybe about fifty times, until I bled inside my mouth,' Chew told me in a calm and matter-of-fact tone. 'The reason why they slapped and not punched was very deliberate. They didn't want to break your jaw. The slaps were very hard, you saw stars.' Chew was made to stand under an air-conditioning vent for twenty-two hours. He was barefoot. 'So cold that your teeth start to chatter.' Then he was asked to write a statement, coming under pressure both to confess his own guilt and implicate others. The statement took the form of handwritten notes. Chew spent months in detention writing, and his account eventually ran to hundreds of pages. 'They are plumbing you for intelligence,' he said. 'You try to minimise going to the dreaded item of meetings, when you are supposed to recall who said what, and who was there.'

There were two waves of arrests under Operation Spectrum, the first in May 1987 and the second a month later. Chew was detained in June 1987 and he speculates that his arrest took place after his name came up in the questioning of the first wave of detainees. He does not know which of his fellow citizens might have yielded his name under interrogation. 'We still keep in touch,' he said. 'But we never went over the painful details of this sort of thing.'

Chia's case haunted the inmates arrested in 1987. Interrogators warned them that, like Chia, they could spend their lives in detention without ever coming to trial. But they knew that state repression had limits. Singapore was not South Korea, where the military had put down student protest with lethal force. 'There was some comfort in know-ing I wouldn't be killed,' Chew said. 'That doesn't happen in Singapore.'

Under interrogation, the detainees were persuaded to

confess. 'If you have three days and nights of no sleep, your mind will be affected no matter what,' Teo said. 'You begin to get persuaded by their story. You sort of say, I'm not the one trying to overthrow the government but perhaps I unwittingly helped.' The interrogations sometimes veered into absurdity. At one point in the questioning of a detainee, her case officer triumphantly declared that George Orwell's *Animal Farm* had been found on her bookshelves, proof of her political beliefs.

Chew says the confession he made in detention was accurate enough, after a fashion. 'Did I have left-wing ideas? Yes I did. What's wrong with that? Did I read Marx? Yes of course I did, I'm a student of social science. I read Marx, I understand Marx ... does that make me a Marxist?' The words came close enough to what his interrogators wanted to satisfy them, but hewed to the truth sufficiently to allow him to retain his dignity.

Videotaped confessions by the detainees were broadcast on Singaporean television. By the end of 1987 all but one, the Catholic worker Cheng, had been released. But the Operation Spectrum detentions had one further twist, the following year, which underlined the Singapore state's determination to bring its black sheep back into the fold. In April 1988, nine of the detainees – including the lawyer Teo – released a joint statement in which they alleged ill treatment in custody and denied involvement in any conspiracy. Chew was not among those who signed the statement. 'I very consciously did not sign it,' he tells me. 'There was a real danger of being re-arrested, which weighed heavy on everybody. The people who signed it were extremely courageous.' Eight of those who signed were arrested again, while the ninth escaped arrest as she was in the UK at the time.

In May of that year, Francis Seow, a lawyer representing

two of the detainees, was himself arrested. The Singapore authorities claimed Seow had been encouraged to run as an opposition political candidate by a US diplomat, Mason Hendrickson. The American embassy official was expelled the next day for allegedly interfering in the country's internal affairs. The US protested that meeting with a potential opposition candidate was part of a diplomat's normal duties, and expelled a Singaporean diplomat in turn.

Singapore's rulers believed the US was naive about the nature of their society. In parliament, the deputy prime minister Goh Chok Tong drew a parallel with the Islamic Revolution in Iran, reaching the conclusion that the regime had been toppled because the Shah had not been sufficiently repressive. The Shah, Goh claimed, had tried to introduce 'American democratic ideals' into a traditional Muslim society, but this worsened the country's upheaval and led to his overthrow. The episode was a reminder of Singapore's determination to steer its own course. 'When the Shah faced domestic problems, the US pressed him to yield ground to his opponents, instead of leaving him to deal with the situation firmly,' Goh told MPs. Singapore, he made clear, would not make the same mistake of looking weak in the face of opposition. He gave a gloomy assessment; in a newborn multi-ethnic nation, a competitive electoral system would quickly fracture along racial and religious lines.

Chew was himself arrested for a second time in May 1988. Although he had not signed the statement, he had complained to the families of some of the other detainees about his treatment in prison and this account was published in the *Straits Times*. This time, he was held for ten months. 'The first time, after I was released, I was very angry, really upset, thinking: what a bloody injustice this is, and so I really came out swinging,' he recalled. 'After the second arrest, after ten months, I suppose they had then achieved precisely the result they wanted. I was sufficiently subdued. I had got it into my thick skull – if I knock my head against the wall, the wall is not going to crack.'

The last of the Operation Spectrum detainees to be freed was Cheng, who was released from prison in 1990, under conditions which included a restriction from engaging in any political activity, a bar on joining any organisation without the permission of the Internal Security Department, and a ban on travelling abroad or changing his address without permission. In the videotape of his confession, broadcast on Singapore state television, questions are put to him by four Singaporean journalists. Cheng's closing words are an eerie parallel of an enemy of the state confessing in a communist regime, with the distinction that he is rejecting Marxism and embracing Singapore's capitalist orthodoxy. He says: 'I realised also that it is very important that I take into account the reality of Singapore, Singapore's vulnerability for example. And that a Marxist state actually is not possible in Singapore.'

Operation Spectrum stands out in Singapore's history. It looks like a moment of supreme self-confidence on the part of Singapore's ruling elite. From a private citizen to a friendly superpower, everyone could be reminded of the perils of overstepping the mark. The dissidents were cowed. Some went into exile, while others lived quiet lives. Chew described what happened to him as a 'political lobotomy'. He went back to running his design business but steered clear of any involvement in politics.

But it also highlighted a few of the cracks in the system. There was open scepticism about the need for these detentions, even in government circles. Though Lee himself remained convinced of the threat, a cabinet minister, Suppiah Dhanabalan, resigned his position in 1992 because of his discomfort with the crackdown. Tharman Shamugaratnam, a senior ruling party politician, said of the detainees in a 2001 interview: 'most were social activists, but not out to subvert the system.'

Tharman, an independent-minded government minister, had been friends and flatmates with Chew when they both studied at the LSE. 'I greatly appreciated his stand,' Chew said. 'He was on his way up [in politics] and one might say: better keep your thoughts to yourself if you don't want to impede your progression up the ladder. It reflected greatly on his integrity and sense of friendship.'

These public disagreements did little to hamper the politicians' careers. Dhanabalan left government but went on to serve as chairman of Temasek, Singapore's sovereign wealth fund. Tharman rose to become Singapore's deputy prime minister. The combination of public dismay at the arrests and disquiet even among senior leaders suggested that Lee had gone too far. In hindsight, Operation Spectrum was a high-water mark of authoritarianism in Singapore, and the state would never be quite as domineering in its treatment of dissent again.

I met Tharman in 2016, when he was deputy prime minister, and we discussed the rise of populism in the West. It was four months after the UK had voted to leave the EU, and on the eve of the US election that would make Donald Trump president. Slim, balding, wearing glasses, he had a detached and slightly chilly air. The essential question, he told me, is whether a system can preserve trust in leadership and in governing institutions, unifying people while respecting their differences. Democracy, he thought, was better at maintaining trust and holding society together than other political systems.

It was an answer that suggested a more collaborative vision than the top-down approach that has dominated Singapore's history. Maintaining the state's legitimacy requires more restraint in the face of peaceful opponents.

In the two decades between Chia's arrest and the Operation Spectrum detentions, Singapore had become a steadily more repressive society. From the media to trade unions, opposition politicians to activist lawyers, any opposing voices were firmly subdued. A hedge of laws surrounds Singapore's citizens, choking off their right to freely act and speak out when it comes to politics. This includes laws inherited from the colonial administration, but legal tools to contain free expression have been enforced and strengthened after independence.

The Sedition Act, brought in by the British in 1948, makes it a crime to stir up discontent, or to produce feelings of ill-will between Singapore's racial groups. The Punishment for Vandalism Act, passed in 1966, introduced caning for graffiti, at a time when far-left protesters were daubing Vietnam War protests on walls and bus stands. The caning of Michael Fay, an eighteen-year-old American convicted of spray-painting cars, attracted international attention and a protest from the US government in 1994. But at the time the law was passed, the government made clear it was targeted at 'anti-national elements' and intended to humiliate adult protesters by caning them like naughty children.

Legislation introduced in 1989, soon after the Operation Spectrum detentions, meant official permission was needed where five or more people gathered for any form of demonstration or campaign meeting. In 2009, the Public Order Act tightened these restrictions, requiring a police permit for any activity relating to a cause, even if only one person was involved.

Hundreds of books are banned under internal security legislation in Singapore. The books include communist tracts by

Lenin, Stalin and Mao, and, more recently, books by scholars of Islam that are deemed a threat to religious harmony. Their printing, sale and possession are all forbidden. Other books, less overtly challenging to the social order, are not officially restricted but can be hard to find in Singapore bookshops; *No Man Is an Island*, a critical biography of Lee Kuan Yew by the Australian priest James Minchin, is one example of this category. Singaporeans speculate that booksellers occasionally censor themselves by declining to stock works the government may disapprove of.

From the 1970s on, the government exerted strict control over the press. The leading Chinese newspaper *Nanyang Siang Pau* – the name means 'South Seas Business Daily' – was targeted by the government after giving coverage to student grievances about the future of Chinese-language education in Singapore. In 1971, four executives of the newspaper were detained under the Internal Security Act, accused of stirring up ethnic chauvinism. Two English-language newspapers, facing criticism from the government that they were fronts for foreign influence, shut down the same year. Domestic newspapers must be licensed, while Singapore law allows the government to restrict the sale of foreign newspapers deemed to be interfering in the country's politics. Singapore's leaders have made vigorous use of libel laws, suing and winning damages or out-of-court settlements from foreign news-papers. In one famous case the *International Herald Tribune* apologised and paid out about US$114,000 for a column that referred to 'dynastic politics' in Asia and mentioned Singapore's prime minister and his father.

The *Straits Times*, founded in 1845, is the oldest newspaper in Singapore and the one with the greatest reach. It functions essentially as a mouthpiece of government. A civil servant was appointed its chairman in 1984, and former ministers or civil

servants have filled the position ever since. A leaked US diplomatic cable from 2009 noted: 'Reporters say they are eager to
produce more investigative and critical reporting, but they are
stifled by editors who have been groomed to tow [sic] the line.'

In the *Straits Times* newsroom, the list of topics deemed off-
limits are known as 'OB markers' – short for 'out of bounds'.
The OB markers, an evolving and shifting set of unwritten
rules, span a range of sensitive areas from race and religion
to security concerns. At times, writing about Singapore's
water supply has been deemed off-limits as a reminder of the
country's reliance on the goodwill of its neighbour, Malaysia.
Singapore's water scarcity has been recast as a triumph. As
ingenious methods of recycling waste water and harvesting
rainwater have reduced dependence on the imported supply, the
topic has emerged from the shadows to be cited as an example
of technological advancement and far-sighted leadership. The
fact that the island's ethnic Malays tend to have a higher birth
rate than the ethnic Chinese majority is another red line, as it
implies the country's demographic balance may tip in future.

I had a small taste of this myself, while writing for the
Financial Times in Singapore, after we published a story about
Singapore which used the word 'censorship'. The day the
story was published, I got a call from a government official
who pushed me to retract the word and then went through
each paragraph of the article, asking me to justify my asser-
tions. I argued my case, and the official backed down, but it
would have been far harder to do if my employer was a news
organisation tied to the government.

Scratch the surface and you will find the same diversity of
opinion that you do anywhere else, but in public Singaporeans
will often skirt around sensitive topics. The political lobotomy Chew talked about after his second bout of detention
seems to have taken hold of a whole country. Life becomes

much easier when you stop struggling to swim against the current. 'It was pointless to beat this thing,' Chew said – 'this thing' being Singapore's controlling state – 'because you would find no sympathy with the rest of society, who were happy to carry on.' Singapore has become a successful and progressive country, but it is hardly an open society. Instead, any questioning of the government will frequently produce a prickly reaction from ordinary citizens.

When I suggested at a party that Lee Kuan Yew was surprisingly intolerant of criticism for a man who had achieved so much, the fellow guest I was speaking to froze. Singaporeans will sometimes ascribe this public caution to being 'Asian', yet in Malaysia or India locals will cheerfully engage in political discussion, whether to praise their leaders or – more often – dismiss them as rogues. Food appears the safest topic of conversation, as the form of culture which is least politically loaded. 'Have you had your lunch?' a Singaporean colleague might ask to break the ice, in the way that a Brit will spark conversation by grumbling about the rain. Consumption, whether of food or luxury goods, is the safest way for people to express individualism.

The design of the city itself has ways of dominating your senses, and numbing your critical faculties. Outdoor advertising boards in the business district train the eye on desirable goods and services – clothes, sports cars, platinum credit cards – or endlessly looping digital tickers of share prices and corporate announcements, names and numbers blinking in neon red. Bland tunes are piped through malls and boom from outdoor speakers, muffling public speech. Through their air-conditioning systems, hotels and shopping centres waft perfumes of musk, bergamot and jasmine to cloak the everyday smells of sweat and cigarette smoke. The streets are not spaces where people linger. Office workers hurry from the transit station exits across crowded plazas to their desks in soaring glass-fronted towers. But despite this regimented, sanitised working environment, Singapore's rebellious streak has begun to reassert itself in recent years.

In December 1998, opposition politician Chee Soon Juan gave a speech without a permit in Raffles Place, the commercial centre of Singapore. Chee, a former psychology lecturer at the National University who has repeatedly criticised the lack of freedom afforded opposition activists in the country, returned to the same spot a week later, in January 1999, to deliver a second speech. Convicted of two offences of making an unlicensed political speech, he was fined. He refused to pay and served two short spells in prison – a first stint of seven days, followed by twelve days for the second offence.

The state's response was unexpected. Lee Kuan Yew discussed Chee's case with an American adviser, Joseph Nye, who suggested creating an outlet for dissent along the lines of Speakers' Corner in London. As a result, Hong Lim Park, a neat little patch of tree-shaded greenery on the fringes of the business district, was designated Singapore's 'Speakers' Corner' in 2001. Singapore citizens need to register with police if they wish to speak there, but they do not need to disclose the subject of their speech in advance or ask for permission. The only forbidden topics are race and religion.

Fittingly for a country that has embraced capitalism without liberal democracy, one of the first large-scale protests in Hong Lim Park came with the financial crisis of 2008, when thousands of ordinary Singaporeans lost their savings. Encouraged by their government to save and invest in financial products, Singaporeans had flocked to place their savings in 'minibonds' linked to the US investment bank Lehman Brothers. The 'mini-bonds' were a speculative investment that offered higher interest than ordinary fixed deposits rates, but were also riskier. The products were sold by local banks including DBS, Singapore's biggest, and acquired by thousands of ordinary savers, many of whom invested their life savings and lost everything when the US investment bank collapsed in 2008.

Investors wiped out by the bankruptcy began gathering for weekly protests at Speakers' Corner. Many of these people were working class and elderly, with poor English language skills and a shaky grasp of financial risk. As public anger focused on the local banks and brokerages which had marketed and sold the products, Singapore's financial regulator stepped in, urging the local banks to prioritise vulnerable clients. In an unusual example of effective people power, many of those who had bought the products went on to receive compensation, though the amounts paid out generally fell short of the original investments.

The past has become a battleground, too. Singapore, a tiny and land-hungry country, has regularly exhumed graves to make way for the living as it rapidly urbanised in the decades after independence. But when the government announced that a new eight-lane highway would cut across Bukit Brown cemetery, and some housing would later be built on the burial ground, it prompted a surge of protest.

The sprawling cemetery was home to some of Singapore's most illustrious ancestors, including tycoons such as Cheang Hong Lim, the nineteenth-century opium merchant after whom Hong Lim Park is named. Campaigners began to document the inscriptions and sculptures on the gravestones. There were no public rallies, but the Bukit Brown activists organised themselves online, and led walking tours to stimulate public awareness – turning a recreational activity into a form of protest.

While some of the graves were well-tended, parts of the burial ground were semi-wild, thronging with fern-covered albizia trees, making it a slice of rustic tranquillity near the heart of the modern city. If the financial crisis had shaken trust in Singapore's banks and financial regulators, the Bukit Brown protest prompted a moment of reflection about the country's relentless drive for urban redevelopment. The cemetery protesters claimed that preserving Bukit Brown would maintain a living connection with Singapore's past, instilling a sense of belonging as the present generation remembered the ancestors whose toil had built the country. As Eugene Tay, an environmental activist, argued: 'The biggest threat to Singapore is apathy, and when Singaporeans do not feel a sense of belonging and are not bothered with what goes on here, then Singapore is in trouble.'

Construction went ahead, and the first section of the highway opened in 2018, but this confrontation with the government raised questions about the nature of citizenship in the city state. Singaporeans had grown accustomed to being deferential subjects of a paternal state that always knew best. This consensus, which had always been fragile, was now being tested. If a grassroots movement could challenge the state over the building of a road, the door to broader change appeared to be ajar.

The fault line in Singapore society between a state determined to retain control and a restive citizenry has been most evident in demands for gay rights. While sex between men is a criminal offence in Singapore, the law is rarely enforced, and there are gay clubs and bars on the island. However, the government regularly insists that Singapore is a conservative society based on heterosexual families. Gay themes in the media are censored, while in vitro fertilisation is restricted to married couples.

A few years ago, a gay Singaporean man fought a lengthy

legal campaign to adopt his own child, fathered with a surrogate mother in the US. A district judge's rejection of the adoption was overturned on appeal in Singapore's high court, where judges decided that while government policy opposed the creation of same-sex families, the child's welfare was paramount. The response fractured along ideological lines. Liberal Singaporeans were supportive of a father's desire to raise the child as his own while conservatives were worried not only about permitting a gay adoption but the use of surrogacy, which is prohibited in Singapore.

Singapore's tolerance of its gay citizens allows it to show a cosmopolitan, liberal face to the world, vital to attract the foreign talent and investment its small and open economy needs. Its rhetoric of family values is directed at conservative households in the island's suburban heartlands, where homosexuality is increasingly viewed with anxiety and hostility by some prominent religious leaders. Every year, since 2009, advocates for gay rights have gathered in Hong Lim Park for the 'Pink Dot' rally. Dressed in shades ranging from cherry blossom to rose, gay men, lesbian women, their families and straight supporters sit on the grass holding placards and balloons. They listen to speeches which shy away from confrontation, placing gay rights in the context of tolerance and honesty.

Numbers attending Pink Dot have grown every year and it attracts an impressive roster of sponsors. From Barclays and JP Morgan to Goldman Sachs and Google, the names of its backers are an illustration of tiny Singapore's powerful appeal to corporate titans. Goldman Sachs even held an LGBT recruiting and networking dinner in Singapore in 2014. But Pink Dot's success was provoking increasingly vocal opposition from Christian and Muslim groups. Matters came to a head in 2016, when the government warned foreign sponsors to stop backing the Pink Dot rally and barred foreign citizens from attending future events. In 2017, for the first time, the event took place with barricades around Hong Lim Park.

Publicly, the corporations had little to say. Google was one of the few to speak up, issuing a brief statement declaring that the company were 'proud supporters of Pink Dot'. Privately, though, there was consternation. Regional executives feared open disagreement with the Singapore authorities, but there was anxiety among senior management about being seen to kowtow to a government taking a hardline view of homosexuality. The tension between Singapore's liberal surface and its controlling instincts had erupted into the open. When I discussed Pink Dot with a government adviser, he smiled, spread his hands to indicate distance, and said: 'We just want to keep the two sides apart.'

Transgender rights, which have become an intensely polarising issue in the West, are gaining increasing prominence in Singapore. The country was a pioneer of sex change surgery, with surgeons performing the first gender reassignment in 1971, a male-to-female surgery on a twenty-four-year-old. It is one of a handful of Asian countries which legally recognises transition. After surgery, a citizen can change the gender recorded on their identity card, though not their birth certificates.

Early in 2021, a transgender student claimed the Ministry of Education and her school had obstructed her from pursuing hormone replacement therapy. The eighteen-year-old claimed her school had threatened her with expulsion if physiological changes took place which left her unable to wear a boy's uniform. The ministry denied her claims, insisting it did not interfere in medical treatment, but the case prompted over 300 teachers and social workers to sign a petition signalling there was a wider problem in Singapore's schools. 'As education and social service professionals, we have witnessed and heard about similar situations faced by transgender students in Singapore schools,' they wrote. A small group of activists protested outside the Ministry of Education headquarters, one of them holding a placard reading: 'Fix Schools, Not Students.' Three of them, who declined to leave when police arrived, were arrested under the Public Order Act. The case prompted a debate in parliament, where minister for education Lawrence Wong noted that gender identity had become 'bitterly contested sources of division' in some countries. The government posed as an impartial mediator, attempting to calm the turbulence. 'We should not import these culture wars into Singapore, or allow issues of gender identity to divide our society,' Wong said.

The idea that strict rules are needed to prevent Singapore descending into chaos has been a persistent thread in the government's thinking. Lee Kuan Yew believed that, as a society, Singapore was too immature to be granted too much freedom. At independence, a narrow elite was responsible for holding together a new nation divided by race, religion and language. Over time, he argued, the educated elite would grow wider and a fragmented society would begin to gel. This is, of course, also a convenient argument for allowing a small elite to wield enormous power over their fellow citizens. On social affairs, while ministers may personally have liberal views, Singapore's rulers have always leant towards conservatism, both as a binding force and because it is believed to sway 'heartland' voters. Material comfort in exchange for circumscribed politics is a deal that most Singaporeans have been willing to tolerate. The country's success since independence appears to vindicate the idea that a sufficiently talented and far-sighted leadership can govern without the checks and balances that correct for mistakes in other societies.

There is the occasional blind spot. For years, there was little public discussion of the role that poorly paid migrant labour played in Singapore society. An OB marker kept most discussion of the topic out of the press. Then, when Covid-19 struck, migrant dormitories proved to be a weak link in the country's defences.

Movements for social change remain strictly policed in Singapore, though the tools the government uses are less draconian than in the past. Since 1987, detention without trial has not been used against a political campaigner or social activist, but public order legislation, libel suits and Singapore's 'fake news' law have all been used to shut down speech that, in most democracies, would be regarded as a normal part of a lively political culture. When the performance artist Seelan Palay commemorated Chia Thye Poh with a work of performance art in front of the parliament building in 2018, he was arrested under the Public Order Act, and sentenced to two weeks in prison after refusing to pay a fine of S$2500. Jolovan Wham, a human rights campaigner, was convicted under the same legislation for hosting an event in which a Hong Kong activist spoke on a video call. Wham served a ten-day prison sentence in 2020. While the consequences are less severe than in the past, chastising a few individuals still has a cautionary effect on Singapore's population. There is little chance of a Hong Kong-style street protest movement gathering force in Singapore.

Restrictions on liberty, easier to justify in earlier decades when Singapore faced hostile neighbours and a world of superpower confrontation, have become increasingly difficult to defend. After significant electoral gains by the opposition in recent elections, the ruling party has promised to listen more and dictate less. The more calibrated repression of recent years suggests that Singapore is opening a safety valve.

The state's actions have become less arbitrary and its punishments less extreme. An activist who invites a Hong Kong protest leader to speak is conscious that he is taking a calculated risk. And while ten days in jail is a disproportionate punishment for hosting a debate, it is far less spirit-crushing than the prospect of a lifetime in detention without being allowed to defend yourself in court.

Singapore is not China. Its democracy may be hemmed in, but it does hold meaningful elections. And in recent years, a substantial political opposition has emerged. The PAP has won every election in Singapore since 1959. In 2020, it took eighty-three of the ninety-three seats in parliament. But the Workers' Party, which criticises the PAP from the left, won ten seats in that year's election, the biggest gain ever made by an opposition party. The burst of activism in recent years has rolled back the boundaries, enabling citizens to openly challenge and question the government. As the penalties for speaking out have become less severe, that trend can be expected to continue. Teo Soh Lung wrote a memoir soon after she emerged from prison, but could not bring herself to read the manuscript. She kept away from politics, focused on her law practice and on building up savings wiped out by legal fees while in detention. But in 2011 she decided to publish her book, *Beyond the Blue Gate*, believing her low profile was doing a disservice to a younger generation. 'We didn't want to repeat the mistakes of the previous set of detainees who didn't tell us what happened,' she said.

When I spoke to Chew, I was struck by the fact that he had been able to resume a successful professional life after detention, and that he appeared to bear no rancour. Once he had bowed to the system by making a confession, the path to reconciliation was open.

Singapore is a small place. After he was released from

detention, Chew bumped into his case officer in the super-market. 'We were very friendly with each other. I almost held a genuine affection for him. He was doing his job. For many years I had explained to my friends when I got out of detention, now that I'm free, I'm not going to make the mistake of being detained mentally.' Chew pointed at his head as he said this. 'It's over, I told myself, if you are going to be really upset about it, obsess about it, you'll still be in prison.'

7

Fighting Disease:
From TB to Covid-19

How the need to control infection
reshaped the city

When the Covid-19 outbreak began to sweep through Asia in the early months of 2020, Singapore appeared to offer the role model of a swift and efficient response. Even as Europe went into lockdown, commuters in Singapore travelled to work on crowded subways, shopping malls and offices stayed open, and few people wore masks. Posters of cartoon characters the 'soaper 5' went up in schools, instructing children to scrub their hands, but the city had a feel of normality, despite the eerie headlines from around the world.

Singapore's earlier brush with mortality during Sars, the virus that tore through East Asia in 2003, meant it was better prepared to cope with the new disease. After Sars, the government stockpiled masks and protective equipment, built a new infectious diseases hospital, and prepared hundreds of general practice clinics across the island to screen patients with flu-like symptoms. The GP clinics had prepared separate isolation rooms, reached through a back door, where doctors wearing protective gear could identify whether specialist hospital treatment was needed. Officials implemented exhaustive efforts to trace the contacts of Covid-19 patients, using skills honed during the Sars outbreak. Their methods combined interviews with patients, trawling through footage from the island's extensive network of CCTV cameras and wearing out shoe leather with house-to-house enquiries.

'Patient 64' in Singapore was a fifty-year-old taxi driver, and police needed to track down one of his passengers with only three clues: the make of the taxi that dropped the man off, the general location of the drop-off and the fact that the passenger was wearing a white top and black trousers. The taxi passenger was only identified after visits to five housing blocks in the neighbourhood and a sift through three hours of CCTV footage followed by knocking on doors.

The government's tone was stern and admonitory, reminding the public of the stiff penalties for breaching quarantine, from fines to prison sentences and in at least one case, stripping a citizen of his passport. But for many, it was comforting to be folded in the embrace of a competent state. Singapore citizens returning from study abroad were quarantined in luxury hotels, which had been vacated as tourism evaporated. They grouched a little at their government's strictness, but quietly felt relief at a system where the state footed the bill for quarantine at hotels with sea views and room service. 'The check-in was smooth and we were shown to our rooms, which were big with double beds,' recalled Yongchang Chin, a master's student at Oxford who returned home to be quarantined at the Rasa Sentosa. 'The first thing we were served was supper from the hotel, and that was quite nice. As we were putting in our key cards, my next door neighbour and

I looked at each other and were like, "Not bad, ah?" "Yeah, quite good." And we weren't allowed to leave our rooms at all after that.'

Chin's room had a balcony, so he could step out and get fresh air, no matter how hot and humid it was. One night, a violinist came out on her balcony to duet with a flute player, serenading fellow inmates with a Taiwanese pop tune. Another night the hotel put on a fire dancer to entertain their involuntary guests, and a fitness instructor came to the poolside to lead people on their balconies through exercise routines. 'Another friend of mine came back to an equally swanky hotel, with better food than me, but his was some kind of room where the windows barely opened,' Chin said. 'So he had no fresh air, nothing, and could only sit and look at the outside world.' Ministers acknowledged the need for shared sacrifice, forgoing their own salaries for a month – later extended to three months – in a show of solidarity with struggling workers. Early on, the government said it would foot hospital bills for Singapore residents who contracted Covid-19.

In the early days of the outbreak, Singapore kept the disease under control while avoiding the disruption of school and office closures. Along with Taiwan and Hong Kong, it showed that early intervention, careful tracking and rigorous quarantine of suspected cases could keep a lid on the disease. Researchers in Singapore were among the first in the world to develop an antibody test, which can identify whether a person has had Covid-19 even after they have recovered. This was a breakthrough, providing a valuable tool to trace the path of the disease. The response combined Singapore's hallmarks: political foresight, bureaucratic efficiency, and the application of science. Kishore Mahbubani, a Singaporean academic and former diplomat, declared confidently in *The*

Economist that the crisis had shown up the difference between the quality of governance in Asia and the incompetence of the West.

But there was a vulnerability in the system, and the virus found it. Singapore's migrant workers, many of them men who came from Bangladesh and India to labour on construction sites and in shipyards, became the source of a new wave of infection which surged across the island.

Between the Sars crisis in 2003 and the outbreak of Covid-19, Singapore banned the subletting of private housing to most foreign labourers, and companies began building dormitories to house them. The move to establish purpose-built housing complexes accelerated after a riot in Little India in 2013, when the death of an Indian construction worker, Sakthivel Kumaravelu, prompted a night of rioting. Hundreds of foreign workers clashed with police and set cars on fire after Kumaravelu, a thirty-three-year-old from Chennai in south India, was knocked down and killed by a bus.

The new dormitories included some gleaming facilities, like the Tuas View complex, which has a cinema screen and a cricket pitch. But it also brings nearly 17,000 workers together under one roof. Elsewhere in the city, more squalid accommodation sprang up attached to factories or above shops, with little space and workers piling into bunk beds. In the twenty-first century, Singapore had reinvented the slum. One of the earliest Covid-19 cases in Singapore was 'Patient 42', a Bangladeshi construction worker called Raju Sarker. After days of suffering from exhaustion, a headache and chills, Raju was admitted to hospital in February and treated in an intensive care unit, unable to breathe without the assistance of a ventilator. The complex where Raju stayed was out on the east coast, five high-rise blocks with amenities including a beer garden and reading room. This block became the centre of a new cluster of infection, as did a shopping centre that he visited before he was admitted to hospital.

By late April one of the world's smallest nations had 13,000 cases, the highest tally of infections in Asia after China and India. At one point that month a single dormitory, the S11 complex – a row of rectangular blocks painted in vibrant colours on Singapore's remote northeast coast – harboured 2000 of the country's 8000 cases. Singapore's spike in cases was a reminder that public health and inequality are woven together. Diseases do not discriminate, and the resurgence of the virus among migrant workers swiftly affected the whole city. By the end of April, Singapore had gone into a partial lockdown, shutting schools and sending workers home. The same month, the government U-turned on the wearing of masks, which it had previously discouraged except for those who were ill. A state famed for its efficiency now seemed to have been wrong-footed.

Unlike Sars, Covid-19 can infect people without them displaying symptoms. Tracing the contacts of people linked to confirmed cases is therefore a less effective weapon against Covid-19 than it is against Sars. It was not until April that Singapore indicated it was shifting to testing at scale, a tool that has been critical for countries that brought the pandemic under control.

Singaporeans wrestled with the fact that the pandemic had revealed an uncomfortable truth about their society, which relied on the labour of a vast migrant workforce. In a nation of 5.7 million, there are around 1.4 million foreign workers. Some, such as the Indian bankers and British IT workers in the city centre, provide professional expertise, but many more provide low-skilled labour, including thousands of maids from Indonesia, the Philippines and other Asian countries who sweep floors and soothe babies in family homes across the island. Many of the men who provide the muscle to build Singapore's malls and office towers are South Asian. On Sundays, the workers' usual day off, they gather for impromptu games of cricket on patches of open land and go out to eat, drink and shop in Little India. Around 300,000 foreign workers in Singapore live in the giant dormitories dotted around remote parts of the island, often twenty to a room, sharing communal cooking facilities and washrooms. 'We owe the foreign workers an apology for the atrocious condition of their dormitories,' Tommy Koh, a former Singapore diplomat, acknowledged in the *Straits Times* as cases among migrant workers soared.

In May ministers announced the mass testing of all foreign workers staying in dormitories. A month later, Singapore announced plans to build new dormitories to higher standards, with sufficient space between accommodation blocks to ensure ventilation. Private squalor had magnified a public crisis.

Singapore's authorities might have seen this coming, as it was foreshadowed in the earliest years of the island's colonial history. When a British doctor, William Simpson, visited the shophouses of Singapore's Chinatown in the early twentieth century, he peered into a row of pitch-dark cubicles that lined the passageway behind a barber's shop and found men living tightly packed together. In one of the cubicles, he found a trader with his goods piled up around him, from soap and towels to boots, pipes and whistles. In a second he found two food hawkers, sleeping on bunk beds, with their supplies of rice, salt and noodles. In a third cubbyhole, windowless like all the rest, he found a man who was suffering from a cough and spitting onto the floor. Simpson, who had served for twelve years as medical officer in British-ruled Calcutta, believed that every part of society was interconnected, and that public health could only be improved by tackling broader environmental and social challenges, from the quality of air to food and drink.

The death rate from disease in colonial Singapore was exceptionally high. The figures were even more appalling when the British took into account the fact that the population was mostly male and youthful. There were few babies and few old people, while the young men disembarking from Chinese junks were physically fit, ready for the exhausting work of hoeing a pepper plantation or hauling a rickshaw. Yet in 1901, out of a population of around 200,000, more than 9000 people died of disease. Malaria was the chief killer, but tuberculosis and beriberi – an easily preventable disease caused by vitamin B deficiency – followed close behind. Infant mortality was shockingly high among Singapore's Asian population, Simpson noted, with around one in three babies dying before they were a year old. 'In all the cubicles, there is an immense quantity of rubbish and filth; a night visit discovered the place to be overrun by cockroaches and other vermin,' Simpson wrote in his report to Singapore's governor.

As always in Singapore, water was a scarce commodity so it was hard to keep clean, and there was no sewage system for the city. Instead, human waste, known euphemistically as 'night soil', was collected in buckets and used to fertilise vegetable gardens. The system of night soil collection was only phased out in 1987.

Neither British officials nor the wealthy merchants of all races suffered the cramped conditions of the men in Chinatown, but disease is a leveller, and the rich were not immune from outbreaks of illness that spread from workers forced into unsanitary conditions. The colonial government and its elected successors made a concerted effort to combat tuberculosis, creating a national register of cases, conducting chest X-rays of the population en masse to discover new cases, and building new housing to allow Singapore's poorest people to escape the overcrowded shophouses. The rate of TB fell dramatically, though the disease has never quite been eliminated.

Singapore's war on disease was fought, in part, by once again expanding the intrusive power of the state and shifting social norms. The Infectious Diseases Act, which came into force in 1977 and was strengthened for the Sars outbreak, gives the government powers to order mandatory examinations of anyone suspected to be a carrier of an infectious disease, as well as the power to isolate them. Violators of quarantine orders face up to six months in prison and fines of up to S$10,000, or both. During the Covid-19 outbreak, a cargo plane pilot who left his hotel room for three hours to buy masks and a thermometer was sentenced to four weeks in prison.

When cleaning Singapore's streets became a national priority, soon after independence, spitting in public – a habit associated with the spread of TB and other diseases – was made illegal. Public health was one motivation for the crackdown, but so was Singapore's reputation. Officials believed that spitting on the street tarnished the country's character and its claim to be modern and civilised.

Beginning in the 1970s, the roadside food hawkers that are a familiar sight across Asia were moved from pavements to purpose-built hawker centres. The hawkers did not always go willingly, and health inspectors sometimes found themselves under attack from determined men who wielded meat cleavers for a living. The centres have nevertheless become a distinguishing feature of Singapore, with small and smoky

stalls selling traditional delicacies such as satay and stir-fried
rice noodles, cooked with theatrical flair in a hissing wok. The
stalls are arranged around a courtyard, sometimes open to the
elements, where diners sit at plastic chairs eating their meals
from laminated tables that are easy to wipe down between
sittings. Like the pub in Britain it has become a touchstone of
ordinary life; Singapore's politicians frequently pose for press
photographs at hawker centre tables. But the original purpose
of moving hawkers off the streets was to curb typhoid and
cholera, diseases which spread when people consume food that
has been prepared with contaminated water.

For many observers, Singapore's drive for cleanliness can
seem like a collection of strange obsessions. Dropping litter
or hawking a throatful of phlegm into the street might be
unsightly, but they seem to have little to do with modernising Singapore. Taken together, however, this battery of
small interventions suggest a 'broken windows' approach to
development, fixing small but highly visible problems alongside a deeper transformation of state, economy and society.
Singapore's post-independence rulers built a health system
that is now among the very best in the world. Average life
expectancy has risen from sixty-six years in 1960 to eighty-
three years now, making its people some of the longest-lived
on the planet. Singapore now has a lower infant mortality
rate than Britain. The government took the lead in healthcare, building new hospitals as well as clinics that provided
day-to-day care in the community. But the system emphasised personal responsibility, making patients contribute
towards the cost of their treatment.

The country's health system is a political hybrid. The government is the largest provider of services – public hospitals
care for around three-quarters of hospital admissions – but
citizens contribute through the compulsory 'Medisave'

scheme, which requires them to divert up to 10.5 per cent of their pay into a health savings account. Requiring citizens to shoulder some of their own healthcare bills is intended to encourage self-reliance, as well as discouraging excessive use of healthcare services and prescription drugs. Patients who get into financial difficulties can apply for support from a government endowment fund which was set up as a safety net for the neediest citizens. Even in public hospitals, there are tiered charges for patients, who can pay more to have their own private room. Singapore's private hospitals, where suites come with antechambers for bodyguards, have treated Burmese generals and Zimbabwe's strongman Robert Mugabe.

Lockdown brought scenes familiar from other cities, as Singapore became a ghost town, with hawker centres deserted and expressways empty of traffic. Supermarkets sold out of flour as people went on a baking binge and parks filled up with people desperate for a blast of fresh air.

But the Covid-19 outbreak also featured a distinctively Singaporean approach to crisis, ushering in a deeper application of technology to track and monitor citizens, justified by the need to fight a mortal threat. Citizens were encouraged to snitch on neighbours who flouted rules with an online form that allowed them to upload pictures. A robotic dog – a remote-controlled machine named Spot that trotted about on four kinked legs – was sent out to enforce social distancing in one of Singapore's parks. Spot played a pre-recorded message in a female, Singapore-accented voice, urging walkers and runners to 'stay at least one metre apart'. Video of Spot was shared around the world, and for some foreign observers it was taken as a herald of a dark future in which bossy robots hector humans. In Singapore, where restaurants have used robots to serve drinks or gather dirty dishes, the machine was mostly regarded as a curiosity.

For the thousands of people made subject to stay-home notices during the pandemic, their phones became a form of electronic tagging. The government sent text messages to people required to stay at home; clicking on a link in the message used their phones' GPS to confirm their location. Officials checked in with random phone calls, sometimes asking people to send a picture of their surroundings. But the Singapore government's introduction of a mobile contact-tracing app, TraceTogether, prompted an unexpected rebellion. The app was launched in late March 2020, using Bluetooth signals to exchange information with other app users to create a digital record of a citizen's movements. Singapore was one of the first countries in the world to deploy app technology to fight the pandemic. 'We've designed it so that we collect very little personal information,' explained Jason Bay, the engineer who led the project, adding that the only time the information would leave a citizen's phone was when a contact tracer asked for it to be uploaded.

This reassurance was not enough. By early June, more than two months after the app was launched, just 1.8 million had voluntarily downloaded it, less than a third of the population. Vivian Balakrishnan, the minister in charge of the government's 'Smart Nation' technology drive, had suggested that a rate of above 75 per cent would be ideal.

One of the reasons for this reluctance is that the iOS version of the contact-tracing app drains iPhone batteries fast, but the low rate of public compliance also highlighted a lack of trust. There was no legal check on official use of the data, as the Singapore government is not bound by the country's data protection act. When, in response, officials expanded the digital tracing programme, bringing in a wearable token – like the app, the tokens worked by exchanging Bluetooth signals – Singaporeans responded with anger. By December 2020, more than 50,000 people had signed a petition in protest. Wilson Low, a mountain bike instructor who launched the petition, revealed the mistrust that lay behind it. 'The government looks to the Covid-19 pandemic as the perfect excuse to realise what it has always envisioned for us – this country's populace: to surveil us with impunity, to track us without any technological inhibitions, and maintain a form of movement monitoring on each of us at all times and places,' he wrote.

Public trust was further damaged in early 2021, when it emerged that – despite the authorities' assurances that data would only be used for contact tracing – it was available to the police under the Criminal Procedure Code, which allows Singapore police to obtain all data within the country's jurisdiction to investigate a crime. Balakrishnan apologised in parliament, saying he regretted 'the consternation and anxiety caused'. The minister introduced a bill which would restrict police use of health data to the investigation of seven serious crimes, including murder and terrorism.

Around the world, the Covid-19 crisis has confronted us with stark choices that raise questions about our values, and the relationship between individuals and the state. Do we accept legal restrictions to safeguard our health or rely on voluntary adherence to rules? How much economic pain are we prepared to accept as the cost of saving lives? In Singapore, the crisis signalled a reset of the relationship between government and citizens. Singaporeans were grateful for their state's efficiency, but openly critical of themselves and their rulers over their neglect of migrants. Ordinary people resisted the attempt to gather intimate data, even in the face of a national crisis.

The state took a softer line with its people than usual. The TraceTogether app was not made mandatory until the end of December 2020, and even then it was only for entry to public venues such as restaurants and offices. Low appears to have suffered no adverse consequences for the launch of his petition.

A healthy society can be created from the top down, through governments providing services and cajoling citizens to eat their greens and dispose of used tissues sensibly. But, as the pandemic has illustrated, public health is also an exercise in community-building, relying on citizens taking responsibility for themselves and others. From campaigns to ban smoking or to urge governments to address the HIV/Aids crisis, reforms to public health around the world have frequently been driven from below. But challenges to the status quo in Singapore have so often come with stiff penalties that most people are reluctant to make themselves a target. In a society where it is risky to take the initiative, people will often do what they are told, but no more. And when citizens express opposition, it is frequently done passively.

Covid-19 was different. The crisis brought an outpouring of communal solidarity. Community groups and non-profit organisations raised funds for migrant workers and supported isolated elderly citizens, creating live-stream events on social media with cooking tips and games. The definition of who belonged in Singapore was shifting. Migrant workers, held at arm's length for years, had suddenly become visible. In a video greeting for the Tamil New Year in April, a minister thanked foreign workers 'for all your hard work in Singapore'. The government pledged to pay their healthcare bills, while a not-for-profit group distributed care packs of masks, soap and hand sanitiser in workers' dormitories. (This was a limited advance: there was also a tightening of controls on migrant labourers, who were required by their employers to install a new app that assigned a colour code to indicate their health status, with 'green' indicating men permitted to go out to work while those flagged 'red' could not.)

Singapore lifted its Covid-19 lockdown at the start of June 2020, and by now it seemed the country had recovered its poise. People returned to restaurants and shops, where squares of duct tape on the floor neatly marked out where they should stand. Singapore's disaster planning had worked, strengthened by the experience of Sars. 'The institutional memory meant that we knew how to do contact tracing. We knew how operational workflows had to be modified,' said Jeremy Lim, an associate professor at Singapore's Saw Swee Hock School of Public Health. 'We knew about making sure hospitals had only a few entry points. How do you transfer a patient from the seventh floor to the basement for an MRI scan without bumping into anyone?'

The country was fortunate too. While its migrant workers had a high infection rate, most were young and otherwise healthy, and they suffered only from mild symptoms of the disease. Raju Sarker, Singapore's Patient 42, made a full recovery from his illness and walked out of hospital in June, quietly thanking health workers for their care.

Governments in the West fumbled their response, and death rates soared, while the crisis accentuated existing inequalities; ethnic minorities in the UK suffered dispro-portionately. In Italy, 3 per cent of those who contracted the illness died. In China, this figure was 5 per cent. In Singapore, nearly everyone who fell ill survived. Despite having more than 61,000 cases by May 2021, there had been just thirty-one deaths. The organisers of the World

Economic Forum – the annual gathering of corporate and political leaders usually held in Davos – announced the event would be moving from Switzerland to Singapore in 2021, because of the enduring risk of coronavirus in Europe. Economic power was already tilting in Asia's direction, and this decision appeared to signal a further shift in the global balance, from West to East.

While Singapore was one of the fastest countries in Asia to roll out vaccination, it remained vulnerable to the emergence of new Covid-19 variants. A surge in cases prompted the reimposition of strict social distancing measures in May 2021, and the WEF cancelled plans to hold its annual meeting in the city-state, one of the reversals we had all become accustomed to as the world stopped and started like a glitchy computer.

Nonetheless, in the shadow of a global crisis, the Lion City felt like a haven. A Singapore hotelier I spoke to likened the psychic impact of this to the Second World War, when people in Asia grasped that European armies were not invincible.

One way to read this outcome is to conclude that societies which value community over the individual are better placed to cope with an emergency. But this ignores the diversity of the states that pulled through best. From authoritarian states like China to democracies like Korea and Taiwan, and ones with hybrid political models like Singapore and Hong Kong, a clutch of radically different east Asian countries all appeared to be in better shape than the West. The result pointed to a level of official competence that cut across systems. It didn't seem to be anything as grand as a shared ideology that had saved lives; instead it was a simple ability to implement effective measures to contain the disease.

8

'No one owes Singapore a living'

Schools, universities and start-ups

The school is a rectangle of hulking concrete, with the children assembled in a central courtyard. The first lesson is one of vulnerability, and of defiant patriotism, drummed into the pupils through giant banners. 'No one owes Singapore a living,' reads one of the hoardings. 'We must ourselves defend Singapore,' declares another. Economic utility and nation-building are the guiding principles of the system. 'What is required is a rugged, resolute, highly trained, highly disciplined community,' Lee Kuan Yew declared in Singapore's early years, as schools focused on producing workers for factories and making a polyglot nation conversant in English.

Alongside its political leadership, education has been the single biggest factor in Singapore's success. In its classrooms, the children of manual labourers have become the skilled workers of a modern economy. The speed of this transition, in the space of a generation, is remarkable enough. But Singapore has achieved something greater. The tiny country's school system regularly earns a spot near the top of global league tables for their proficiency in maths, science and literacy. Singapore's schools tell a revealing story about the country, but they also offer an example that educators around the world, from the UK to Chile, have been eager to copy.

The transformation is sometimes ascribed to Confucian values or disciplinarian parenting, but the secret is simpler and the change happened relatively recently. When Singapore achieved independence, education had been the preserve of the affluent. A majority of its workforce were low-skilled labourers on docks or plantations, and two-fifths of the population in 1965 were illiterate. The city state began developing its distinctive approach to maths in the 1980s, when a group of researchers led by maths teacher Kho Tek Hong were given the task of strengthening children's basic numeracy skills by the country's Ministry of Education. Kho and his colleagues visited other countries including Canada, Japan and Israel as well as absorbing the latest theories in educational psychology.

Singapore maths in the 1970s was 'mechanical', Kho recalled, with students learning by memorising. The team's work was influenced by Jerome Bruner, the American psychologist who argued that people learn in three stages – first by using real objects, next through pictures and then through symbols. This approach became embedded in the Singapore approach to basic maths, which begins with concrete representations like folding pieces of paper to demonstrate fractions. Children in Singapore frequently make use of the 'bar modelling' technique, which encourages them to model verbal problems like 'Sam has twice as much money as Sally'. Drawing these problems out as sets of bars – Sam has six bars to Sally's three – helps the children see the mathematical structure behind the words.

The maths curriculum in Singapore is also simpler than its Western counterparts, covering fewer topics with greater depth. Andreas Schleicher, head of a programme which measures school performance globally for the OECD, a group of wealthy countries, told me: 'Mathematics in Singapore is not about knowing everything. It's about thinking like a mathematician.'

At the heart of Singapore's education system is an inspiring idea. Unlike many of its counterparts in the West, the system is built on the belief that every child is capable of learning, depending on how a concept is presented to them and the effort they put in. Singapore emphasises whole-class teaching, rather than letting the teacher explain the concept first and then breaking the children up into groups for work. At Admiralty Secondary School, near the northern tip of the island, I watch a maths class in which the teacher gets children up out of their seats to stand at the whiteboard and solve algebraic equations in front of the class. The atmosphere is one of happy competition. Throughout the day, the children are absorbed in their lessons, but they never come across as drones. Instead, they are animated and occasionally cheeky. As one boy makes a hash of solving an equation on the whiteboard, then goes back to correct it, a classmate shouts out cheerfully: 'Still wrong!'

The school's principal Toh Thiam Chye tells me the school steers its pupils towards science, framing the decision in economic terms. Singapore has a 'manpower constraint', he notes. Robotics is a cross-curricular theme at Admiralty, bringing together design, science and technology. In the science class I watch, the children are being taught programming with a circuit board hooked up to an LED. They learn how to vary the lines of code to change the colours of the LED. The year before my visit, the students built a robotic arm. This year's project is to build a miniature driverless car, essentially a small robot with wheels. The projects require the students to think about designing solutions to a real-world problem, as well as learning how to integrate coding and electronics. 'Ambitious goals – broken into small steps,' says the principal as he observes the class. When I discuss this bias in favour of science with a spokeswoman for the Ministry of Education, she says that children are encouraged to pursue their strengths, and while Admiralty emphasises science, other schools lean towards the humanities. (This is fair: other schools offer pupils a greater emphasis on arts subjects such as drama or vocational skills such as journalism.)

Primary education in Singapore begins at six, though children will typically attend a pre-school from the age of three. Pupils transfer to secondary schools aged twelve. The medium of instruction in most mainstream state-run schools is English, but children from each ethnic community are also expected to learn Malay, Tamil or Chinese, according to their heritage, while children of mixed parentage can apply to study one of these Asian languages.

Singapore inherited a system divided between English-language schools and schools that taught in an Asian language, but non-English schools were phased out in the 1980s. This partly reflected parental choice, as families believed their children's career chances would be improved by learning English. But it also reflects the political fault line that runs through language in Singapore, between the English-educated elite like Lee and his circle and the radicalism of students who attended the country's Chinese-language schools. Lim Chin Siong, the left-wing politician detained in 1963, was an alumnus of the most famous of these schools, the Chinese High School.

*

The National University of Singapore, usually referred to by the initials NUS, is one of two public universities on the island and among the highest rated universities in Asia. Both NUS and the other major university, Nanyang Technological University, teach in English – the latter has a sharper focus on science and technology, as its name implies, and grew out of an institution founded to train engineers, established in 1981. The NUS is the more venerable of the two, tracing its ancestry to Singapore's first medical school, the King Edward VII College of Medicine, founded in 1905.

Singapore was the home of the only Chinese-language university in Southeast Asia, Nanyang University. Known as 'Nantah' in Chinese, this was founded in 1955 by the businessman and philanthropist Tan Lark Sye, whose fortune was made in rubber exports. Nantah was a community endeavour. Donations came in from across the Chinese communities in Singapore and Malaya to support the new venture, from tycoons and ordinary workers alike. The Hokkien Huay Kuan – the clan association for Hokkien speakers – provided a vast tract of land for the campus while tuk-tuk drivers and cabaret dancers gave what they could afford. Like the Chinese-language high schools, Nantah nurtured political activism. Dozens of Nantah students were arrested and around a hundred were expelled from their degree courses for suspected involvement in communist politics. The university was shut down in 1980. Officially, it was merged with NUS, but it effectively ceased to exist. Its extensive grounds were used to set up the precursor of Nanyang Technological University.

Though the political passions of the 1960s had ebbed by the time the schools were phased out and the university was shut, there was an enduring legacy of mistrust between older Singaporeans educated in English and those schooled in Chinese. The government defended the closures as simple pragmatism in a society where families preferred an English education. Their opponents suspected an act of score-settling. Many alumni of the university were furious.

Around two dozen of Singapore's Chinese-language schools became bilingual state schools, under a scheme known as the Special Assistance Plan. The survival of these schools was intended to ensure that a section of the population retained a high level of ability in the Chinese language and an understanding of Chinese culture. The Chinese High School, now known as the Hwa Chong Institution, was one of the schools absorbed into the scheme. Hwa Chong occupies a large campus in the leafy Bukit Timah neighbourhood, with an ornate Chinese gateway leading to a neo-classical school building with a clocktower. As China's economic strength has waxed, mastering the language has opened career opportunities too, boosting the fortunes of the bilingual schools. Hwa Chong is now one of the most sought-after schools in the country.

The government wanted Singapore's working language to be English, the language of commerce from Hong Kong to Houston. But ministers were anxious about losing touch with their Asian roots entirely, believing they needed a counterweight to Western cultural influence. This anxiety helped inspire the state-led push to encourage Chinese Singaporeans to coalesce around a single version of Chinese. Mandarin, China's official language, was adopted in 1979 to replace the southern Chinese dialects spoken among Singapore's Chinese: Hokkien, Teochew, Cantonese and Hakka. Though known as dialects, these are cousins in the Chinese language family, diverging from each other like French from Italian. A Cantonese speaker will struggle to understand Mandarin without some formal instruction.

In the twentieth century, Mandarin was established as the most prestigious of these languages, the version of Chinese used in formal school and university instruction, but dialect was the everyday language of Chinese Singaporeans in homes, shops and workplaces. The Speak Mandarin campaign launched in 1979 restricted the use of dialect in television and radio shows, while civil servants were asked to refrain from speaking dialect in the office, and parents were discouraged from giving their children dialect names. It was effective, with dialect-speaking households dropping from 76 per cent of the population in 1980 to 48 per cent in 1990.

Singapore has also become one of the most Anglophone societies in Asia, with around a third of the population mainly speaking English at home. But many Singaporeans favour a hybrid version of the colonial tongue, known as Singlish, combining Chinese syntax with a blend of English, Malay and Chinese vocabulary. A familiar Singlish question would be: 'Makan already?' – 'have you had lunch already?', borrowing the Malay word for food, 'makan', and slotting it into a Chinese word order, with the topic of the sentence coming first. The government has sought, less successfully, to suppress this too, with a 'Speak Good English' movement launched in 2000 to encourage Singaporeans to be grammatically correct.

The use of dialects has been eroded, partly because younger people have grown up learning Mandarin in school and partly because Singaporeans have grasped the value of speaking standard Chinese for business. But people have clung to the use of Singlish as an expression of their identity. From attempting to stamp it out, ministers have reconciled themselves to letting Singlish live alongside formal English, acknowledging through gritted teeth that the local patois is 'fun'. Alongside Singlish, everyday speech comes peppered with acronyms, the sign of a society which is both in a hurry and has a high level of assumed knowledge. Everyone knows that public housing is an 'HDB', that the highway spanning the island is not the Pan-island Expressway but the 'PIE', and that Lee Kuan Yew is invariably referred to as LKY. This last has a touch of blasphemous avoidance about it, as if saying the patriarch's name in full may summon his ghost.

For years, the country's schools have emphasised high academic achievement. Passing exams is the gateway to the most prestigious universities and the best-paid jobs, in a society where there are few alternative templates for a successful life. The 'iron rice bowl', a secure and well-paid post in the public sector or with a Singapore-based multinational, remains the goal for many.

The idea that Singapore is a meritocracy is deeply ingrained. Every year, Singapore students with outstanding academic results compete for government scholarships that pay their university fees in full, often to study overseas at Oxford, Cambridge or an Ivy League university. On their return, these high-flying scholars join the administration or the armed forces and the most suitable candidates are drafted into jobs as cabinet ministers. Speaking at a public debate to mark the fiftieth anniversary of Singapore's separation from Malaysia, prime minister Lee Hsien Loong even referred to a 'natural aristocracy' without which society would suffer.

The romantic ideal of Singapore meritocracy is that the poorest boys and girls can make their way into the elite through spectacular exam performance, and this was true in Singapore's early years. But after a generation in which the country's middle class has grown, these advantages are most likely to accrue to the children of already wealthy families. In recent years, Singaporeans have become increasingly aware of the barriers between them, and how seldom different worlds meet, even on such a small island. Singaporean citizens rarely encounter migrant workers, with the exception of the maids who labour in their homes. Few families who live in public housing have friends who live in grander privately owned homes.

A handful of elite schools dominate the top echelons of Singapore society. The Raffles Institution, named after its founder Sir Stamford Raffles, tends to produce top politicians. Set on a sprawling campus in central Singapore, Raffles is the alma mater of Lee Kuan Yew and his successor as prime minister, Goh Chok Tong. Its whitewashed walls, sharply inclined terracotta roofs, grassy quadrangles and lavish facilities suggest a tropical variant of an English public school.

The Anglo-Chinese School, established in 1886 by the Methodist church, grooms the sons of the business elite. Both are boys' schools. 'RI boys run the country,' goes the saying. 'ACS boys own it.' Raffles and ACS are among a handful of independent schools in Singapore, which are allowed autonomy but receive some state funding. The schools forge lifelong bonds. 'They do something right with regard to their alumni spirit,' said Wee Teng Wen, a Singapore businessman and ACS alumnus. 'I go to some weddings, there's always a corner that would erupt with the School Song. I roll my eyes, I'm sure the wives roll their eyes, but it's impressive that an institution is able to create that degree of loyalty.'

Chan Poh Meng, principal of the Raffles Institution, is among those who have acknowledged how divided Singapore society has become. 'A long period of conditioning means that we often fail to see elitism even when it is staring us in the face,' Chan said in a speech at the school's Founder's Day in 2015. Wealthier families had been able to dominate the school because they could afford to coach their children for admission, the principal conceded. When he sought to recruit students from less wealthy backgrounds, he was told that some parents did not want to send their children to RI. This was not because parents feared their children could not cope academically, but because they feared they would not fit in.

In 2014, the Singapore government reduced state funding for six leading independent schools, including Raffles and ACS, and warned these schools they would need approval from the Ministry of Education if they wanted to fundraise for 'non-standard' features such as swimming pools. At least two of the schools already had Olympic-sized swimming pools, but this was a belated acknowledgement that the gulf between the elite and the rest should not be allowed to widen any further.

A few years ago, Singapore's prime minister warned of the risk that some of the country's most sought-after schools could become 'closed circles' that perpetuate elitism. He insisted the government would work to ensure this never happened. But a telling statistic in his speech revealed how far the change had already gone. In a country where the overwhelming majority of households live in government-built flats, just 53 per cent of Raffles Institution's students lived in public housing. At home and at school, there were two Singapores.

Privately, many Singaporean parents express concern that the system places too much emphasis on passing exams, with many children facing long hours of tutoring after school. Assessments by the OECD have found that in Singapore, as in some other East Asian societies, high achievement is bound up with high anxiety over failure. Fear may be a spur to short-term achievement, but it can also lead to burnout. An anxious student is more likely to duck a challenge.

NO ONE OWES SINGAPORE A LIVING 175

Grade anxiety can have tragic consequences. In 2016, an eleven-year-old boy – referred to in the press as Master H – committed suicide on the day he was due to show his parents his disappointing mid-year exam results. According to a report in the *Straits Times*, witnesses who saw the boy's mother grieving at the scene heard her saying in Mandarin: 'I only ask for seventy marks. I don't expect you to get eighty marks.'

Two years after Master H's death, a Singaporean woman named Liang May posted a picture of herself on Facebook, sitting on a daybed with her smiling husband and children and holding up a card with her Primary School Leaving Examination score: 190. May, a mother of two, is the author of a blog about parenting, A Million Little Echoes, which gives a frank account of the daily struggle for advantage and status in Singapore, from the chauffeurs hanging around outside school gates to pick up princelings, to the choice between weekends spent in playgrounds or tuition centres.

The PSLE is an exam taken by every Singaporean child at the end of their final year of primary school, P6, when they are eleven. The four subjects a child takes, English, maths, science and their mother-tongue language, are aggregated to give what's known as the T-score, a number that will have a decisive influence on their lives. 'When we moved house at P6, we changed school too,' May wrote in her Facebook post. 'It contributed to my first academic failure and threw my school performance out the window.' The T-score indicates how well a student has performed relative to his or her peers. The higher the score, the more likely a pupil is to gain admission to their first choice of secondary school. A score of 200 and above secures a place in the 'Express' stream for secondary school, a pathway expected to lead to a university education. The maximum number of points is 300.

Lower scores mean a pupil enters the 'Normal' stream. At the lowest level, from 151 and below, a pupil will enter a variant of the 'Normal' stream which leads to a vocational education in a subject like food science or tourism. The model for the PSLE was the eleven-plus exam in the UK, hated for dividing children at an early age. May's post was part of a coordinated campaign by a group of Singapore parents under the name Life Beyond Grades. The posts featured both high and low scores, with high and low achievers sharing regrets that ranged from lost hours of play to emotional scars, alongside the conviction that academic achievement mattered less than qualities that were harder to measure. 'I am saying that grades are only a part of learning. Beyond that, our children will need adaptability, grit and resilience to survive,' wrote Jaelle Ang, an entrepreneur.

At a family level, the battle for advantage often requires an investment of time by mothers. Middle-class Singaporean women frequently speak of the need to drop out of the workforce around the time their children have crucial exams. Some of the fundamental neuroses of Singapore's society are crystallised in the T-score: the emphasis on individual competition, and the high cost of academic success or failure. 'Once you are streamed into the normal technical stream you become someone that society writes off from ever going to university, ever becoming a professional,' I was told by Dr Johannis Auri bin Abdul Aziz, an adviser to Singapore's Ministry of Education.

Singapore has begun to implement a succession of changes aimed at making the system less intense. This includes phasing out streaming in favour of letting students tackle individual subjects at differing levels of difficulty. Schools have brought in applied learning programmes to teach practical skills such as coding and encourage pupils to experiment in areas where there are no tests or grading. Mid-year exams in the first two years of primary school have been abolished. From 2021, the grading of the PSLE is being changed. Instead of the T-score, which ranks pupils against each other, children will be placed in one of eight bands according to how well they have achieved against the objectives of the curriculum. Instead of racing to finish first, children will be aiming for a personal best. This change has brought relief for some parents, though many feel the exam remains a heavy burden for young shoulders.

Pragmatically, it can be hard for an individual family to fight the constraints of the system. If grades still matter to universities and to employers, parents remain likely to push their children hard. Inevitably, Singapore's education reforms have met with resistance. 'There's a lot of pushback. Parents and teachers – who were survivors of the system – still feel that push towards getting their kids the highest grades possible,' said Johannis.

There is a growing appreciation that an era of rapid technological change may require workers with a greater appetite for risk. This could mean launching a start-up to take advantage of new opportunities, or considering a radical career change in middle age as shifts in consumer habits hollow out old industries. But this is where Singapore's school system, for all its accolades, can be a barrier.

The Singlish word *kiasu* means a grasping or selfish attitude driven by a fear of missing out. The word encompasses both trivial examples – grabbing the choicest dishes at a buffet – and a description of a national culture that gears Singaporeans up for intense competition from an early age. Singapore's *kiasu* culture is also reflected in a sense of national vulnerability, which is partly justified by the occasional sabre-rattling of Singapore's neighbours and partly amplified by a leadership for whom it is an effective means of mobilising public loyalty. The banners on display at Admiralty Secondary School are a reminder that this thread of paranoid patriotism is woven into children's minds at an early age.

The emphasis on Singapore's vulnerability filters into lessons too. Social studies, the class in which Singaporean children are taught about citizenship, draws lessons from the fates of other nations. The rise and fall of Venice is an exemplar of the need for capable leadership and an enterprising spirit. Northern Ireland and Sri Lanka illustrate the violent consequences of racial or religious tensions.

Kuik Shiao-Yin, co-founder of a cluster of Singapore businesses including a café, design studio and training consultancy, who served as a nominated MP, an honorary position in Singapore's parliament, has suggested that the *kiasu* mentality can hinder progress. This aversion to hazard was the reason that entrepreneurship in Singapore lacked originality, Kuik suggested in a parliamentary debate in 2016, describing many Singapore start-ups as 'copy-and-paste work of little worth'.

'The *kiasu* entrepreneur is driven by the anxiety to make short gains rather than a mindful desire to win at the long game,' said Kuik. 'So he will only take the risks that everyone is already taking and innovate what everyone else is already innovating.'

When I first arrived in Singapore, I walked through the business district from the palatial headquarters of a regional bank to the cramped offices of a digital lending start-up, on the seventh floor of a dishevelled 1950s office building. Kelvin Teo, co-founder of Funding Societies, told me how difficult it was to employ people in Singapore. 'The talent will come in, and we will like them ... and then they will speak to their boyfriend or their wife,' he said, with a rueful smile. The employee's partner would usually deliver a firm nudge: why work for a start-up when you could enjoy the security of working for a bank?

Three years later, Teo's start-up has moved to a glass-fronted tower, has around 350 employees and is lending around US$50 million a month (it was lending less than US$1 million a month when I first met Teo). The entrepreneur says he has found a few ways to compete for staff with more established companies. 'The advantage for us is that we don't quite follow the career ladder. You don't have to wait until a manager leaves before you get promoted. We're happy to promote you at an accelerated pace, if you're ready to solve bigger problems.' Culture is an advantage too. Start-ups are less hierarchical than the typical Singapore corporate. 'We send our own calendar invites, take our own notes. We either do or we die,' says Teo, who began his career as a management consultant at Accenture and McKinsey.

Some of Singapore's most successful new businesses have been founded by outsiders. Sea, Southeast Asia's biggest gaming company, was co-founded by three men from mainland China. Two of the founders, David Chen and Gang Ye, were drawn to Singapore with scholarships for study. Lazada, an ecommerce business, was founded by a German, Maximilian Bittner, and backed by the Berlin-based technology investor Rocket Internet. The Chinese online retailing giant Alibaba bought a controlling stake in Lazada for US$1 billion in 2016, its biggest deal outside China at the time and a mark of confidence in the success and growth prospects of the business.

Grab, which fought off competition from Uber to become the dominant ride hailing business in Southeast Asia, was founded by two Malaysians: chief executive Anthony Tan, a member of a Malaysian Chinese business dynasty, and co-founder Tan Hooi Ling, who was raised in a middle-class household in Malaysia's capital, Kuala Lumpur. Insiders at Grab say that their founders display a flexible approach to challenges that is uncharacteristic of their more single-minded Singaporean business counterparts. Grab has thrived amid relentless competition from rival platforms, and a messy regulatory environment.

State-backed efforts to nurture more home-grown start-ups have been less successful. Overly generous government funding has provided a lifeline to anaemic businesses, many of which have generated little growth and few jobs. A degree of risk aversion appears ingrained in many Singaporeans. Teo suggests that the high cost of failure may go some way to explaining this: 'Singapore is not a country of second chances, or at least not yet. If you have a negative record historically, you're black-marked for quite a long period of time. It's why small businesses cannot get funded if ten years ago they went bankrupt or they missed a few credit card payments.'

Failure in Silicon Valley is celebrated as a rite of passage on the road to success. The consequences of failure in Singapore are stark, and this lesson is inculcated early on. 'For civil servants the high flyers are usually from the best universities, and if you're not from that category you're streamed out early,' another businessman told me. 'To that extent your history follows you for quite a long period of time.'

Singapore's schools are one of the most remarkable aspects of the system Lee Kuan Yew and his allies devised. They have been a success story, not just in domestic terms but globally. But from top to bottom, Singaporeans are now conscious that a system which has served them well in the past has become excessively rigid. The country's schools must demonstrate a capacity to evolve and meet new demands. It can be hard to make bold changes when so many people are heavily invested in the status quo. But in the past, when faced with intense challenges, Singapore has gone through radical transformation.

Singapore is keen to encourage more 'deep technology' ventures, developing tech in areas like artificial intelligence. Jui Lim, chief executive of SGInnovate, the government agency backing local scientists who want to build deep tech start-ups, concedes that foreign entrepreneurs are 'hungrier' than comfortable Singaporeans. 'With prosperity we have to find new ways to entice, to cajole people to look at entrepreneurship as an opportunity,' he says.

Lim argues that conditions in Singapore are unique. On a small and expensive island where the system emphasises self-reliance, taking a gamble with your career may be disastrous. 'If you're an entrepreneur in the US and you fail repeatedly in Silicon Valley, you can move to Wyoming, buy an acre for a dollar, grow vegetables, raise chickens and you're not going to die,' he says. An escape to the countryside is not an option for Singaporeans. Lim compares his country to Scandinavia, where he argues that a well-educated population cradled by a nurturing state has turned to invention out of a desire to beat boredom. 'We have to find our own way,' he says. 'We have to keep experimenting.'

9

Taming the Internet

How Singapore brought social media to heel

The boy has a tangled mop of black hair, dark-framed glasses, narrow shoulders and a voice that rasps on the threshold of manhood. 'Lee Kuan Yew is dead – finally,' he exults, in a video clip posted online days after the death of Singapore's founding father in 2015.

Hands waving as if to shake off an excess of nervous energy, sixteen-year-old Amos Yee hunts out the words that will inflict the greatest damage. 'Lee Kuan Yew was a horrible person,' he declares. 'Everyone is afraid that if they say something like that they might get into trouble . . . but I am not afraid.' The monologue is heavily salted with swear-words and indulges in the grossly sexual imagery favoured by some teenage boys.

Lee is not the only icon to be toppled in Yee's rant. Jesus is described as 'power-hungry and malicious' and the schoolboy is contemptuous of parents too. Not just his own, but the older generation in general, who are 'delusional and ignorant and stupid' for believing in the official story of Singapore's transformation under Lee.

The style is puerile. But the essence of Yee's criticism, targeting the former premier for his tight grip on the media and for pushing 'nationalistic propaganda' through the education system, might not be out of place in the report of a human rights watchdog.

The consequences of Yee's sacrilege were swift. Weeks after the video was broadcast, in an atmosphere made more tense by a national convulsion of grief over Lee's death, the teenager was convicted on charges of hurting religious feelings and obscenity, and sentenced to four weeks' detention. In many other countries, Yee might have been dismissed as a gadfly, a minor irritant whose rant could be waved away as the outbursts of an internet basement-dweller. In Singapore, the authorities chose to slap him down in a manner that illustrates the country's complex relationship with the internet and the potential it offers to accelerate the flow of information.

Singapore's government has embraced the internet as an essential technology for economic growth. But it is wary of its ability to spread dissent. This was underlined to authoritarian regimes worldwide during the Arab Spring, which established the power of social media as a tool for documenting oppression, coordinating anti-government protest and magnifying the reach of protests. Ordinary people became angry at their governments, marched against them, and realised that others were marching too.

Middle Eastern autocracies have tended to use clumsy means of repression, blocking websites and jailing bloggers. Singapore offers a test case for a more subtle model. Its system of media control is indirect, with reporters pressured by their editors to ensure their political coverage never challenges the government. 'You're not supposed to ask questions in a difficult way,' one former Singapore journalist, who worked for a business publication, told me. 'The government will complain to your supervisors about that. But you're allowed to write what you want to write. After that, the editors will change it so much that you can't recognise it any more.'

This system cannot simply be transferred online. It was Facebook, Twitter and YouTube that let protesters across the Middle East share images of police brutality, fuelling public anger and bypassing government monitoring of domestic newspapers and television. Unlike reporters for the Singapore press, bloggers like Amos Yee can broadcast directly to the public from their bedrooms.

For the Singapore government, strengthening techno-logical skills and encouraging the flow of ideas that can be commercially exploited are high priorities. One consequence of this desire to maintain an open and dynamic internet is that, unlike China and other authoritarian regimes, Singapore makes little attempt to block political content online. The OpenNet Initiative, an advocacy group that tracks attempts at online control and surveillance, finds that Singapore practises 'extremely minimal' filtering of internet content, restricted to pornography sites, sales of banned drugs and religious extremism. Instead, the government has been pushed to cede some ground on the internet, allowing voices that would never be heard in Singapore's neutered main-stream press. From heritage campaigns to activists against the death penalty, social media has created new spaces for debate.

It was a blogger named Alex Au, a softly spoken man in rimless glasses, who gave one of the earliest demonstrations of the power of the new media. Au is a writer, whose blog Yawning Bread is an elegantly crafted series of observations on culture and politics in Southeast Asia. Just ahead of the 2006 general election, Au went to a rally of the opposition

Workers' Party in Hougang, a bustling northeastern suburb of malls and housing estates. Finding the rally so crowded he could not reach the front, Au headed to a nearby tower block instead, climbing thirteen floors up the stairs as the lift lobby was full of people with the same idea.

From this vantage point, he took a photograph that has become famous, showing tens of thousands of people gathered in a floodlit field. He published the picture, along with an account of the rally and a speech by an opposition politician attacking the government over healthcare costs, on his blog. The picture and blog post 'On Hougang Field' was shared with delight by Singaporeans, accustomed to a tame media dominated by the ruling party's perspective. No one could recall seeing wide-angle pictures of opposition rallies in Singapore's mainstream media, which favoured close-up shots that concealed the size of the crowd.

By the time of Singapore's 2011 general election, the power and reach of social media was becoming clear. The election that year was unusual. Voters were worried about the rising cost of living and openly critical of the government over an influx of foreign workers. The public complained of overcrowding on trains and buses, where the system had failed to keep pace with growth in the population. Social media amplified this dissent. The youngest candidate in the election, a twenty-four-year-old advertising executive named Nicole Seah who ran for one of the opposition parties, became an unexpected star on YouTube, with fiery speeches calling for a more inclusive society.

During the campaign, prime minister Lee Hsien Loong displayed contrition, telling a rally: 'If we didn't quite get it right, I am sorry.' The ruling party held onto power, but their 60 per cent share of the vote was their worst outcome since independence. It seemed as if the internet was living up to its

promise of creating a new space for conversation that highlighted the gaps between official rhetoric and reality, even
in one of the most carefully managed societies in the world.

The government appeared caught off-guard, with the
prime minister acknowledging that ministers had to work
harder to engage voters online. He expressed an Olympian
disdain for the unruly qualities of the internet. 'It is anony-
mous, it is chaotic, it is unfiltered, unmoderated and so the
medium lends itself to many negative views and ridiculous
untruths,' he complained. Singapore's elite had grasped that
allowing people to gather in the untamed space of social
media could be as risky as allowing them to gather in the
streets. The question that perplexed them was: how were they
going to bring this new medium to heel?

Remy Choo Zheng Xi was fourteen when Speakers' Corner
at Hong Lim Park was opened in September 2000. A student
at the Anglo-Chinese School, he had acquired an interest in
debating in his second year, and that got him interested in
political news from the region. He read about the student
protest that culminated in the fall of Indonesia's President
Suharto, and about demands for reform in Malaysia. 'I
started relating a lot of that to how things were different in
Singapore . . . Singapore was exceedingly tightly controlled,'
he told me.

In the first week that Speakers' Corner was open, Choo
decided to give it a shot. Speaking to a crowd of about
seventy mostly elderly folk, he gave an impassioned speech
about democracy. 'I said public participation was important
in getting the government to improve the lives of ordinary
Singaporeans. As Singapore is a one-party state, it is not as
attentive to the citizenry as it could be.'

It was thrilling. 'The crowd were kind of excited,' Choo recalled. 'When you are a kid, you have the courage to say things that make you cringe on hindsight.'

Halfway through what Choo describes as a 'very privileged' upbringing, Sars hit Singapore. Air travel slumped, pummelling industries that relied on tourists. His father's restaurant business was wiped out, and the family sold their car and moved from private to public housing. He shrugs off its impact on him – 'children are very adaptable' – but that shift in perspective feels significant. Choo became a lawyer, dividing his time between commercial litigation and legal cases likely to have a broader impact on society. While at law school, he helped found a blog site, The Online Citizen, one of the first outlets to cover taboo topics, from migrant workers' rights to rising inequality.

A slim, handsome man, now in his mid-thirties, Choo is gay and he has taken up legal challenges to Section 377A, the section of the penal code which criminalises gay sex, as well as championing free speech. When he speaks about his life, discrimination against gay people in Singapore and its intolerance of free speech feel like two sides of a coin, illustrating the corrosive impact of secrecy. 'The biggest unspoken impact of 377A is just not being able to be out, not being able to be fully comfortable with being out. It certainly has an impact on the confidence with which members of our community can express ourselves, with even loved ones who may have a different world view,' he says. Choo was thirty-one when he came out to his family. He was outed by someone who created a website that combined images of Choo kissing a man with a legal case that he had handled, about a website accused of stirring up racial hatred. 'I'm not sure whether it was my political views or my sexual orientation that they were targeting,' he says.

After its setback in the 2011 election, Singapore's ruling party promised to listen to its citizens and address their complaints. But in the years that followed, the government began to exert a firmer grip over the flow of information online. In 2013 Singapore introduced a licensing scheme for news websites, extending the system that regulates broadcasters and newspapers. These licences require news sites to remove content deemed 'in breach of standards' within twenty-four hours. They are also required to post a bond of S$50,000, creating a financial forfeit for non-compliance with the regulator. The Online Citizen was one of those required to register.

Singapore's government has frequently used libel suits against foreign media, suing and winning damages from the *New York Times*, Bloomberg and *The Economist*, among others. The country's leaders insist on their right to defend their reputation, but their eagerness to turn to the courts to police criticism of the government has troubled human rights advocates.

Under Singapore law, libel is not just a civil matter, but a criminal offence which can be punished with up to two years in jail. As in Britain, it is up to the person defending a libel claim to prove that their statement is true, which tends to put newspapers and campaigners on the back foot. Government ministers sue for libel in the Singapore courts, where they have never lost. The foreign press soon grasped that stories about the Lee family tended to be sensitive, particularly any suggestion that younger members of the family had not earned their position purely on merit.

Personal blogs, too numerous to police individually, were excluded from the formal licensing scheme. Instead, Singapore has used legal tools to pursue a handful of dissidents, like a gardener plucking dandelions from a stretch of lawn. A defamation suit was deployed against a blog for the first time in 2014, when the prime minister sued blogger Roy Ngerng, a slender young man in dark-framed glasses who had been a dogged critic of the government and whose blog, Heart Truths, probed the reasons for the persistence of poverty, especially among the elderly, in what had become one of the world's richest countries.

Inadequate retirement income is an emotive topic in Singapore. Although people make substantial mandatory contributions to the state-run retirement savings kitty, the Central Provident Fund, the fact they are allowed to withdraw money to pay for housing, healthcare and other needs often means their savings are eroded by the time they retire. Pensioners often find they need to keep working in old age. A government survey in 2011 found that 29 per cent of Singaporeans over the age of sixty-five were still working, up from 15 per cent in 2005. Most were working from financial necessity rather than the desire to stay active. Many very old women, in their seventies, were working as cleaners or low-paid service staff. Singaporeans had grown indignant at the sight of old people gathering cardboard to sell for recycling or carrying stacked trays in fast food restaurants.

On his blog Ngerng effectively accused the government of misappropriating pension funds, comparing it to a case in which the leaders of a Singaporean church had been charged with fraud. The comparison was absurd – government ministers had not stolen public money – but the consequences for Ngerng were disproportionate to his offence.

After receiving a warning letter from the prime minister's lawyer, Ngerng took the blog down and apologised. But he kept pressing the government over pensions. One Saturday in June, three weeks after the blog was published, he was among the speakers at a rally which drew around 2000 people to

Speakers' Corner under the slogan 'Return our CPF'. There were loud cheers as Ngerng asked probing questions about the government's management of its financial assets. It looked like a dangerous mix. A blogger was asking troublesome questions on an issue that triggered a strong public reaction.

The prime minister's lawyers sued for damages. 'Freedom of speech does not come free from the need to be responsible for what one says,' the premier observed on Facebook. Days later, Ngerng was sacked from his job as a patient coordinator at a government hospital after his employer said his conduct was incompatible with 'their values and standards'. He was convicted of defamation and ordered to pay S$29,000 in legal fees. The court later imposed damages of S$150,000.

The blogger raised thousands of dollars from the public to help fund his defence, after making an appeal on his site. The successful fundraising implied that at least some fellow Singaporeans felt the government's tactics were heavy-handed. But his case had underlined the severe financial penalties that an individual who challenges the Singapore government can incur. A few months after the prime minister sued Ngerng, Alex Au was convicted of contempt of court over a blog in which he wrote about legal challenges to Section 377A. Au was fined S$8000. It was not quite the life-changing punishment meted out to Ngerng but the conviction disturbed human rights activists for its use of an archaic corner of the law.

The offence of 'contempt of court' is usually meant to prevent people interfering in the course of justice. In most countries it curbs the kind of speculation on high-profile court cases that can prevent a fair trial. In Au's case, he had raised modest questions about the scheduling of two cases that both involved the legal ban on gay sex. He was found guilty of 'scandalising the judiciary', a legal provision that

protects judges from ridicule. Singapore has since strengthened its contempt of court law, using it to crack down on
what the state regards as unjustified criticism of judges.
Relatively mild comments posted on Facebook have resulted
in convictions for a human rights activist and an opposition
politician. The prosecutions have a cumulative effect, says
Choo, who represented Au in the contempt of court case,
obliging people to watch their words.

I was struck by the fact that Ngerng, Au and Choo are all
gay. This might just be coincidental with their activism, but
it reminded me of George Bernard Shaw's line about progress through friction. 'The reasonable man adapts himself
to the world: the unreasonable one persists in trying to adapt
the world to himself,' Shaw wrote. 'Therefore all progress
depends on the unreasonable man.' In a society where gay sex
is officially illegal (though, for practical purposes, tolerated),
gay men and lesbians have to break with conventions just
to exist. After that, it's a relatively small step to questioning
other aspects of your society that don't seem to make sense.

A year after he was convicted and jailed for his Lee Kuan
Yew video, Amos Yee was back on YouTube. This time,
his emphasis was more overtly on religion, with videos
attacking Islam and Christianity. The films were delivered
with panache, but they also reflect an adolescent prurience,
obsession with swear words and a crude desire to shock. In
one scene, Yee mimes sex with a crucifix. He was arrested
and sentenced to six weeks' jail on eight charges, including
offending the feelings of Muslims and Christians. Underlying
Singapore's tough attitude was the official fear that comments
like his might spark religious discord. Jailing him, the judge
warned: 'his contemptuous and irreverent remarks have the
tendency to generate social unrest.'

This official view was not necessarily shared by religious

believers in Singapore. When he was first arrested and held on remand in 2015, he was bailed by a Christian family counsellor, Vincent Low, who wanted to demonstrate his tolerance of criticism even when it was couched in juvenile terms. But the initial sympathy for Yee began to wear thin as his antics grew more extreme. Just before Christmas 2016, Yee flew to the US, where he was granted political asylum. Yee's YouTube channel and videos were taken down by Google in 2018. He was charged with solicitation and possession of child pornography in November 2020, pleading not guilty.

In a society more accustomed to robust debate, Yee might have been no more than a pinprick. His crudity and deliberate provocation make his output tough to watch, but equally easy to ignore. The intensity of Singapore's allergic reaction to him suggests an unwarranted degree of anxiety about the fragility of the country.

At the heart of Singapore's efforts to tame the internet is a battle over the truth and whose version of it prevails. For decades, the government had told a story of how Singapore had been created by Lee Kuan Yew and his allies, and how this transformation had been threatened by communists and malign foreign powers. There is an element of truth to this account, but like all national stories there is a dash of myth-making too. Singapore's leaders insist that the threat of a violent communist insurrection in the 1960s was a genuine one. But many Singaporeans are sceptical of this version of events, noting that fear of a radical left takeover, and the government's repeated insistence on Singapore's vulnerability, have helped the ruling party to consolidate their hold on power.

This struggle burst into the open when Singapore drew up its fake news law in 2019. While plenty of countries around the world have acted to curb misinformation online, Singapore's legislation, the Protection from Online Falsehoods and Manipulation Act, is exceptionally harsh and unusually broad. Known simply as 'Pofma', the law sweeps across a range of potentially sensitive topics, from public health to Singapore's relations with other countries, including anything which might diminish public confidence in the government. For individuals, publishing false statements can, in the most extreme cases, attract a jail term of up to ten years, a fine of up to S$100,000 or both. Companies that participate in the spread of online falsehoods or fail to comply with a correction notice can face fines of up to S$1 million.

The historian P. J. Thum, who is managing editor of the news website New Naratif, posted a video to YouTube in which he argued that the law defined falsehood so broadly that every statement could be considered false in some way. 'This definition is so broad that the omission of a fact, accidentally or otherwise, is sufficient for something to be considered misleading,' he said.

Thum had been asked to give evidence at select committee hearings which paved the way for the law, and these hearings underlined how vigorously the government intended to defend its own version of the truth. He was cross-examined by a government minister who focused on the historian's research into Operation Coldstore, the 1963 security sweep which had detained leading left-wingers. The cross-examination turned into a marathon six-hour session, in which the minister accused Thum of falling below 'the standard of an objective historian' and ignoring or suppressing inconvenient evidence. During the hearings, the government painted a picture of a nation encircled by predators. 'We are a small and multiracial society that can be easily overwhelmed by a larger adversary taking advantage of our societal fault lines,' communications and information minister Yaacob Ibrahim said.

The film remains online, along with a notice that says it contains 'several false and misleading statements'. But the first use of Pofma targeted an opposition politician who questioned the independence and investment decisions of state investment funds. The same month, Singapore extended the use of the law beyond its borders, ordering Facebook to correct a post by a user in Australia, Alex Tan. Facebook complied. For his YouTube video questioning the law, Thum was issued with a directive under Pofma, requiring him to publish the government's 'corrections' to his argument.

The martyrs of free speech in Singapore include some extreme and unsympathetic figures, like Amos Yee, but many more of those who have fallen foul of the law have been moderate voices asking thoughtful questions, like Roy Ngerng and Alex Au. Ngerng moved to Taiwan and continued to post critical commentary on Singapore. Au continued to write and speak out. The country's independent media has been buffeted, but it has escaped a knockout blow; blogs that question the official narrative are still operating.

For a well-entrenched ruling elite with little by way of significant political challenge, running a well-resourced and organised state, Singapore's government can seem surprisingly anxious. But it is an anxiety which makes sense when you observe the speed at which apparently stable regimes have collapsed once they lose control of both the internet and the streets. Singapore had demonstrated that a determined and well-resourced national government could effectively impose its will on the internet, without taking the extreme steps of shutting down the flow of information entirely or building up a patchwork of censored websites. The country's rulers could instead use an armoury of laws to pick off targets one by one, and remind everyone of the risks of asking too many questions. It did not matter that platforms like Facebook and Twitter were not directly under state ownership or control. They could be forced to bow to Singapore's laws, even outside the country.

In Lee Kuan Yew's years in power, the government created a deferential public culture, ruthlessly eliminating awkward voices by controlling the press and hounding opposition politicians. Singapore seemed to have become a placid place in which citizens were content with their lot. The internet opened up channels through which a rebellious uproar became audible to the world. Singapore's application of legal restraints has succeeded in muffling this uproar, but not choking it altogether.

10

Singapore Inc

Family businesses and the state-run economy

When the property developer Kwek Leng Beng joined forces with a Saudi prince to buy the Plaza Hotel in New York in 1995, the deal signalled the global reach of Asian wealth and underlined the extraordinary resources which could be marshalled by the upper echelons of Singapore's business elite. The famous Manhattan hotel, owned by Donald Trump, had filed for bankruptcy. As commercial real estate prices tumbled in the early 1990s, the buyers acquired it for US$325 million, which was US$75 million less than Trump had paid seven years earlier. 'My father believed in Asia,' Kwek told an interviewer in 1997. 'I believe in the world-wide markets.'

From designer labels to football clubs, hotels to landmark office blocks, Singapore's richest men and women have gone on a shopping spree over the past three decades. Singaporean investors have acquired London's former stock exchange tower, the British luxury goods maker Mulberry and the Spanish football club Valencia.

These trophy purchases are the most eye-catching evidence of a broader shift. Asia has overtaken North America in its concentration of high-net-worth individuals, meaning those with assets of US$1 million aside from their main home. Asia's tycoons are destined to play an increasingly prominent role in the century to come.

Discovering what makes them tick can be a challenge. The owners of the country's family businesses form an aristocracy whose discreet style is shaped by the struggles of their early years. Their demeanour in person is conservative, modest and guarded. 'If you're a stranger, they will be perfectly nice to you when you meet, but under that is a level at which they consider: is this person a "threat" to me in any way?' said a friend of a leading business family. 'Is this person going to hit me up for money, or name-drop me? Is this encounter a net-positive for me?'

Families played a central role in the development of Asian commerce, founding and leading powerful multinational businesses such as India's Tata group and Samsung in South Korea. Across the continent, family ownership and control was a way of building trust and pooling resources. Placing a family member in a position of authority was often a safer bet than hiring a stranger. Funds could be raised within a family when stock markets were embryonic or non-existent. The creation stories of Singapore's founding business patriarchs are a blend of hard graft, trading acumen and the ability to take skilful advantage of opportunities, in good times and bad.

Kwek Hong Png, father of the Kwek who bought the Plaza Hotel, came to Singapore from China's Fujian province aged sixteen, boarding the ship with nothing more than his ticket, a sleeping mat and quilt. After a family connection secured him an apprenticeship in a hardware store, Kwek saved enough money to start his own trading business, going into partnership with his three younger brothers. He prospered during the Japanese occupation, procuring steel and other raw materials for the Japanese military. When the British came back, he turned to cement production and profited from the post-war construction boom.

Keeping businesses under family control, rather than out-sourcing management to professionals, means the source of a clan's wealth stays firmly in their grip across generations. In a Singapore business, the eldest son will usually inherit, rather than dividing a corporate empire between heirs. But even after the reins of a business have been handed over, it is common for the patriarch to stay on as chairman. When Wee Ee Cheong succeeded his father as chief executive of the family-run bank UOB, aged fifty-four, he was known as the 'young son'. His father Wee Cho Yaw stayed on as chairman for another six years and only stepped down from the board when he was eighty-nine. Father and son occupied separate wings of the bank's headquarters, two slender skyscrapers by the Singapore River, and the older man retained significant influence. 'I think fundamentally their values are the same,' said a bank insider. 'Conservative, long-term – ensuring the business is there for the next generation.' But the father favoured keeping a lower profile.

The heads of Singapore's elite families exercise tight control over their clans. Some manage their children and grandchil-dren by ruthlessly controlling the purse strings. Others, like the Wee family, have found creative ways to nourish family ties. Wee Cho Yaw gave his children adjoining parcels of land, so that their gardens abut each other, and he hosts a Sunday afternoon family lunch that all must attend 'on pain of death', one associate said. The family has a reputation for being particularly close-knit. 'No matter how polished and friendly they are to outsiders, at a certain point in the evening they fold in on themselves,' said a friend, meaning that the family always closed ranks, forming a unit that clearly had strong internal bonds. 'It's like watching droplets of mercury coalescing into a single drop.'

Singapore is often feted as a free market dream, a success story built on global exports, low corporate taxes and a minimal welfare state. In Brexiters' imagination it is a role model for the UK outside the EU, in which entrepreneurial zeal would be unleashed by deregulation. This depiction looks plausible at first glance. From its bustling food courts to its cavernous fashion stores, the city is vibrant with commercial activity. Its successful business families resemble Hong Kong's tycoons. But this impression obscures the central role that is played by Singapore's interventionist state.

In the early decades of transformation, the country's leaders mobilised the entire island's resources in their drive to build an industrial society. As well as inviting foreign multinationals to base themselves in Singapore, the government established businesses that filled gaps in private expertise, from a national shipping line to defence industries. After the British withdrew from the Sembawang naval base, it was converted into a government-linked commercial shipyard. In 1968 the government created a bank, DBS, which would provide long-term finance to companies to support Singapore's growth as a manufacturing hub. DBS moved into broader commercial and retail banking and is now the biggest bank in Southeast Asia.

Singapore defied the economic orthodoxy in the West, which said the state had no business running companies. The phrase most often used to deride government interference in business was 'picking winners'. While other Asian economies such as Taiwan and Korea also had states with active industrial policies, none went as far as Singapore with wide-spread government ownership of businesses. Unlike Hong Kong, where tycoons dominate the political system, it is the government that is supreme in Singapore.

Singapore's business families played their part. In the 1960s, the government turned to private developers to build malls, office blocks and hotels in the city centre, replacing the run-down and low-rise shophouses that had characterised the city until then. To encourage the creation of commercial property in the early post-independence years, when Singapore's economic outlook still seemed uncertain, officials had allowed developers to pay for land in instalments and thrown in tax concessions to sweeten the deal. As Singapore's export-driven economy roared through the 1960s and 1970s, these investments paid off handsomely. Private fortunes that had already been substantial became astronomical. 'The big Singaporean families grew up with Singapore, they helped Singapore develop,' said one insider. 'They are tuned into what needs to be done.'

The state was willing to work hand-in-glove with commerce, but businessmen who stepped out of line were running a risk. The independent-minded rubber tycoon Tan Lark Sye, who championed the cause of Chinese-language education and backed left-wing politics in the 1950s, was stripped of his citizenship after the PAP government accused him of supporting communism.

Property developers regularly gripe about the way taxes on purchases are used to rein in the housing market. Lobbying of this kind falls on deaf ears if it does not suit the government's masterplan. 'You know the Singaporean idea of feedback,' said someone familiar with Singapore's family-run businesses. 'They call everyone into the room, you give your feedback, and then they get a bunch of scholars to run the numbers.

If your feedback doesn't fit the model, your feedback isn't taken in.'

The government plays a strategic role in the economy. In the 1980s, Singapore made a concerted push to focus on hi-tech industries that needed skilled workers, such as the manufacture of computer components and pharmaceuticals, becoming one of the world's biggest exporters of hi-tech goods.

Goods were not the only thing Singapore had to trade. Despite its lack of charismatic wildlife and natural beaches, the city has thrived as a tourist destination. Singapore has built its appeal on artificial attractions, with millions of visitors drawn to its casinos, infinity pools and designer fashion boutiques. More recently, Singapore has head-hunted leading research scientists from Western universities, and expanded the research capabilities of its own institutions in an effort to encourage science-based entrepreneurship. In 2019, a Singapore university hired the British scientist who won the Nobel Prize in Physics for his experiments with graphene, the super-thin material with a range of exotic applications.

For a country smaller than New York, Singapore's economy is surprisingly diverse. The row of black-hulled supertankers regularly anchored off the island provides one clue about the source of its wealth. Rooted in its historical rubber and tin industries, commodities trading remains one of the linchpins of Singapore's economic success, buying and selling the raw materials that have powered Asia's economic transformation. When the world economy slows or a glut of oil builds up, a line of tankers gathers off the coast. The ships drop anchor in the Singapore Strait as they wait for demand to pick up again, before discharging their cargo here or sailing on around the world.

As well as trading in oil, Singapore acts as a hub for

transshipment and a base for manufacturers who transform petroleum into industrial chemicals. Jurong Island, a man-made pile of sand off Singapore's western shore, is forested with the steel towers of chemical refineries. A network of caverns has been hollowed out beneath the seabed to create more storage for crude oil.

The city state is also one of Asia's leading centres for currency trading, and for wealth management, the delicate business of financial planning for the super-rich. It is a launchpad for multinationals seeking to cater to Southeast Asia's booming middle class. From IBM to Exxon, Facebook to Novartis, hundreds of Western multinationals have their Asia-Pacific headquarters on the Southeast Asian island. Singapore is an ardent suitor. 'Top companies in each sector of interest are constantly identified and revised and Economic Development Board officers will cold-call them,' one former government official explained. 'But Singapore's branding is good enough that many companies will also reach out independently to us.'

The headline corporate tax rate has been cut steadily over the years and is now 17 per cent, but behind this figure is an array of incentives to reduce tax bills further. Companies that set up regional headquarters in Singapore can apply for a concessionary rate of 5 per cent for the first five years. Low taxes continue to attract companies to Singapore, with prickly political consequences. In 2018, the world's biggest mining company BHP Billiton settled a tax dispute with Australian authorities over sales channelled through its Singapore marketing arm, agreeing to pay over US$386 million in additional taxes. For years raw materials such as iron ore which BHP Billiton mines in Australia had been sold to the Singapore hub, which then sold the commodities around the world.

Microsoft, Apple and Google have also booked revenues from Australian operations through Singapore. Defending the practice at an Australian Senate inquiry in 2015, a Google executive said: 'We are not opposed to paying tax, but we are opposed to being uncompetitive.'

In 2018, Facebook announced plans to invest US$1 billion in a data centre in Singapore, its first in Asia. Data centres are power-hungry complexes that require round-the-clock cooling, which means a tropical island without its own energy sources is far from the ideal location (data centres are, by contrast, a boom industry in Iceland where they benefit from a subarctic climate and plentiful geothermal energy). Then, in 2021, the social network revealed that it would build two new subsea cables, Echo and Bifrost, linking Singapore to the West Coast of the US.

The plans underlined Singapore's ability to build on historic advantages. As with oil, the country was able to profit from its political stability, talented workforce and location in an important region in order to lure investment, even though it did not possess a wealth of natural resources. The regional resource to be tapped in this case is not hydrocarbons but the attention and online spending power of Southeast Asia's growing middle class, while Echo and Bifrost will be the hi-tech equivalents of the Suez Canal, the artificial channel through which this valuable commodity will flow between east and west.

Increasingly, Singapore plays a pivotal role for Chinese businesses too. At a time when the Chinese tech industry is facing setbacks in the US and India, companies like Alibaba, Tencent and ByteDance, the Chinese owner of TikTok, have turned to Singapore as a route to regional expansion. The country's predictable politics, an important aspect of its appeal as a business hub, has been underlined by the violent confrontation between pro-democracy protesters and police in Hong Kong. Though the US remains the most important source of foreign investment for Singapore, China is its biggest trade partner. The ethnic and linguistic heritage of Singapore's Chinese majority has helped strengthen business ties.

One executive who spent time with Chinese government officials said: 'They always take comfort in the fact that you are Chinese at heart. They trust you a little bit more because you understand the culture, and the language is very important.' At banquets, Singaporean Chinese understand the protocol of 'who walks first, who walks behind, how you introduce people', the executive added. 'It was quite instinctive for me, but some of our staff had to be coached. Even the gift presentation had to be rehearsed, you know, what you are giving, who's going to give it, who are you going to pass it to after receiving it?'

Business people who win the trust of political leaders are invited onto government boards, while civil servants and army generals will be drafted into roles in businesses where the government has an investment. The executives of international businesses that establish themselves in Singapore are welcomed into the cosy network that links the country's business elite with its governing class. Corporate leaders and government officials fraternise at a circuit of dinners and country club golf sessions. The effort to avoid any perception of sleaze keeps these dinners sedate. 'From time to time you might drink a nice bottle of wine, but it's hard to deviate from the norm of what's considered acceptable for senior civil servants,' said an executive at a government-linked Singapore business.

The men who attend these events are frequently less prim in their private lives. Socialising at karaoke bars is a normal part of business life in Singapore. These bars, known in Singapore as 'KTV bars', aren't just an excuse for belting out cheesy hits, but often places where attractive hostesses are — illicitly — paid to perform sexual services.

Singapore is a node in a broader network of ethnic Chinese businessmen in Southeast Asia, many of whom keep homes in the city but have second homes, and sometimes second families, in Indonesia and Malaysia. Outside Singapore, deals are struck in the traditional way, with an emphasis on personal relationships and the building of trust through drinking sessions and karaoke. The 'standard unit of currency' in exchange of gifts used to be Château Lafite, an expensive Bordeaux red; now it is Macallan 18, one of the world's most sought-after Scotch whiskies (a few years ago a bottle of 1926 Macallan was auctioned at Sotheby's for US$1.9 million). Across Southeast Asia, the golf course is the universally accepted place to do business: 'Golf, spa, massage, karaoke, dinner – and model-looking female caddies,' said one executive.

Politics and business are closely aligned. Through a fund called Temasek, which was established in 1974 to manage the state's investments, the government owns large chunks of major domestic companies like Singapore Airlines and SingTel, the leading telecoms operator. The major shareholder in about a third of companies in the *Straits Times Index* – the biggest publicly listed companies in the city state – Temasek is now a leviathan with a portfolio worth S$306 billion in 2019. The fund has invested abroad and more than three-quarters of its assets are overseas.

The apex of business and politics in Singapore remains largely, but not exclusively, male. One of the exceptions is Ho Ching, Temasek's chief executive since 2004, who is widely considered the most powerful woman in Singapore. Ho, who is married to the prime minister Lee Hsien Loong, never gives interviews but posts prolifically to Facebook, serving up a welter of wildlife pictures, inspirational quotes and the occasional flash of insight into the ruling circle's views – including an angry denunciation of racism after social media posts criticised the hiring of Indian nationals at Temasek. Ho announced in February 2021 that she would step down from Temasek by the end of the year.

In 1981, Singapore created the Government of Singapore Investment Corporation, now formally known by its acronym GIC, to manage its reserves and make long-term investments. Funds like these are usually set up to invest surpluses from national budgets in oil-rich nations like Kuwait and the United Arab Emirates. GIC was the world's first sovereign wealth fund that was not based on excess profits from oil.

The state does not pick winners from among businesses. Instead, the state-owned companies of 'Singapore Inc' are expected to turn a profit and compete with the private sector and each other, whether they sell electricity or mobile data plans. In ordinary times, they receive no favours from the state, and many are listed on the stock exchange where they are accountable to shareholders. Academic observers suggest this lies at the heart of why state capitalism in Singapore has been so successful.

Ministers say there is no political intervention in commercial decision-making, but the existence of a state fund with deep pockets gives Singapore the resources to ride out a crisis. As the pandemic pummelled airlines worldwide, Temasek stepped in with a lifeline for Singapore Airlines, ensuring the survival of a business critical to the country's future.

Despite its small domestic economy, the country's regulators have encouraged an over-supply of nearly every business. Fierce competition between rival providers keeps prices low and maintains backup systems. Where another country of Singapore's size might have one or two telecoms operators, Singapore has four. It has seven power generating companies. The exceptions to the rule are the stock exchange, the airline and domestic media, which are all monopolies. All three have strong ties with the government, either through state investment or through links between their management and Singapore's political masters.

Singapore's foreign workforce is a significant factor in its economic success. The fact that over half the workers in its manufacturing sector are migrant labourers helps keep the prices of its exports competitive. Three-quarters of its construction workforce is foreign, keeping down the cost of building new offices and factories. This puts Singapore in a stronger position to compete with regional neighbours such as Malaysia and Thailand for investment, unlike other rich countries which have lost manufacturing jobs to lower-wage economies.

Not all of Singapore's foreign factory workers are low-paid. At Rexadvance Technologies, a precision engineering manufacturer, foreign hires are paid around S$3000 a month as machine operators. 'No one wants to get their hands dirty,' the company's founder Jessie Chen said. In 2018, the average gross monthly salary was around S$4400, meaning many Singaporean citizens work for much less than Rexadvance pays its staff, but a Singaporean desperate for income is more likely to opt for takeaway delivery than work in construction.

Singapore's response to unrest among its low-paid workers has remained punitive. A group of bus drivers, migrants from mainland China, went on strike in 2012, in protest at being paid less than Malaysian drivers for the same company. One of the drivers was jailed and twenty-nine others were deported. After the migrant workers' riot in Little India a year later, more than fifty men were deported. The government brought in restrictions on the sale of alcohol in the neighbourhood, and stepped up the police presence and use of surveillance cameras.

In contrast, the foreign white-collar workers who are often brought in at senior levels live a privileged existence, enjoying a comfortable lifestyle of beers by the pool and long Sunday lunches at seafront restaurants. The occasional scandal – Nick

Leeson, the Singapore-based rogue trader whose multimillion dollar bets triggered the downfall of Barings Bank, is the most prominent example – has done nothing to diminish the appeal of bringing in foreign talent. In Singapore's financial sector, 16 per cent of employees are foreign nationals, a proportion that rises to 36 per cent in senior banking roles. Chief executives of Singapore companies are regularly recruited from abroad, including a New Zealander as head of industrial conglomerate Sembcorp and a German boss at the country's postal service. Singapore's most prestigious country club, the British-founded Tanglin – which has a S$100,000 joining fee – caps Singaporean membership at 51 per cent of the total, with the result that a substantial proportion of the club's members are European and North American.

Among Singapore's business elite, the connection to the US in particular runs deep. The high school of choice for the sons of Singapore business people is the Anglo-Chinese School, founded under British rule and where doing poorly at Mandarin is, for some boys, an ironic badge of pride. The heirs of Singapore business dynasties usually head to US business schools for the last lap of their education.

Global acquisitions by Singapore's tycoons have not faced the same hostility as deals involving Chinese companies. The anglicised elite, coupled with the fact that Western businesses are now so familiar with Singapore, helps explain the affinity. Closer to home, government-linked companies have run into hostility when on the acquisition trail in other Asian countries. A tie-up between SingTel and Hongkong Telecom failed in 2000 because, according to bankers and diplomats who followed the deal, Beijing did not want a Singapore state company controlling a major utility in its backyard.

Competition for jobs has spurred growing anxiety about migration in Singapore, an issue which has surfaced repeatedly in election debates. The government has been tightening restrictions on low-paid workers for years. More recently, it has raised the minimum salary threshold that foreign professionals must clear to have the right to work in Singapore and put pressure on companies to ensure that vacancies are advertised to Singaporeans. The brutal economic contraction that accompanied Covid-19 is likely to harden attitudes. During the election campaign in 2020, Singapore's foreign minister declared: 'The only reason we have foreigners here is to give an extra wind in our sails when the opportunity is there. Now we are in a storm and we need to shed ballast.'

The ceaseless quest for commercial advantage has occasionally brought risky business to Singapore. Leeson's downfall embedded Singapore in the public consciousness as a place where speculative fortunes could be made and lost. The controls at Barings were notably bad – Leeson, who was twenty-eight at the time, occupied a dual role, both in charge of trading and as a manager who monitored the trades. The culture clash at Barings between the old-school aristocratic bank and its new generation of hungry young 'barrow boy' traders has been well-documented. Leeson, the son of a plasterer from Watford, could not have been more different from the blue bloods at the top of Britain's oldest merchant bank. Its demise was also a story of the lure of Asia for European bankers. The perch in Singapore allowed Leeson to trade between two Asian markets. The idea was, at its simplest, to exploit price differences between the same contract in the Osaka and Singapore exchanges, buying in one market when the price was lower and selling in the other market when the price was high.

Instead of sticking to this, his strategy shifted to the riskier and more potentially lucrative one of betting on the long-term rise of the Japanese stock market. When he sustained losses, he took greater risks in an effort to win these back.

The collapse in Asian markets after the Kobe earthquake in 1995 exposed him, and the bank, to massive losses.

It would not be the last time that a European financial institution was stung by the risks of doing business in a new and distant market. In the wake of the global financial crisis, as many Western governments stepped up pressure on private banks over tax evasion, a number of Swiss banks expanded their operations in Asia. The combination of rapidly growing wealth in the region and relatively light scrutiny from regulators was a recipe for abuse. The venerable Swiss bank BSI, founded as Banca della Svizzera Italiana in the late nineteenth century, established a Singapore foothold in 2005. But the business mushroomed in 2009 when two senior executives from rival Coutts quit to join the Swiss bank, and dozens of Coutts staff resigned to follow them. Jho Low, a pudgy Malaysian businessman who became the biggest customer of BSI's Singapore branch, is alleged to have played a central role in a vast international corruption case involving billions of dollars siphoned from a Malaysian government fund, called 1MDB. Low has consistently denied wrongdoing and says the charges are politically motivated.

The scandal was global in scope. Looted government funds were used to buy artworks and property in Beverly Hills and Manhattan, according to US prosecutors, as well as allegedly financing the Hollywood film *The Wolf of Wall Street*. The case became a graphic illustration of the ethical pressures faced by private bankers in Asia. As BSI and other banks pushed for rapid expansion in their Singapore offices, setting high targets for their staff, questions about the sources of funding were dismissed. The bank became the custodian of US$2.3 billion in funds channelled from the Malaysian government. Yeo Jiawei, a wealth manager at BSI who had been lured away to work directly for Low, appeared to have been another intoxicated by a dream of stratospheric wealth.

Yeo, a slim young man with clean-cut good looks, sent his former supervisor at BSI a picture from a flight on a private jet and bragged about attending a boxing match in Las Vegas, where he took a selfie with Mike Tyson. In a society where so many had prospered in the space of a generation, the prospect of a short-cut to the top must have been irresistible.

Regulators around the world began to probe the affair after British journalist Clare Rewcastle Brown uncovered the first indications of wrongdoing in 2015. Singapore's authorities shut down two Swiss banks in the city, including BSI, and fined other banks after the scandal highlighted loopholes in their system for fighting money-laundering. As authorities cracked down, bankers implicated in the affair found themselves in court. In a dark wood-panelled courtroom in the down-at-heel state court building, I watched as Yeo, dressed in a purple prison jumpsuit and wearing shackles that clinked as he moved, was convicted of offences relating to the corruption case. Yeo was eventually sentenced to four and a half years in prison for money-laundering.

Singapore's regulators conceded that the scandal had tarnished the city's reputation, and vowed more intrusive inspections of banks for suspected money-laundering. The country's efficiency and political stability, the qualities that make it so attractive for legitimate businesses, also make it a target for the proceeds of white-collar crime. A bank executive described the affair as: 'a wake-up call for everyone ... everything tightened.'

Fu bu guo san dai – 'Wealth never survives three generations' – is the Chinese version of the saying, but many cultures have some version of this adage, reflecting the fact that grooming heirs to a family business is frequently a messy affair.

Unlike Japan, where family businesses lasting centuries have mastered generational transition, Singapore's family-controlled titans are heading into uncharted waters. The founding generation is dying out, while a second generation which successfully stabilised and expanded their inheritance is looking to the untested ranks of their sons and daughters. Meanwhile, a new generation of mainland Chinese entrepreneurs are making Singapore their home. In 2019, Zhang Yong, who was born in a small town in China's Sichuan province and made his fortune through the hotpot chain Haidilao, supplanted homegrown tycoons as the richest man in Singapore.

The founding fathers of Singapore businesses earned a reputation for being fierce and workaholic deal-makers. Born into poverty, they often retained penny-pinching habits; one tycoon is reputed to have carried his papers in a plastic bag in preference to a briefcase. Their grandchildren, raised in comfort, can be forgiven for having less fire in their bellies.

To understand the outlook of this new generation, I spoke to Wee Teng Wen, whose great-grandfather founded UOB in 1935. Wee launched a hospitality business after graduating from Wharton, the University of Pennsylvania's business school, opening a rooftop bar and then a private members' club. The club, Straits Clan, focuses on a younger crowd more interested in hearing adventurous ideas than enjoying country club facilities, Wee said. It has invited speakers willing to tackle potentially divisive issues such as gay rights.

We spoke on a video call, during a partial lockdown to curb the spread of Covid-19. Wee had a floppy fringe, which looked expensively cut, and a gym-honed physique. He was softly spoken, but firm about deflecting unwelcome questions. 'The country clubs were always more about prestige,' he told me. 'Not everyone can afford the S$100,000 to join and play golf.' His own version of a private members' club was set up to 'attract and promote diversity', with what he described as a relatively low fee, S$3000, around two-thirds of the average monthly salary in Singapore. The starting capital to set up the bar came, Wee says, from the sale of his own country club membership.

Did he come under pressure to go into banking? 'I was always fortunate because it was never direct pressure,' Wee said. 'It was always indirect or implied. I always had flexibility to carve my own path. In my generation the reins loosened considerably.' A year earlier, Wee's father – the chief executive of the family-owned bank – had said he would be willing to look outside the family for a successor, though his second son Teng Chuen had started working for the family business.

A cynic might say that running bars and clubs is a playboy's diversion before settling down to the family trade. For Wee, though, a hospitality business is a way of bridging divides. 'I've always been fortunate to be exposed to various networks,' he told me. 'Old business, having grown up in that world, and then the restaurant and lifestyle sector. I do quite a bit of investing so I'm plugged in to the start-up scene. No one was coming together and mixing and mingling.'

The older generation made their fortunes in more cut-throat businesses. The shift in style brought about by this generation reflects the more comfortable place Singapore has become. It is, perhaps, also what Singapore now needs.

11

Asian Values

Defending Singapore, with guns and ideas

Military top brass, defence officials, arms dealers and spies from East and West gather once a year at Singapore's Shangri-La hotel to size each other up, gossip and conspire. It's a scene of military theatre, with rifle-toting Gurkhas in body armour manning the checkpoints outside. Inside, gold-starred generals in shades of khaki and olive mingle with admirals in gleaming white beneath the vast chandeliers of the ballroom, a hangar-sized chamber decked out in cream and gold. The Shangri-La Dialogue, as the forum is known, has become the sumptuous setting for an increasingly fractious power struggle on Asia's high seas.

This is the Asian century, when the continent is forecast to retake its historic place as the economic heartland of the world. But it is also an era in which Asia's growing economic might and its hunger for more resources is fuelling military competition.

In the ballroom of the Shangri-La, the threats come cloaked in diplomatic jargon. Speakers refer to a 'rules-based order' and 'Freedom of Navigation operations'. But in recent years, the meaning beneath the clunky phrasing has become increasingly plain. China's determination to be a great power in Asia, backed up by increasing military might, has raised America's hackles and sown disquiet among US allies in the region, from Australia to Japan. For decades, the wealth and security of non-communist Asia has rested on the US military, which has kept the seas open to trade and sheltered its allies. This has not been a purely altruistic deal. American businesses have prospered greatly from investments and trade across the Pacific rim.

This calculus is changing. On reefs and atolls in the South China Sea, within a sweeping arc that Beijing calls the 'Nine-Dash Line', China has built radar facilities and runways for fighter jets. The zone China claims runs close to the coastline of several of its neighbours.

Vietnam, the Philippines, Taiwan, Malaysia and Brunei all have overlapping claims here. US warships and aircraft regularly cross through sea or airspace claimed by China, engaging in so-called 'freedom of navigation' patrols that assert their right of passage. The stakes are high. These are not just some of the world's busiest shipping lanes but waters teeming with fish, while vast natural gas and crude oil reserves lie beneath the seabed. Backed up by Chinese coastguard ships, Chinese fishing vessels have raided waters where Indonesia claims exclusive economic rights. China's coast guard has also confronted Malaysia and Vietnam over oil and gas exploration in the area.

In a usual year, the choreography of the Shangri-La Dialogue takes on a familiar pattern. America and its Asian partners hector China over its high-handed claims. The Chinese delegation indignantly push back. But the 2017 forum, the first of these diplomatic gatherings after Donald Trump was elected US president, was different.

Delegates gathered in the ballroom to hear the US defence secretary Jim Mattis, a former Marine general with a permanently sombre cast to his features, offer reassurance that America would continue to stand with its allies. 'Bear with us,' he told the assembled military men and spooks. 'Once we've exhausted all possible alternatives, the Americans will do the right thing.' His remarks fell flat, with friendly nations openly voicing scepticism about US intentions in the region. For Singapore, the forum's host, the tension between the West and a rising Asian power is particularly acute.

During the Cold War, Singapore's allegiance was plain. Though it has never been a formal US ally, the country was fiercely anti-communist. When the US was forced to withdraw from military bases in the Philippines, Singapore offered to host them instead. The island was too small to be of practical benefit – the Philippines bases had been America's biggest overseas military outposts – but the gesture was a signal of friendship. The war in Vietnam 'bought precious time for capitalist countries to gather strength in Asia', Singapore's prime minister wrote in 2020, offering a remarkably glowing assessment of a conflict now seen as hubris in the West.

For decades, Beijing was the sponsor of Singapore's ideological opponents. China provided arms and training for communist insurgencies across Southeast Asia through the 1950s and 1960s. Although this support began to wane from 1972, following Beijing's rapprochement with the US, China's conversion to capitalism has complicated the relationship. The US remains Singapore's most valued investor and the two countries have close defence ties, but trade ties with China are now essential to Singapore's prosperity, as is the case for all of America's allies and partners in Asia. As Mao's successors steered China on a new economic course,

Singapore could pull off a balancing act between the two powers, benefiting from China's growth while keeping close ties with the US. But China's growing inclination to flex its military and diplomatic muscles makes that balancing act an increasingly precarious one.

Unlike many of its neighbours, Singapore makes no claim to disputed waters in the South China Sea. But the island nation is stiff-necked about its attachment to international law, fearing the consequences for small nations if great powers do as they please and the risks to its own maritime trade if access to sea lanes becomes restricted. Singapore has urged China to respect a UN court ruling that rejects Beijing's claims in the South China Sea. As China's foreign policy has grown more assertive, Singapore has expanded defence cooperation with the US, allowing US surveillance aircraft and littoral combat ships – small warships designed for operations near the shore – to use its facilities. This has created a prickly relationship between the Chinese motherland and its distant kin in Singapore.

China is making determined efforts to court its global diaspora, including Singaporean Chinese. Young people have been encouraged to take part in 'root-seeking' summer camps in which they explore their heritage and learn about Chinese martial arts and calligraphy. Militaristic propaganda videos, uploaded to YouTube and shared on WhatsApp groups, boast of China's strength. An older generation of Chinese Singaporeans, who were educated at Chinese-language schools and feel a close affinity with China, are particularly susceptible to these films. Their impact is to encourage viewers to side with China in foreign policy arguments. Over the South China Sea, for example, they are likely to argue that China is simply setting right a historical injustice.

In 2020, Google deleted thousands of YouTube channels as

part of an investigation into 'coordinated influence operations linked to China'. A number of these channels uploaded information about Hong Kong, and the US response to Covid-19, Google said. While some ordinary Singaporeans have been swayed, such propaganda efforts have had no discernible impact on the government.

Conscious that it leads a multicultural and multiracial society, Singapore's government is wary of being perceived in the region as an agent of Chinese influence. Singapore was the last country in Southeast Asia, aside from Brunei, to establish diplomatic relations with the People's Republic, and it still maintains close official ties with Taiwan, which China regards as a part of its territory. Troops are sent from Singapore to Taiwan every year for military training, while in 2013 the two countries signed a free trade agreement. Late in 2016, six months before Jim Mattis addressed the massed ranks of generals in the Shangri-La's ballroom, these tensions burst into the open when Hong Kong customs officials seized nine of the Singapore military's armoured troop carriers, en route from Taiwan following a training exercise. Beijing made an official protest to Singapore over its military ties with Taiwan, urging Singapore to adhere to the 'One China' principle, the diplomatic acceptance that there is only one Chinese government. The armoured cars were released a few months later and shipped back to Singapore, but China's point had been made: when superpowers collide, smaller countries need to pick a side. *Global Times*, China's nationalist tabloid, suggested that the 'special bond' between the two countries was being eroded by Singapore's defiant stance over the South China Sea.

Pressure is likely to grow. Singapore has already been the focus of unconventional assault. In 2018, a cyberattack of 'unprecedented scale and sophistication' targeted a health database, extracting the personal details of 1.5 million patients. Prime minister Lee Hsien Loong's personal medication details were 'specifically targeted and repeatedly accessed', the Singapore government said. The government described the attacker as having the characteristics of an 'advanced persistent threat' group – in other words, a state or state-sponsored organisation.

And there are indications that the Chinese state has made use of Singapore as a cover for anti-US espionage. In 2020, a Singaporean man named Dickson Yeo pleaded guilty to acting as an agent for Chinese intelligence in the US. Yeo was accused of using a false consulting firm to lure Americans – including government employees and an army officer – who might be of interest to China. US officials say Yeo was recruited in 2015, when he was studying for a PhD in Singapore.

As a new superpower conflict beckons, Singapore, a city that has always faced both East and West, finds itself in a precarious position. Singapore was built by Asian migrants who brought with them the culture and languages of their homelands. Many were uneducated young men who knew little of their own heritage beyond traditions handed down through families, but as these communities grew richer, they established schools that revived and maintained ancestral learning. Their rulers were an English-speaking elite. George Brown, a British foreign secretary, once described Lee as the 'best bloody Englishman east of Suez'. The last three words were a reminder, if one were needed, that Lee would never be seen as a true Englishman, for all the British values he had absorbed.

After the fall of the Berlin Wall, Lee emerged as an unlikely champion of Confucius. The timing was not coincidental. The end of the Cold War sent a shiver down the spine of authoritarian regimes across Asia, offering a reminder of how rapidly a powerful system could crumble. The removal of the West's chief competitor made it easier to see democracy and liberal values – free speech, a free press, the right to protest – as universal ideals, rather than just one option in a contest of ideologies. In search of a stabilising influence, Singapore turned to ancient tradition.

A Chinese philosopher from the sixth century BC might not, at first glance, appear to have much to offer the modern world. Confucius disdained merchants and soldiers, yet the rising nations of Asia modernised their militaries and transformed their economies along Western lines. Confucian ethics stress filial piety and bearing children to continue the family line; across East Asia, birth rates have been declining, often at the behest of governments that wanted to contain population growth.

But elements of his philosophy appeared useful. Lee argued that Confucian traditions imbued Chinese Singaporeans with a strong allegiance to the group, a reverence for education and respect for scholarly leaders. This was a rewriting of Singapore's turbulent past. It might have accorded with Lee's vision of a perfectly ordered society, but it is hard to reconcile this with the violent labour disputes of Singapore's early days. Still, these strands of Singapore's heritage would be woven together into a narrative that challenged what Lee called 'the unlimited individualism of the Americans'. When it suits them, Singapore's rulers like to emphasise the importance of community and nation, at times when the people are being exhorted to submit to wise leadership and accept the sacrifice of some freedom for the common good. At other times, the pursuit of individual wealth and power is lauded, even when it is built on inherited privilege, as is the case with many of the young men groomed for leadership in the country's elite schools.

In 1991, Singapore crystallised these ideas in an official government statement, 'Shared Values', which explicitly put loyalty to the nation and community above individual freedom as well as emphasising the importance of family and the idea of racial and religious harmony. It was taught in schools as a new subject, civics education. The statement was Singapore's spin on an ideology which became known as 'Asian Values'. At home, Asian Values became a way to inoculate the population against the Western ideas that flowed in alongside Singapore's embrace of capitalism. Investment by foreign multinationals was welcome, but the West's bohemian culture and pursuit of individual liberty was regarded with suspicion. The last thing that Singapore Inc needed was workers who wanted to drop out of society.

Singapore's leaders feared the growth of two tribes, sometimes dubbed 'cosmopolitans' and 'heartlanders'. Cosmopolitan Singaporeans were at ease with a more globalised nation, comfortable speaking English. They had higher education levels and skills that were valued in a global market. They had smaller families and shared the attitudes of other metropolitan cultures, from acceptance of homosexuality to scepticism towards religious faith. The heartlanders, by contrast, made a living as taxi drivers or stallholders, and were more comfortable speaking Singlish or an Asian language. They were judged to be more conservative, more deeply rooted in their traditional cultures. The ruling party like to present themselves as mediators between the two, understanding the need to embrace modernity while preserving the country's values.

Tolerance of homosexuality is one of the perceived dividing lines – in 2014, a picture book about two male penguins rearing a chick together was withdrawn from the shelves of children's libraries in Singapore, out of concern that it clashed with conservative values. The book, *And Tango Makes Three*, has been equally controversial in the US. Since it was published in 2005, more people have requested its removal from US schools and libraries than any other publication.

Singapore's rulers were not the only ones in search of a new creed. The early 1990s were an optimistic time in East Asia. For three decades it had been the world's fastest growing region, and the four Asian tigers – Singapore, Hong Kong, Korea and Taiwan – were leaders of the pack. It seemed obvious that the region would not just catch up with but outstrip the West, achieving economic dominance and offering a rival political vision. In 1993, representatives of more than thirty Asian nations, from leviathan powers like Japan and India to minnows like Bhutan and the Solomon Islands, gathered in Bangkok to offer a challenge to the idea of a global liberal order. The Asian states agreed that human rights were universal, but warned they should not be a condition of development aid or 'an instrument of political pressure'. They rallied around the idea that human rights needed to be seen in the context of differing historical, cultural and religious backgrounds. The statement gave cover for governments seeking the latitude to pile pressure on political opponents or harass human rights activists.

This rhetoric found an eager audience across the former Soviet Union too. Vladimir Putin has placed conservative values and the suppression of liberal opposition at the heart of his system. Putin's protégé Dmitry Medvedev openly admired Singapore, as did leaders of post-Soviet nations from Kazakhstan to Georgia. Singapore's rapid economic growth and social harmony, combined with tightly controlled political freedom, appeared to offer a third way to a clutch of autocratic regimes who wanted to open up to capitalism while resisting democracy.

Singapore's magnetism for strongmen and dictators was on display once again when North Korea's leader Kim Jong-un arrived for a summit with US President Donald Trump in 2018. The night before the summit meeting, Kim toured Gardens by the Bay, the lush flower gardens on Singapore's waterfront, and the Marina Bay Sands hotel and casino complex. Highlights of his visit featured in a North Korean television broadcast which praised 'clean, beautiful and advanced' Singapore. One of Asia's poorest and most isolated nations was being offered a deliberate glimpse of one of the continent's richest and best-connected, in images that swept from the romance of its glitzy skyline to the cargo handling capacity of its port. The forty-two-minute film quoted Kim saying that he was eager to learn Singapore's lessons.

Emulating Singapore is easier said than done. Closing down the space for political opposition is insufficient, as admirers of the Lee model soon find. Kazakhstan's president Nursultan Nazarbayev regarded Lee Kuan Yew as one of two eminent founders of a nation (his other hero was Charles de Gaulle), but while the Kazakh leader succeeded in keeping a chokehold on dissent, the giant post-Soviet country built fragile prosperity on the back of its oil wealth and is plagued by corruption. Instead, copying Singapore's economic success and social stability requires a government that can success-fully carry out systemic changes such as improving schools and tackling sleaze in public office.

Aside from China, there is one curious example of a coun-try that has successfully adopted elements of the Singapore model, and that is Rwanda. On the face of it, few coun-tries are more different than a landlocked and mountainous African state and an island at the crossroads of Asia's mar-itime commerce. Yet Paul Kagame, the rebel commander who ended the genocide in 1994 and has ruled ever since, describes Singapore as an 'inspiration'. Rwandan officials have studied Singapore's urban design and the training of its civil service. The tiny African country has recovered from devastating communal violence to achieve political stability and rapid economic growth. The streets of the capital Kigali are clean and crime rates are low, while official corruption has been kept at bay. Poverty and child mortality have fallen and the government has introduced a national health insurance scheme.

There is a dark side to this achievement. Rwanda is intolerant of dissent. The media is tightly controlled and human rights groups report that the government operates a pervasive network of informants. The country, which remains heavily reliant on foreign donors, poses a Singapore-style dilemma: testing the degree to which it is acceptable to trade human rights for development.

But it is China that has been the single most important student of the Singapore model. China has been obsessed with the tiny city state for decades. On a tour of southern China in 1992, Deng Xiaoping urged the Chinese to learn from Singapore, praising the island nation's orderly society. 'We ought to use their experience as a model and we ought to manage things even better than they do,' he declared. Like Singapore, China has a state-led economy with state-owned enterprises dominating key sectors. Two masters' degrees at Singapore's Nanyang Technological University – courses in managerial economics and public administration – became known as the Mayors' Class because of the number of Chinese officials they attracted. In November 1991, months after Singapore published its statement emphasising subordination to the state, China issued its own white paper on human rights, which again placed the rights of the individual below those of society and the state. Alongside Singapore and

Malaysia, China became a public defender of the concept of Asian Values.

Singapore's rhetoric had helped pave the way for the rise of an autocratic superpower. Yet the emergence of such a powerful proponent of Asian Values has, paradoxically, exposed some of the weaknesses at the heart of this ideology.

There isn't much evidence that Singaporeans are as conservative in their values as their rulers make out. The existence of Pink Dot and dissident bloggers such as Roy Ngerng suggest that Singaporeans want the freedom to express their identity and question their leaders. They may be attached to family life, but as the gay father who sought to adopt a child born through surrogacy indicates, their idea of what constitutes a family does not necessarily equate to a heterosexual couple with two children. It is true that there is some distinction between liberal 'cosmopolitans' and more conservative 'heartlanders', but this is likely to erode as Singaporeans attend university in growing numbers.

While the US was the sole superpower, Singapore's leaders were free to reject its values while benefiting from a global system that rested on American strength. Beijing's aggressiveness has pushed Singapore deeper into a club of Asian democracies, strengthening its defence ties with Japan and India. In a sea of larger powers, a small nation like Singapore makes a tempting morsel. In a 1966 speech, Lee Kuan Yew suggested two possible defence mechanisms, making itself a 'poisonous shrimp' that would give a predator indigestion or swimming in the wake of a bigger fish for protection. The country has since embraced both strategies, aligning itself closely with the US while building up its own armed forces.

With 59,000 active personnel, the Singapore Armed Forces is dwarfed by most of its neighbours, but it is the most lavishly equipped in Southeast Asia. 'Poisonous shrimp' may have been an appropriate description in its early years, but the SAF is now a more deadly beast designed for a defence strategy that can hold a larger power at bay. Singapore boasts the region's biggest air force, including around sixty F16 combat aircraft, a plane that can fly over 500 miles from its base, strike and return to its starting point, as well as a fleet of unmanned drones, used for reconnaissance, that can stay aloft for up to fourteen hours. The US has given Singapore approval to buy up to twelve stealth fighters, while its navy operates a fleet of four submarines, a weapon that lends itself to asymmetric warfare, the ju-jitsu of enabling a smaller nation to resist a bigger one. A submarine, so long as it is quiet enough to stay hidden in the deep, can provide a powerful deterrent to a much larger fleet of surface warships.

Since the 1980s, the country has practised a doctrine of 'total defence', which involves preparing the population psychologically for emergencies, building a strong economy that can pay for its military expenditure as well as creating a highly trained professional force capable of rapid mobilisation. 'Not if, but when' is the sombre slogan that appears on posters simulating the gory aftermath of a terrorist attack.

With limited space, Singapore's military routinely trains far beyond its borders. The Shoalwater Bay training area in Queensland, northern Australia, which is also used by Australian, US and New Zealand troops, is about four times the size of Singapore. Its air force pilots train at bases in Arizona and Idaho, where a substantial portion of Singapore's combat aircraft are permanently based, as well as the US Pacific territory of Guam.

Singapore's forces have taken part in humanitarian,

peacekeeping and medical missions overseas but have fired shots in anger just once, in 1991, when commandos stormed a hijacked Singapore Airlines flight. Flight SQ117 was hijacked by four Pakistani militants shortly after take-off from Kuala Lumpur, Malaysia's capital, for the short trip to Singapore's Changi airport. The hijackers, armed with knives, demanded the release of detainees held in Pakistan, and threatened to make an American passenger their first victim. All four hijackers were killed when commandos seized the grounded plane in an operation that lasted thirty seconds. All of the 126 passengers and crew survived. 'It was really surgical,' said one of the commandos, Fred Cheong. 'So we just have to be very clear, shoot very straight, and let's do it.'

The hijacking is a faded memory, but the government constantly reminds citizens of the need for vigilance. A military thread runs through public life in Singapore, which requires all male citizens and permanent residents to perform two years of national service once they turn eighteen. National service was intended to compensate for Singapore's size by making use of all available manpower, but it had the unintended consequence of creating a binding institution in Singapore society. Unlike schools, whose make-up is often skewed by privilege, the military brings all classes and races together.

For Ravi Alfreds, who grew up in a middle-class household and attended one of Singapore's elite schools, national service gave him a chance to mix with a radically different social circle. He trained with the sons of people who drove taxis or worked as food hawkers. 'There were people whose families were struggling to make ends meet, people for whom English wasn't their first language,' Alfreds told me.

Even in the levelling environment of the armed forces, however, privileged sons are widely believed to get an easier ride. The sons of politicians and senior executives, known as 'White Horses', are reputed to be spared punishments such as disciplinary bouts of push-ups or weekend confinement to camp. It was not until 2009 that Singapore's armed forces appointed its first general from the Singapore Malay community, when Ishak Ismail became a 'one-star' general, the lowest rung of the senior command. By the end of 2020, he remained the sole Malay to have achieved this distinction.

Numerous senior government ministers and heads of government-linked companies are drawn from the army, including the prime minister Lee Hsien Loong, who was promoted to the rank of brigadier-general aged thirty-one, a year before he entered parliament. Ordinary Singaporeans can sometimes be derisive about the men – and occasional women – who parachute from the military into the highest reaches of civilian life. Given Singapore's largely bloodless post-independence history, its generals lack combat experience. 'Paper generals' is a common insult. But Singapore's elite regards the military as a valuable training ground, taking men and women who excel academically and fostering their leadership skills. A Singapore reservist who joined a rescue mission to Taiwan after an earthquake described it to me as a 'camaraderie, forged through difficult moments, that warms the heart'.

The importance of the military in national life was underlined by the hapless candidacy of Ivan Lim in the 2020 general election. Lim, a shipyard manager selected to run for the ruling People's Action Party, was undermined by critics who accused him of high-handed behaviour in his professional life. Among the most wounding accusations was a Facebook post by a man who said he was the regimental sergeant major of the unit Lim commanded during his national service. The RSM drew attention to an episode in which

Lim told junior officers they were not permitted inside the air-conditioned tent being used for a briefing, a vignette that added to perceptions he was condescending to subordinates. Lim issued a statement in which he said that 'people can have different perspectives of the same incident', but the damage was done and he withdrew from the election soon after.

'The RSM and commanding officer usually get along. It's a symbiotic relationship,' said Alfreds, who did his own national service from 2000 to 2002. 'If the RSM doesn't respect the CO, it's hard to see the men respecting the officer. It's quite telling.'

The emphasis Singapore places on its military might be seen as the embodiment of Asian Values. By its nature, the armed forces emphasise community and nation over the individual. But the Lim affair suggests a contrasting reading: the military is also a place where individuals are put to the test and personal character is revealed. The backlash against his candidacy, in which ordinary voters defied a traditionally hierarchical political system, was a democratic moment.

In the West, the Cold War was a frozen conflict of espionage and propaganda, punctuated with assassination and ending in an unequivocal victory. In Asia, the struggle between communism and capitalism had a more ambiguous outcome. For China, 1989 did not mark the dawn of freedom, but Tiananmen Square and a grim confirmation of the Communist Party's grip on power.

China is now at the heart of a political and economic project that is knitting the Eurasian landmass together. Railways, pipelines, ports and power plants are being built with Chinese investment and Chinese contractors. The 'Belt and Road Initiative', as it is called in English, is creating a network that embraces countries as far afield as Kazakhstan and Sri Lanka, Oman and Belgium. From Kunming in southern China a rail line is snaking its way into northern Thailand, a tentacle of the Belt and Road project. Ultimately the line will run all the way down into southern Malaysia. At the centre of the network is a power that stifles debate, controls the information its citizens receive, and is resolutely opposed to democracy. It seems the ultimate triumph of Asian Values that a China inspired by the idea of state and community above the individual is now the dominant force of a continent. Singapore can bolster its defence ties with the US to strengthen its security and insist on international rules, but its economic linkages with China will only grow more important. The risk of being independent-minded while needing Chinese trade is that an angry China responds with economic sanctions, as it has done against Australia. In the years to come, Singapore's diplomats will need to be honey-tongued to defuse the tension.

Early in 2017, I toured the glossy apartment blocks and arcades of a new city being built on reclaimed land at the southern tip of Malaysia, just across the strait from Singapore. The unusual thing about this settlement, called Forest City, is that many of the residents will not be Malaysians or Singaporeans. Every week, busloads of prospective buyers from mainland China were brought in to take a tour. In China, the project was pitched as a way for investors to move money abroad. Its location in a trop-ical country near Chinese-speaking Singapore added to its lustre. The city is expected to house 700,000 people when it is complete.

Among the buyers was Xing Han Jiang, aged sixty-two, a businessman from Shanghai who had bought two apartments. 'I fell in love with the greenery, the beach and the weather,' he said. 'In Malaysia, there's no winter – but China gets very cold in winter, which is no good for my body.' Runze Yu, chief strategy officer of the property developer Country Garden, joined the economic dots. 'It's like gravity,' he told me. 'Once you have two very heavy economies close to each other timewise, you will see bigger GDP being generated.'

12

The Art of Resistance

Art, a changing society and the boundaries of expression

'Nothing to do?' the sign asked in white lettering on brown. Swimmers padded past in flip-flops, heading for the beach on Sentosa, the resort island off Singapore's southern coast. 'Go fly kite,' was the instruction below. And then, below that: 'Actually, cannot. Sorry. Find something else to do.'

It was the perfect spoof of Singapore's rule-oriented culture, dangling the promise of sanctioned fun before snatching it abruptly away. So perfect that tourists frequently confuse it with the real thing and share the picture online as an example of bureaucratic absurdity. The giveaway that it might not be the work of a ministry is the use of Singlish, where 'cannot' is used to mean 'no', and the closing mockery of an official apology.

If the purpose of art is to imagine alternate worlds, it becomes a particularly fraught activity in an engineered society. Public art in Singapore is routinely unthreatening, with a tendency either towards idealised human figures or smooth abstractions. Art is sometimes a form of investment, as with the Dalí sculpture on display outside the headquarters of UOB, the Singapore bank, and occasionally simply decorative. It is startling to find anything even mildly irreverent.

The work on the beachfront is by Sam Lo, an artist who first came to public attention when they were twenty-four and had just been arrested. (Lo is non-binary and uses the pronouns they/them.) Their crime was to post stickers on pedestrian crossing buttons – 'press for time travel', one read – and for spray-painting the words 'My grandfather road' on a busy street in the city centre. 'My grandfather road' is a jibe aimed at drivers who act as if their family owns the tarmac under their wheels. 'Does this road belong to your grandfather?' is the rhetorical question being asked. The answer, of course, is that public spaces in Singapore are strictly policed by the state. Their use of Singlish is also a reminder of Singapore officialdom's uptight attitude to English: even a misplaced apostrophe can be an act of rebellion.

Under Singapore's Vandalism Act, Lo faced up to six months in prison or a S$1000 fine. Women are spared corporal punishment but caning is mandatory for men convicted of vandalism. The disproportionate severity of Lo's treatment for creating playful street art drew attention around the world and a clamour for leniency at home. Lo was nicknamed 'The Sticker Lady', and the hashtag #freestickerlady took off on Twitter. Arriving in court dressed in a dark suit and sunglasses, the artist pleaded guilty to seven counts of 'mischief' and was sentenced to 240 hours of community service.

Lo's experience of the arrest and trial made them realise how powerful art could be. 'The papers called me a vandal on the first day,' they told me. 'On the second day they called me a street artist.' Lo, a slender figure in a black T-shirt, arms wreathed in tattoos, spoke to me from their studio, surrounded by half-finished works of sculpture. 'We know that graffiti is illegal,' Lo said. 'But the reason why we use the street is that it's the biggest gallery there is, and it's where the public is. With every sticker I put out, it made people smile.' The idea that Singapore has no cultural life is a myth. Artists have been the antennae of a nation in transition, registering and interpreting the changes in the air.

As Singapore was transformed into an industrial society in the 1960s and 1970s, people were cut loose from their traditional culture and associations. Men who had earned an irregular living as casual labourers were now working in factories. Many women left the home to find paid employment for the first time. Children went from playing in ramshackle villages where chickens pecked the dirt to apartments on the upper floors of high-rises.

Singapore was a newborn nation, but its culture was not a blank slate. Chinese migrants brought with them a conception of art as a vehicle for social and political reform. The art of Singapore's first postcolonial decades reflected the abrupt wrench of a society in transition. Kuo Pao Kun, whose family moved to Singapore from China when he was ten, became one of the country's foremost dramatists. Kuo, who wrote in Mandarin, targeted exploitative capitalism and celebrated workers who stood up to unscrupulous bosses. *The Struggle*, his 1969 play about families evicted from their homes to make way for industrialisation, was banned a fortnight before it was due to be performed for the first time. 'The tickets were sold, the stage was rented and the show had to go on,' actor Yong Ser Pin said years later, recalling how the cast filled the gap by throwing together an impromptu poetry recital. The play was Kuo's second, but he had already acquired a reputation as a seditious writer with a debut work critical of Singapore's nascent tourism industry, featuring a tour agency that lures a young woman into prostitution. Written at a time when Singapore's government was eager to attract foreign investment, and had just pacified trade unions after years of labour unrest, it is easy to see why *The Struggle* attracted official hostility.

With his wife Goh Lay Kuan, a dancer and choreographer, Kuo founded the Singapore Performing Arts School, where she taught ballet and he taught drama. Their daughter Kuo Jian Hong said her parents believed life and art were 'inseparable ... They felt it important to speak for people who don't have a voice, or can't be heard. The underdogs.'

In 1976, both Kuo and his wife were detained under the Internal Security Act. According to a *Straits Times* article headlined 'The Faces of Subversion', the couple's performing arts school had been set up 'to propagate leftist dance and drama'. Goh, nicknamed the Red Ballerina in the press, was released a few months later after giving a televised confession, but Kuo would be detained for over four years and was stripped of his Singapore citizenship on release. He learned languages in prison, becoming fluent in Malay and starting to learn German. He joked that if he had been detained for longer, he would have become fluent in German too. His writing changed in prison, his daughter said, becoming more complex. 'Before detention it was more black and white, and after that, rarely.'

Singapore's Chinese-language artists were a straightforward political foe but the West's youth culture was a more complex threat, seen as corroding personal morality but also associated with the street protests and radical politics of Europe and the US. Censors banned The Beatles' 'Lucy in the Sky with Diamonds' and, with less obvious justification, 'Yellow Submarine'. It took decades before

restrictions on these songs and other tracks thought to celebrate drug-taking were lifted. The drug references were not
the only problem. The defiant individualism celebrated in
Western rock music was at odds with the conformist credo
of Asian Values.

By the 1980s, however, Singapore's government was focusing on the need to shift beyond manufacturing and turned
a calculating eye to art as a way to diversify the country's
economic base. The arts had trophy value too. Singapore
aspired to be a global city and the presence of artists put a
cosmopolitan gloss on that aspiration. If the country sought
to be a hub for commerce and finance, like New York or
London, attracting and hosting artistic talent was an essential
mark of sophistication. For the most part, nudity and profanity remained off-limits, deemed unacceptable by censors
concerned to uphold family values. Naked bodies were rarely
seen on Singapore stages, until in 1986 the Ballet National
du Senegal were permitted to perform traditional African
dances, bare-breasted, at the Singapore Arts Festival. 'The
director of the culture ministry took the official view that
toplessness is not allowed,' recalled Arun Mahizhnan, one of
the festival's organisers. 'The story is that when this reached
the ears of Lee Kuan Yew's wife, she said: "are we such
prudes?"' Political writing, meanwhile, was only permitted
if it referred to other countries, such as criticism of apartheid
South Africa. Any reflections on domestic politics needed to
be in code.

Through the 1960s and 70s, Chinese-language theatre had
commanded substantial audiences, but by the 1980s it was in
decline, partly because of the political constraints on writers
and partly because English was supplanting Chinese as the
dominant language among younger Singaporeans. Visitors
to Singapore complained of its cultural desolation, knowing

little of its former abundance. When Kuo returned to drama after his release from detention in 1980, he began writing in English as well as Chinese. The use of English made Kuo more palatable to English-educated cabinet ministers, who saw and appreciated his work. His first play after detention, *The Little White Sailing Boat*, about a young man who gives up family wealth to pursue his socialist ideals, was scrutinised closely by censors. 'I argued that we should see it through an artistic lens, and not a political one, and in the case of Pao Kun it worked,' said Mahizhnan, who staged the play at the Singapore Arts Festival.

One of Kuo's best-loved works, *The Coffin is Too Big for the Hole*, dates from this period. First performed in 1985, the monologue is narrated by a man whose grandfather's traditional Chinese coffin will not fit a standard-sized plot. In the struggle with inflexible bureaucracy that follows, Kuo hints at the constraints imposed on individuals and Singapore's traditional cultures by its transformation. In 1989, in a remarkable reversal of fortune, Kuo was awarded the Cultural Medallion, Singapore's highest award for the arts. A decade later, his 1995 play *Descendants of the Eunuch Admiral* made the Singapore compromise even more explicit. The eunuch admiral of the title is the fifteenth-century Chinese seafarer Zheng He, who was castrated to serve the Ming emperor. In Kuo's allegory, modern Singaporeans have lost their vitality and intellectual spark. They have become slaves, but are lulled into submission by material success.

In recent decades, Singapore has built a spectacular arts infra-structure, including the Esplanade performance space, which opened in 2002, and the National Gallery, a conversion of two colonial buildings, the Supreme Court and City Hall, which opened in 2015. But these gleaming new spaces lack new ideas to fill them. The National Gallery's collection does however feature important artworks from Singapore's history, including pieces by Chen Wen Hsi, who migrated to Singapore from China in 1948. His paintings, influenced by Cubism as well as traditional Chinese art, draw on observation of nature to create abstract forms. A Chen painting of gibbons dangling from tree branches – a glorious swirl of tree and monkey limbs – is featured on Singapore's S$50 bill.

The gallery touches on historic controversy, too, featuring works from a group of social realist artists calling themselves the Equator Art Society, active in the 1950s and 1960s. The group's work, though less overtly political than Kuo's drama, hints at communist sympathies. One famous work, *Epic Poem of Malaya*, features a youth declaiming from a book with a red cover. Alongside these historical works, the gallery tends to feature international blockbuster shows by artists like Yayoi Kusama.

Tiny and expensive, Singapore is a difficult place for an artist to survive, lacking the dilapidated buildings and run-down neighbourhoods that often become creative and bohemian spaces in other countries. Arts philanthropy is growing, but the state is by far the main source of funding. Under a state-backed cultural plan, Renaissance City, launched at the turn of the millennium, the government opened the purse strings for artists. It had an economic rationale: ministers wanted to establish Singapore as an attractive destination for creative industries and the talented individuals these industries needed. But there was also a political purpose behind it. Ministers talked of 'cultural ballast' that would strengthen Singapore's sense of national identity. Through the creation of shared stories and images of Singapore, the arts were to be an instrument of nation-building.

Artists pushed for a relaxation of boundaries too, but this proved a little more complicated. The trouble lay in squaring the official desire for art that would bolster the national narrative with artists' own interest in giving an alternative account of affairs. 'The Renaissance City report is an example of the government stepping in, regulating, searching for what they want,' said Lim Tzay Chuen, a Singaporean artist. 'But they don't know what they want. We, the arts community, are a digit, a statistic, to serve their purpose: "How many artists do we have? How many museums do we have?"'

For Singapore's entry to the 2005 Venice Biennale, Lim proposed a wholesale relocation of the Merlion, a statue of a fantastical beast with the head of a lion and the tail of a fish, spouting water from its mouth, that stands in front of the commercial towers of Marina Bay. The lion's face is turned east, the direction that according to feng shui principles brings prosperity.

'The story of the Merlion is a ridiculous story,' Lim says. 'What was important to me about the project for the Venice Biennale was having the statue move out of Singapore, so that kids would be able to rethink and rewrite the story of the Merlion. I imagined primary school kids going to the Merlion park, without the statue, and teachers saying, "it's gone for a swim, it's gone for a vacation". And then you could have the kids come up with their own, better stories.' Lim, in dark-rimmed glasses and a flowing black beard, chain-smokes and swigs green tea from a glass as we speak.

It's a compelling idea, removing a state-sponsored mascot and creating an absence that would allow Singapore's people to use their own imaginations, but his vision never became a reality. The request was declined by the Singapore Tourist Board, which is responsible for the Merlion. Instead, the artist designed two luxury toilets as Singapore's entry to the Biennale. Along with the washrooms, visitors to the Singapore pavilion were greeted by a sign reading: 'I wanted to bring Mike over' – Mike was Lim's codename for the Merlion. An attempt to transplant the Merlion from Asia to Europe had become a conceptual piece about the clash between art and bureaucracy, and Lim's failure to achieve his goal. To its credit, the Singapore government went along with this provocative work. Gallingly for Lim, a few years later, Denmark temporarily relocated the Little Mermaid to the Shanghai Expo, attracting the controversy and admiration that should have been his.

Lim continues his negotiation with Singapore's slowly shifting attitudes to art. In one discussion with the management of a Singapore gallery, he proposed a text-based work with the letters P, A and P (the initials of the ruling party) printed in fading pigment on a white sheet of paper. 'The idea would be that the red pigment of the letters would fade. And after fifty years, the work is just a white, blank paper,' Lim told me. 'But the director of the arts space said that this work would require too many years of commitment. Which was my point.' Even in privately owned art spaces, art that directly confronts Singapore's politics is hard for curators to stomach.

Singapore has done an effective job of controlling the past. When I speak to younger Singaporeans, I am struck by how much is left out of their historical knowledge. You will hear that Singapore is a conservative society, but not that it had a radical past that was vigorously suppressed. Pivotal

episodes in history are stamped with the government's inter-
pretation. The detentions of Singapore's early decades will
occasionally be defended as a necessary measure to stem the
communist tide.

Sonny Liew, a cartoonist, had the same experience when
he began to delve into Singapore's past. Liew had always been
interested in Singapore's history, but in his late teens he was
startled to come across James Minchin's *No Man Is an Island*.
It was the first time that he had read a book that was critical of the system and its founding father. Liew was a fan of
2000AD, the British science-fiction comic where the future
was often an allegorical version of contemporary racism, religious bigotry and authoritarianism. The two interests came
together in *The Art of Charlie Chan Hock Chye*, which retells
the country's history through the story of an imaginary
comic artist named Charlie Chan.

Published in 2015, the comic undercuts the official version of Singapore's story in which the PAP transformed
the island from a swamp into one of the world's wealthiest
nations. Instead, competing histories of Singapore are fed
through a science fiction blender. In one strand, the British
colonial rulers appear as green-skinned alien overlords, the
Hegemons, who force humanity to adopt their language,
Hegemonese, for all official business. Lee Kuan Yew appears
as a lawyer who defends workers' rights, but alongside him
is Lim Chin Siong, the left-winger with whom he joined
forces to win power in 1959. The graphic novel imagines an
alternative future in which Lim, rather than being detained
in Operation Coldstore in 1963, becomes prime minister
and Singapore develops under left-wing leadership while Lee
becomes a vociferous critic in exile.

Instead of a straightforward riposte to the standard narrative, the graphic novel becomes a kaleidoscopic vision of

counterfactual Singapores, with surreal retellings of history. In one sequence a giant robot defends student protesters from brutal colonial police; in another, British army officers are portrayed as monkeys while invading Japanese soldiers become growling dogs. The 'out-of-bounds markers' that indicate the limits of what Singaporean journalists are allowed to write become a whiteboard marker that can turn a cartoon character's smile into a frown. 'Lim Chin Siong . . . I hadn't read about him before I did the research,' Liew told me. 'He was considered Lee's biggest political opponent. It's interesting how he has been erased over the years. Alternate takes on history have been semi-erased.'

When I met Singaporeans who asked difficult questions, they often had an element of the outsider in their background, and this was true of Liew, who was born in Malaysia before moving to Singapore to study. He studied abroad, reading philosophy at Clare College, Cambridge. After *The Art of Charlie Chan* was published, Singapore's National Arts Council withdrew an S$8000 grant, an official saying that Liew's version of the country's history 'potentially undermines the authority or legitimacy of the government and its public institutions'. The book was not banned however, becoming a bestseller in the country and winning Singapore's most prestigious literary prize, the first time a graphic novel had done so. Liew continued to use a state-subsidised studio. A few years later, the artist was awarded a grant from the same government funding body, which he returned. 'There's nothing on the scale of Kuo Pao Kun, but the fact that it's still always there in the background compels you to self-censor,' Liew said. 'What happened in the past gets you to behave in the present without having the same sanctions again.'

An artist is less likely to be jailed or exiled than in the past.

But in a more comfortable society, writers and artists worry about whether being seen as troublemakers will affect their careers. An exhibition of original artwork from Liew's book featured at the Angoulême International Comics Festival in France, one of the world's biggest comics events, in 2018. The festival organisers approached the Singapore government for funding, but were declined, Liew says. 'They didn't turn them down right away but kept them wondering for a long time. It's never explicit and you are never really sure about what's happening.'

The end of the Cold War, and the end of a generation of a Chinese-educated writers and artists, has decreased antagonism between artists and the state. But the relationship remains unpredictable, and the authorities are vigorous in tackling artists who stray too far into a direct challenge to authority. Government officials argue that their approach is not ideological, but instead focuses on holding together the common ground. This is a familiar refrain for the PAP, which still fears the prospect of culture wars over hot-button issues like abortion or gay rights that have split societies in the West. 'You look at where social norms are, and you try to gauge what society, by and large, finds acceptable,' Rosa Daniel, chief executive of the National Arts Council, told me. 'Our objective is to ensure Singapore stays together including all the newcomers co-existing with local-born Singaporeans.'

Daniel suggests that artists are able to 'explore all topics, whether it's religion, nudity, profanity, sexuality. It's all there. It's always about the treatment and the motivation.' The treatment is sometimes objectionable if the artist takes a very skewed and divisive view, Daniel adds. 'We may object to funding that, but this does not stop the artist from putting out the work as long as no law is broken.' Our conversation turns to *The Art of*

Charlie Chan, and she tells me bluntly that her agency should not have funded the book. 'I am very short of funding dollars,' Daniel said. 'If I have two works and one ticks all the boxes, why would I fund the one that doesn't tick all boxes?'

A few years ago, Singapore politicians and officials began eagerly discussing the theories of Richard Florida, the urban economist who argued that a 'creative class' of knowledge workers was drawn to living in diverse and tolerant cities. Florida suggested that more bohemian cities were more likely to attract these workers. On the face of it, Singapore does not seem to fit the bill of a city open to eccentricity. Yet in recent years, Singapore's creative industries, from performing arts to advertising and design, have been growing faster than the economy as a whole. Florida himself identified Singapore as the world's leading country for the percentage of workers whose jobs require them to think and innovate.

But it is tax and regulation that have enabled the growth of this economy. Singapore's rigorous protection of intellectual property, skilled workforce and low taxes have attracted games designers such as Electronic Arts and Ubisoft, as well as the film production company Lucasfilm, which moved into an eight-storey complex shaped like a space-age boomerang and nicknamed the Sandcrawler. As well as customising products for the region, these offices employ international teams of artists working on visual effects for games and films. Kathleen Kennedy, president of Lucasfilm and a veteran Hollywood producer with credits including *E.T.* and *Jurassic Park*, said the Singapore operation was 'comparable to exactly what we are doing in San Francisco or Vancouver'. In other words, like those cities, Singapore had become a place where talented artists chose to live.

Here, Singapore offers a challenge to the idea that a society with fewer restrictions will earn an artistic dividend. While the most provocative and disruptive creative forms, from graffiti to performance art, seem to need a liberal democracy in which to thrive, it may be that a more authoritarian state can harness the economic energy of the creative industries in the same way that it once attracted manufacturers: through education, discipline and a business-friendly environment. Singapore's rigorous legal protection of intellectual property is a significant advantage for creative businesses. China, by contrast, has been accused by the FBI of 'stealing innovation' in sectors ranging from agriculture to hi-tech.

It's true that Singapore lacks a homegrown cultural export. It has nothing like K-pop to offer the world, but the global popularity of Korean youth culture is a phenomenon few countries can match. So far, the biggest cultural export that Singapore has reared domestically is One Championship, a promoter of mixed martial arts – the term 'cultural' is used loosely in this context.

If Singapore's authorities have cautiously relaxed boundaries in recent years, it may not be a sign of growing liberalism. Instead, you could see this as a recognition of their victory in setting the limits of acceptable challenge. There is no one who offers the same degree of defiance to the ruling order that Kuo once did. Yet Singaporeans remain remarkably persistent at attempting to free themselves from the constraints imposed on their minds.

A year after 'Sticker Lady' Lo was arrested for placing stickers at pedestrian crossings, they were commissioned to produce the public artwork on Sentosa. They parodied Singapore's rule-driven idea of fun. 'My biggest theme is escapism, or release,' Lo said. 'I've always believed that although as a city we are rather progressive, we are at heart a rather conservative society steeped with deeply instilled Asian values that we brought over from previous generations. If people were to truly realise who they are without the need for societal constructs, they might find a true version of themselves. Maybe there'd be a lot of chaos and that's the price to pay, it's whether we want to pay for it or not. Those signs were a parody of how those walls are keeping us in.'

13

Sin City

Sex work, gambling and illicit drugs

The shopfront was decorated with a silhouette image of peasant women in conical hats and *ao dai*, the traditional Vietnamese tunic dress, indicating the nationality of the workers inside. A few doors down, red lanterns hanging outside another brothel showed that the women here were from mainland China. The air was ripe with the aroma of tropical fruit, mingled with cooking smells from food stalls. It was late, but the night air was still muggy. We stopped at a restaurant that was little more than an alcove facing onto the street, and which specialised in dishes of creamy white soy milk soup accompanied by sticks of fried dough, like dipping churros into bowls of panna cotta. Down a shadowy passageway between shops, away from the neon-lit façades of brothels, dozens of men could be glimpsed gathered around a card game. Some of the players were seated on plastic chairs while others squatted on their haunches. Lookouts kept watch for police.

This is a side of Singapore the authorities would prefer to keep hidden, diverting tourists instead to the gardens and

theme parks of Sentosa and the air-conditioned malls that
provide family-friendly entertainment, while food hawkers
are zoned into courts and legal gambling is restricted to casinos or the state-run lottery. Geylang, a grid of narrow streets
on the eastern fringes of central Singapore, was as exotic to
my Singaporean friends as it was to me. We were out on a
culinary tour, sampling traditional Chinese sweets and bowls
of durian, the toffee-sweet and perfumed Southeast Asian
fruit. But this was also a glimpse of an older Singapore, a port
city of migrant labourers and sailors in search of casual sex
and the thrill of a card game.

The way that countries manage their relationship with
vice, from prostitution to gambling and illegal drugs, offers
an insight into the kind of society their citizens want to live
in. Like all societies, Singapore's ethical boundaries have
shifted over time. Unlike most democracies, Singapore's
rulers have taken a hierarchical approach to deciding how
rapidly society should be allowed to change.

At first glance, Singapore appears profoundly conservative in
its attitude to sex. The government openly regards heterosexual families as the cornerstone of society, with public housing
policies that encourage people to marry before starting a
family. Childbirth outside marriage remains exceptionally
rare, at less than 2 per cent of births (the average for rich
countries is now over 40 per cent). When the extramarital
dating site Ashley Madison announced plans to launch in
Singapore, the country's internet regulator announced that
access to the site would be blocked because of its 'flagrant
disregard of our family values and public morality'. A legal
amendment that came into force in 1996 makes it an offence
to be naked in your own home, if you can be seen from a

public place. One of the driving forces behind this change in the law was Singapore's high-density living, and an official belief that private lives had to be restrained to bind society together.

Singapore's treatment of relatively innocuous entertainment can seem prudish. A brief lesbian kiss was cut from the Star Wars film *The Rise of Skywalker*, a decision made by Lucasfilm's owners Disney to prevent government media regulators giving it a higher rating. *Sex and the City* was banned for years, and when the series was finally aired in 2004, scenes showing actress Kim Cattrall's bare breasts were censored. *Brokeback Mountain* was screened uncut in Singapore but restricted to viewers over twenty-one (the film was rated 15 in the UK).

In economic affairs, Singapore's government wants to be in the vanguard, pre-empting rivals by rapidly adopting new technology and encouraging the growth of new sectors. Social changes are deliberately taken at a slower pace. The official policy, articulated by prime minister Lee Hsien Loong in 2007, is to stay 'one step behind the frontline of change'. These two desires, to seize commercial advantage while staying buttoned-up, come into conflict over the depiction of sex on film, where censorship preserves conservative values but runs the risk of stifling creativity, and the sex industry, where the demand created by tourists and business visitors clashes with the desire to preserve a nation's modesty.

Prim Singapore has a disreputable history. A 1979 Hollywood film, *Saint Jack*, shot in Singapore's red light district, offers a startling glimpse of this past. Banned in Singapore for its graphic detail, the film recalls a world in which Chinatown gangsters dominated the brothel industry, while the city centre thoroughfare Bugis Street was nicknamed 'boogie street' and was famed for the glamour of its transgender women, some of whom walked the street in drag. Photographs from the era show young Caucasian men, with the wild-eyed look of servicemen off the leash for the night, dancing naked on the flat roof of a Bugis Street public toilet, cones of burning newspaper clenched between their buttocks.

The wild side of the city was tamed with the same determination that Singapore's rulers brought to tackling disease and clearing slums. The authorities began to restrict transsexual prostitution on Bugis Street in the 1980s, and in 1985 the original street was demolished to make way for a subway station. The letters pages of Singapore newspapers, gripped by fear of HIV/Aids, showed relief rather than regret at the decision. When the street reopened in 1992, running between the buildings of a new retail complex, transvestite street performers were banned. Memories survive through places as well as people, and the physical transformation of the city, turning Chinatown into a tourist attraction and Bugis Street into a shopping destination, has helped to erase its bohemian past. Two years after Bugis Street was demolished, one of the first references to 'sterile' Singapore appeared in the *New York Times*'s travel section. The piece alerted travellers to some of Singapore's hidden charms, but took for granted the fact that most tourists thought of it as a dull city of yuppies.

The endurance of a red light district in Geylang, further out of the city centre, is a reminder that Singapore's straitlaced public image is blended with pragmatism. Prostitution is not illegal in Singapore, though soliciting, pimping and running a brothel are, and the brothels of Geylang and Singapore's other red light districts are tolerated. The official view of the sex trade is one of expediency, summed up by a government minister who said in parliament over two decades ago that attempting to eradicate prostitution would fail and criminalising it would drive it underground. Wong Kan Seng, who was home affairs minister at the time, admitted to the existence of a state-sanctioned sex industry: 'It is better that the police know where these areas are and enforcement action can be taken, rather than to disperse these brothels to the whole of Singapore and we have a cat-and-mouse game chasing after them.'

Singapore passed a law to deter and punish human trafficking in 2014, but it has seldom been used. Three traffickers were convicted under the law in 2019, including a married couple who brought women from Bangladesh to work as nightclub dancers and forced one of them into prostitution. There were no convictions under the law the year before. The US, which conducts an annual review of worldwide efforts to combat human trafficking, has urged Singapore to strengthen efforts to identify sex trafficking victims, including training police officers to spot signs women have been coerced into the sex trade.

Geylang is an older and shabbier slice of the city. The buildings here are low-slung, rising one or two storeys high. Unlike much of the rest of Singapore, land ownership in Geylang is fragmented, slowing down the consolidation of plots which allows for rapid development. At its food stalls, customers sit at formica tables, eating from melamine bowls. Many of the dishes are traditional ones that have fallen out of favour with middle-class Singaporeans, such as offal soup and frogs cooked in a claypot.

Sherry Sherqueshaa began working in Singapore's sex trade soon after she decided to transition from male to female at the age of eighteen. Someone who never felt they fitted in, either with their male or female classmates, Sherqueshaa dropped out of school at sixteen without qualifications. She worked on the street, beginning at Woodlands, a district on

Singapore's northern periphery near the border checkpoint
with Malaysia, before moving to Geylang. The fact that she
was born male added to the risk she faced, as she could be
charged by police with violating Section 377A of the penal
code, which criminalises sex between adult males. 'I knew
that I was putting myself at big risk,' Sherqueshaa told me.
'These clients could rob me or even assault me. I know that
I can't make any report. I thought that I should be doing
anything they ask me to. If I can't do it, I have to come up
with excuses.'

Sherqueshaa, a slender woman with elfin features, said
that when she first got into the trade, sex workers got their
understanding of the law from speaking to each other. Life
on the streets changed after volunteer activists began advising
women on how to deal with the authorities. 'They were telling us how to talk to the police, what to answer when we are
found with condoms in our bag,' Sherqueshaa said. 'Things
changed for good.' Sex workers learned that it was acceptable to carry condoms, rather than fearing that police would
pounce on this evidence of their trade. Sherqueshaa told me
that she understood and accepted Singapore's conservatism,
but also knows that 'demand will never end'. 'Our clients are
fine with transgender women,' she said. 'But they would not
be an ally publicly because they have to be discreet.'

I spoke to Sherry Sherqueshaa at the offices of Project
X, an advice and advocacy organisation for sex workers, at
Orchard Mall, an eighteen-storey tower block near the main
designer shopping district. Orchard Mall offers an incongru-
ous mix of electronics stores and garish bars. When the shops
close for the day, the bars open up and the tower's atmosphere
changes. It is a favoured location for prostitutes to pick up
Western clients, often sailors or business travellers in town
for just a few nights.

Singaporean women like Sherqueshaa, however, are rarely commonly seen soliciting sex on the street these days. Over the years prostitution has become stigmatised and the sex trade in Singapore has become dominated by foreign workers. Just as the construction of roads and other infrastructure is undertaken by male migrant workers from mainland China and South Asia, female migrants from the same regions have been drafted into the sex industry. This echoes the gender divide of Singapore's colonial era, when men from China and India laboured on docks or farms, while women from China and Japan were trafficked to work in brothels. The Japanese women were known as *karayuki-san*, meaning 'woman who has gone to China'.

One of the spurs of this shift from a domestic to an increasingly foreign workforce is Singapore's post-independence ideal of meritocracy, which encourages the view that Singaporeans stuck in less appealing jobs only have themselves to blame. 'Sex work started to be looked down upon and many Singaporeans started to transition out,' said Vanessa Ho, executive director of Project X. 'In the past there was an understanding that you do whatever you need to do to survive.'

Geylang is the best-known of modern Singapore's red light districts, but alongside it there is a thriving sex industry at Keong Saik Road in Chinatown and Desker Road in Little India. While they attract the occasional crackdown on gambling and street soliciting, these zones are officially tolerated. There is a degree of state regulation in the sex trade as the women who work in Geylang's brothels carry yellow cards requiring them to go for health check-ups, limiting the spread of sexually transmitted diseases. In spite of regular police raids, meanwhile, illegal brothels thrive across the island, from the many massage parlours and karaoke

joints which are a front for sexual services to entire apartment blocks rented out by pimps. The 'licensed' sex trade in
Geylang and other red light districts is far smaller than the
illegal industry. 'There are around 800 licensed sex workers,'
Ho said. 'I'd estimate that unlicensed there are 10,000 to
15,000. It's huge.' New technology allows crime syndicates
to operate remotely, hide their identity more effectively and
communicate more discreetly with each other and with clients. In 2018, more than 1400 foreign women were arrested
for offering sexual services through online platforms.

The Women's Charter, the act which brings together laws
protecting women and girls, was strengthened in 2019 in an
effort to deter international vice syndicates. The measures
included enabling the police to take action against websites
offering sexual services in Singapore, even if the sites are
hosted abroad, and strengthening police powers to pursue
landlords who let out flats for prostitution. The strategy
behind these measures was to curb the involvement of organised crime and drive prostitution out of Singapore's suburban
residential neighbourhoods, the 'heartlands', back into the
red light districts.

Life in an officially sanctioned brothel is safer but more
restrictive than working for an illegal set-up. Women in the
red light districts' official businesses have to work seven days a
week while half of their earnings go to the brothel manager.
Women who work in the unlicensed sex trade tend to have
more personal freedom, including the opportunity to take a
day off from work, but often face exploitative deals, such as
contracts in which the agent takes all the earnings from their
first thirty clients. 'Some women get arrested before they hit
thirty customers, and there is no criminal compensation,' Ho
said. 'Even if the agents and pimps are caught, the women are
deported, as criminals.'

Women working outside tolerated brothels face a greater risk of being attacked by a client. Gesturing at a photograph of a man pinned to the wall behind her, Ho told me: 'He's been attacking sex workers for the last three years. He will call every single one of them to see who falls for his tricks. He is physically abusive. Someone got punched in the stomach, someone else got punched in the face.' An 'Abuser Alert' programme set up by Project X has catalogued dozens of cases of physical assault, rape and blackmail against sex workers every year. Women fear reporting harassment to the police as they risk being charged with soliciting. Ho argues that Singapore should offer sex workers immunity from prosecution, noting that when it comes to dealing with crimes against these women 'there's still a victim-blaming mentality'.

The sex trade in Singapore is regarded as a necessary evil. The policing of the business relies on sexual and economic inequality. It is easier to control the supply of sexual services, as this involves a group of poorer women, than to manage the demand and tackle the behaviour of the men who pay for sex.

Sex, drugs and gambling are unlike other industries. All three challenge a conservative view of society that is centred on the family and underpinned by thrift and personal responsibility. Prostitution and the drug trade, especially in societies where they are illegal, rely on a vulnerable swath of workers to service clients or ferry drugs. Drugs and gambling threaten to tip into destructive addictions, with a potentially corrosive effect on a society where discipline is prized. Singapore has taken radically different approaches to managing the potential harm from all three vices, while absorbing some of the benefits. The government's shifting attitude to gambling, in particular, shows how the state is open to change when it is driven by an economic imperative.

In the early years of this century, Singapore eased up. A government-appointed committee reviewed censorship laws and recommended lifting a ban on *Cosmopolitan* that had lasted for two decades. A new film classification was introduced, PG13, which allowed movies with mild bursts of coarse language and discreet glimpses of nudity to reach a younger audience. Police raids on gay bars stopped and the government promised there would be no harassment of the gay community. Franchises of the Parisian topless cabaret Crazy Horse and the London superclub Ministry of Sound opened, a splash of hedonism after decades in which this kind of Western decadence had attracted disapproval.

Singapore's permissive moment did not always translate into business success. The Ministry of Sound got into a legal dispute with its London parent and closed; the Crazy Horse franchise shut its doors after less than two years, blaming poor attendance on the government's tight restrictions on advertising, which were intended to safeguard public morals but meant that few tourists got to hear about it; the local edition of *Cosmopolitan* closed after four years, struggling to make an impact in a crowded market for lifestyle publishing. Casinos were the exception to this trend. Gambling has boosted Singapore's economy and created significant wealth for its business backers.

Lee Kuan Yew opposed gambling for years. His father, a storekeeper and depot manager for the oil company Shell, was a problem gambler who pestered his wife to let him pawn her jewellery in order to feed his habit. Lee feared gambling would encourage a get-rich-quick mentality and erode the Singaporean work ethic. For years, proposals to open a casino in Singapore were turned down and Singaporeans' only legal option was to head either for Macau or one of the 'floating casinos', cruise ships that lurked in international waters just off the coast and offered day-trips spiced with games of roulette and poker. Then, in 2005, the government changed its mind. Ministers had become anxious that Singapore was losing appeal as a tourist destination, dismissed by travel writers as safe and unimaginative. Sanctioning the opening of casinos would transform visitors' perceptions as well as helping to diversify Singapore's economy, they believed.

Lee, by then the minister mentor of a government led by his elder son, gave the decision his seal of approval. His reforms had created a First World city, Lee said. One that was clean, wholesome and safe. But a new Singapore was needed that combined this efficiency with sufficient panache to attract global talent. It was time for the country to let off a little steam. Christian churches protested, arguing that tax revenues would not outweigh the economic and social damage of gambling, and a petition against the casinos attracted more than 29,000 signatures. But the government pushed ahead regardless. In 2010, two casinos opened. Both were vast complexes, combining gambling with dining, shopping and other entertainment.

The casinos are aimed primarily at attracting tourists and wealthy expatriates. Singapore seeks to deter its own people with a stiff entrance levy, which was raised to S$150 a day in 2019. Singaporean visitors who are deemed financially vulnerable can be banned from entering by the government, while casinos are prohibited from advertising to the domestic market. Singapore's casinos are camouflaged. Their architecture blends in with the decorous style of its conference centres and business hotels, rather than imitating the gaudy façades of Macau or Las Vegas. Even the word casino is scrubbed out. They are officially known as 'integrated resorts'. Marina Bay

Sands, the more lavish of the two, is one of the world's most
profitable, and generates about a third of the total operating
income at its US parent company, Las Vegas Sands, which
also runs seven casinos in Macau and two in Las Vegas.

Remarkably for a country which once showed die-hard
opposition to gambling, the Sands complex has become an
emblem of Singapore. Its three fifty-five-storey towers are
linked at the top by an aerial bridge lined with restaurants
and an infinity pool, making the building's outline resemble
a wicket in a game of cricket. Alongside the hotel and casino,
the complex contains a shopping centre and a combined art
gallery and science museum shaped like a lotus. The multi-
storey casino has carpeted floors elaborately patterned with
red and gold swirls; in the open central space, there are hundreds of stations with a variety of tables and games, including
blackjack, baccarat, roulette wheels and numerous forms of
poker. Waiters, both humans and robots that resemble cabi-
nets on wheels, make the rounds serving free non-alcoholic
drinks. The smell of cigarette smoke hangs in the air.

Vernon Leow, forty-seven, a Singaporean who runs his
own design and photography business, used to visit Marina
Bay Sands a few times a week for the 'thrill of getting good
cards'. 'You get to have a shot at the combined jackpots, and
it can be quite a lot,' Leow said. 'I've seen one guy win S$1
million in five minutes. So I always think the money is there
to be won. If you don't try, you don't get it.' Leow had an
annual pass, which meant that he often popped in if he was
passing. 'If I was around the area, in between meetings, I'd
just go in there, whether it's for a meal or gaming. Or maybe
I'm free in the afternoon, I'll just go for a few hours and play.
It's just somewhere to go to kill the time.'

The S$150 entrance levy for locals is meant to deter
Singaporeans from impulse gambling, but Leow is sceptical

about how effective this is. A single bet can be higher than that, he points out. 'In fact, a lot of gamblers fall into the trap of chasing their losses because there's this 24-hour period that you already paid for,' he says. 'Sometimes your luck is down but you might stay longer to make the most of your time. If your luck is bad that day, it can get quite bad.'

But the evidence suggests Singapore has managed to profit from gambling while keeping its toxic side-effects under control. Surveys indicate that less than 1 per cent of the population in Singapore are 'problem gamblers', who may get into difficulties paying bills or quarrel with partners because they cannot control their habits, which places the country at the low end of the spectrum globally. And, while the UN has warned that Southeast Asia's booming casino industry is the 'perfect partner' for organised crime groups seeking to launder money – one spectacular case involved a multi-million-dollar electronic heist from Bangladesh's Central Bank, which was funnelled through the Philippines casino industry – there is to date scant evidence to show that illicit cash is flowing through Singapore's casinos.

Of all the vices, Singapore takes the most implacable moral line on drugs. As global moves to legalise the recreational enjoyment of cannabis gather pace, including more tolerant official attitudes in neighbouring Malaysia and Thailand, Singapore stands out for its refusal to countenance any softening of the line. In 1975 the death penalty became mandatory for the manufacture, import or trafficking of controlled substances including cannabis, amphetamines and opioids, above certain quantities. The quantities involved are tiny and likely to attract the mildest sentences in western European countries: being caught with more than 200g of cannabis resin or more than 30g of cocaine brings mandatory execution in Singapore. The use of the death penalty has been on the wane in recent years but as recently as the 1990s, Singapore was hanging more than seventy people a year, making it the world's most prolific executioner in proportion to its size.

Opium smoking was rampant in colonial Singapore, where around a third of the Singapore Chinese population were habitual opium smokers by the mid-nineteenth century. Exhausted dock-workers and rickshaw-pullers would often buy the residue left by another smoker, seeking a cheap fix at the end of a day's labour. Before the Second World War, opium had come under the control of the colonial government and was only available to registered users, under a policy intended to diminish use of the drug. After the war, when the possession of opium and opium pipes was declared illegal, Singapore became the centre of an illicit trade run by crime syndicates, shipping opium out of India, Burma and Thailand and into Singapore and the surrounding countries. Now even imported poppy seeds, commonly used as toppings for cakes and bagels, must be submitted for testing to ensure they are not contaminated with traces of opium alkaloids.

The harsh nature of Singapore's drug laws was underlined in 2007, when the country hanged Nigerian footballer Iwuchukwu Amara Tochi. Twenty-one-year-old Tochi had been arrested at Changi airport three years earlier carrying 100 capsules containing just over 700g of heroin. The young man, who grew up in a village in rural Nigeria, hoped to win a contract with a Singapore football club. He claimed that he did not know the capsules contained heroin, and said he had been paid to carry 'herbs' by a man in Pakistan, who asked him to deliver them to a sick friend in Singapore. At his trial, his defence counsel pointed out that he had made no effort to dispose of the drugs, even when he knew that police were coming to interview him, and made no serious attempt to conceal them. The judge at his trial accepted there was 'no direct evidence' that Tochi knew the capsules contained heroin, but ruled that he had 'wilfully' turned a blind eye to the contents of the capsules.

Singapore brought in reforms in 2013 that gave the courts discretion over sentencing. If a defendant could prove his role had been to act as a courier, there was a chance he would be spared the noose. But the country continues to carry out several executions a year, the majority of them for drug offences though murder and the use of firearms are also crimes punishable with death. The sentence is always carried out by hanging, at dawn, inside Changi prison.

Singapore has argued fiercely in favour of maintaining capital punishment. Speaking at a UN event in 2016, foreign minister Vivian Balakrishnan described capital punishment for drug-related crimes and murder as a 'key element' in keeping the country drug-free and safe. In the Tochi case, Singapore ignored an appeal for clemency from Nigeria's president. The country has been resolute in the face of similar appeals from the leaders of other nations whose citizens have been convicted of trafficking drugs into the city state. A government-run research agency in Singapore is funding the study of cannabis for medical treatments, and in recent years the use of a cannabis-based medicine was approved for a girl with epilepsy. But officials made clear that this medical usage did not mark a shift in their thinking on drug use.

Compared with illicit drugs, the official view of alcohol is liberal. Booze is heavily taxed, making Singapore one of the world's most expensive places to get a drink, but the city has no shortage of rooftop bars where a gin and tonic will cost you S$22, while families gathered for a banquet of Chinese dishes will regularly share a bottle of good wine.

Social attitudes to drinking are driven by class and money. Expat bankers drinking Guinness in a waterfront bar will not draw a second glance, while a South Asian migrant worker unwinding with a can of beer will attract disapproval. Many of the workers involved in the Little India riot in 2013 had been drinking, and the police were pelted with empty beer and whisky bottles. Since then, authorities have enforced a ban on drinking in the street in Little India over weekends and public holidays.

Prostitution is tolerated in Singapore as a fact of life. Casinos have now been embraced as a source of revenue. On drugs, the prevailing wisdom remains: 'Just Say No'. This risk-averse official attitude may be understandable, given the historic damage that opium in particular has inflicted, but it also suggests a lack of faith in its people.

14

The Demographic Challenge

Dating, ageing and migration

Michelle Goh specialises in speed dating. The couples usually meet at a European restaurant – a German café where menu highlights include crispy pork knuckle and Black Forest cherry torte is a favourite option – as Chinese restaurants with their large family-sized tables tend not to cater for romantic encounters.

The singles fill out a questionnaire in advance. The questions are designed to be playful, and draw out personality: 'if I had a superpower, what superpower would it be?' Her agency, CompleteMe, tries not to focus on careers as this can warp an encounter. 'If someone says they are a lawyer or doctor, the next thing is: this person is very rich,' Goh says.

Behind the dynamics of coupling up are the economics of a small and expensive city, where professional status can be a romantic trump card and men in particular often spend much of their youth getting ahead in their career before thinking of a mate. 'I don't want the average worker to be judged on their employment,' Goh says of her efforts to keep encounters focused on personality over bank balance. 'To prevent that from happening, I say that if you want to share what you do, please do so, but it's not on the questionnaire.'

The dating habits of Singaporeans have never mattered more. Currently, around 12 per cent of Singapore's people are aged over sixty-five, which makes it slightly more youthful than the US and most western European countries. But Singapore has one of the lowest birth rates in the world, lower even than Japan. At 1.1 births per Singaporean woman, this is far below the level needed to replace the existing population. Coupled with one of the longest life expectancies in the world, the country is due to become one of the world's oldest nations within a few decades, alongside Japan, Korea, Taiwan and a swath of Mediterranean nations where the demographic outlook is equally sobering.

These numbers are the outcome of a government policy that was spectacularly successful. In the 1970s, like many developing nations, Singapore's planners feared the consequences of a population explosion that might unravel all of their social and economic progress. Large families were branded irresponsible, straining education and healthcare systems. As Asia's giant nations launched campaigns to curb fertility, often coercing some of their poorest citizens into sterilisation, Singaporeans were encouraged to postpone starting a family, and to space out the birth of their children. The message was drummed into children in classrooms and into adults through penalties for those who strayed from the approved number of offspring: 'stop at two' was the message. Mothers lost paid maternity leave after their second child while bigger households fell down the waiting list for state housing. The government set up the Family Planning and Population Board in 1966, to provide contraceptive services and public health education. The state made it easier to access abortion and encouraged sterilisation.

Singapore introduced a Eugenics Board in 1970 to consider applications for sterilisation. The name is shocking to modern ears, but the belief in encouraging couples with 'desirable' characteristics to reproduce remained popular with Singapore's leaders, even after the science behind eugenics had been discredited in the 1930s and the word permanently tarnished by its horrifying association with the Nazis' mass murder of people with disabilities. At the time, Britain still had a Eugenics Society, founded by the geneticist Sir Francis Galton, who had coined the term (the UK society changed its name to the Galton Institute in 1989).

The main purpose of the Eugenics Board was not to filter out 'undesirable' parents but to be sure that applicants understood the consequences of the operation. But the government also introduced measures which encouraged less well-off families to be sterilised, such as waiving hospital delivery fees if either parent agreed to the procedure. The state regarded sterilisation as a convenient contraceptive method for poor or uneducated women, who would not want to incur the recurring costs involved in buying oral contraceptives and might, ministers suggested, struggle to understand how babies were made.

The board was abolished after just four years and sterilisation became a matter to be decided between a patient and her doctor. Measures to discourage fertility among the poor or less well-educated remained a theme of Singapore's government, however. Lee Kuan Yew feared that if fewer graduate women had children it would lead to a 'more stupid' society. Graduate mothers who had three or more children were allowed priority admission to their first choice of primary school, a policy launched in 1983. The idea was to encourage women with degrees to have bigger families, but after lacklustre take-up from the women it was aimed at, and a furious response from less well-educated parents, the idea was binned a year later.

Singapore's transformation in the 1960s had radically altered women's lives. The expansion of industry created more opportunities for women to work outside the home, and the Women's Charter introduced by the PAP ended polygamy and established marriage as an equal partnership. Greater economic and social freedom has been accompanied by an increasing reluctance to settle down. The proportion of Singaporean women who remain unmarried in their late twenties rose to 69 per cent in 2019, up from 63 per cent a decade earlier. As Singapore has grown wealthier, childhood mortality has fallen and education has become increasingly important as a gateway to a good job, parents have focused on investing more time in fewer children.

Singapore's birth rate declined so rapidly that the government was forced into a course correction. For two decades, beginning in 1984, the state even turned matchmaker, setting up an agency called the Social Development Unit to promote marriage. This was aimed exclusively at graduates, while a sister organisation to do the same for non-graduates was created a year later. The two agencies laid on tea dances, wine tastings and cruises to encourage romance, as well as offering tips on courtship (men were advised to 'bathe regularly' and pay women compliments). In nearly two decades, almost 30,000 graduates married through the Social Development Unit. Gallingly, the non-graduate network had a far higher hit rate, with more than 100,000 members getting married.

The emphasis on graduate fertility faded, giving way to an all-out push to raise the birth rate. Parents receive cash bonuses from the state for their offspring, currently S$8000 for the first and second child, rising to S$10,000 for the third and every subsequent birth. There is a government subsidy for IVF treatment, with no upper age limit. The policy tweaks were accompanied by a publicity drive. In a poster campaign on Singapore's subway a few years ago, cheerful cartoon images of eggs and sperm with cute human faces warned commuters that 'fertility is a gift with an expiry date.' The sweetmaker Mentos chimed in, with a rap video urging Singaporeans to do their patriotic duty that was timed to coincide with National Day celebrations in 2012. The Mentos rap combines explicit imagery, adolescent humour and passion-killing references to Singapore's demographic difficulties. Over a stuttering beat and synthesiser chords, a male voice raps: 'I know you want it, so does the SDU.' Combining two Singapore allusions in a single creaky couplet, he adds: 'Like a government scholar I wanna cram real hard/Tap you all night like an EZ-Link card' (EZ-Link cards are used to tap in and out of public transport).

The two separate matchmaking agencies were merged in 2008 and turned into the Social Development Network, which accredits commercial dating agencies rather than matchmaking directly. As well as vetting dating agencies, the SDN promotes subsidised events once a year, encouraging single Singaporeans to make connections over kayaking trips, hip-hop dance classes and weekend breaks.

Singaporeans now find a partner through a mix of dating apps, agencies and introductions by family and friends. Arranged marriages negotiated between the parents of the bride and groom, once traditional among all of Singapore's Asian cultures, are now largely extinct among Chinese and Malays and declining among Indians. Alongside US apps such as Tinder, there is a Singapore version, Paktor, named after the Hokkien Chinese word for going on a date, while Muslims often use bespoke apps such as Muzmatch and Minder to meet Muslim partners. Reflecting a society where social mores are more conservative than in the West, Paktor's advertising emphasises socialising rather than casual fun. Goh, whose business is accredited by the Social Development Network, offers coaching to prep her dates, in some cases helping them manage their expectations. 'I tend to educate ladies to up their dating game because we have a bio clock running,' she says. 'One Thursday I was running a ladies' workshop and during that event I was encouraging the more mature ladies to consider divorced guys.' One of the women at the workshop confessed she had found a match through one of Goh's events, but was hesitating as the man was divorced. Goh told the woman the experience was likely to make him a better partner, convincing her to accept him.

Men are usually told to narrow their desired age gap. 'Earlier on in life, guys will build up financial stability. By the time they have done that, in their late thirties, early forties, by then they realise that family formation is important, and they want two to three kids, so they want to date women in their thirties. Ladies will typically look for intellectuals as communication is a big factor for them,' she adds.

Goh discovered a knack for making connections when she was single herself and launched a Facebook group to enlarge her social circle. After her son was born, she quit her job in business development to launch a dating agency. 'There's not many jobs out there that make a difference in people's lives,' she says. 'A successful couple, every time they have an anniversary they remember you. In Maslow's hierarchy of needs, it's self-actualisation, finding a calling in life.'

For all of Singapore's efforts, the birth rate keeps slipping down. Singaporeans are staying single for longer, with men marrying at around thirty on average, and women at twenty-nine. The Chinese majority, who make up about three-quarters of the population, also have the lowest birth rate of any community. The country is preparing to go silver as gracefully as it can. The government is urging companies to hire older workers, with subsidised training to brush up their skills, and is even bringing retirees back into the workforce. 'Tap into a wealth of experience,' ran the tagline on a government advertising campaign featuring a seventy-six-year-old inventory manager at a jewellery store and a sixty-year-old salmon filleter. It's increasingly common to see elderly people stacking trays and clearing cutlery at food courts. At the official retirement age of sixty-two, employers are required to offer their workers a new contract, renewable annually, though it comes with a twist – the salary and perks must be renegotiated and a senior member of staff may find themselves downgraded to a more junior role.

The city's design is changing to accommodate the shift to a greyer population. Wellness hubs scattered across the city offer tips on graceful ageing, from healthy eating and exercise to spotting signs of dementia. 'Silver zones' on the streets feature narrower roads, forcing motorists to take more care of pedestrians, and extend the time for which the green man flashes at crossings. Prison cells are being fitted with grab bars to cater for the rise in elderly offenders. In the last few decades, new state-built apartment blocks have come with fitness equipment that spans generations, with toddlers scrambling to be first down a slide while their grandparents quietly flex their legs on static exercise equipment nearby.

Without new blood, all of this will simply be a managed decline. Fewer workers means slower growth, and a need for higher taxes to fund pensions. But the biggest impact of an ageing society, economists argue, is lower productivity growth – the rise in the economic output per hour worked that is key to making countries richer. Productivity growth is often driven by rising education levels or the deployment of better technology – think of how advances in our understanding of genetics have raised the yield of crops from farmland. But an ageing workforce appears to be linked to lower growth in productivity, for reasons that are unclear. It may be that older workers are less adept at using new technology, or their presence makes companies less inclined to adopt it. Whatever the cause, Singapore faces an uncertain future without an infusion of new blood. And this is a vexed question.

When I arrived in Singapore at the end of 2015, assimilation seemed easy. Sponsored by my employer, collecting my employment pass took a matter of minutes. Since many professional Singaporeans had been educated abroad and often had a special fondness for the UK, making new friends was straightforward. I noticed the occasional double-take triggered by my skin colour. Once, a lettings agent blurted it out when I arrived for a viewing: 'I thought from your voice that you were Caucasian,' she said, laughing with apparent embarrassment.

For the most part though, this was a gilded experience of Singapore, as it is for most foreign professionals who move to the city state. The surge in migration over the last generation has been dramatic. Migrants now make up about 30 per cent of the population, up from 10 per cent in 1990, prompting anxiety over the disappearance of Singapore's distinctive identity – expressed in its fusion Chinese-Malay-Indian cuisine and Singlish language. The migrants from mainland China and elsewhere in Asia on whom Singapore relies for much of its dirty, dangerous or low-paid work have no legal route to becoming citizens, and for them the experience is very different. A few years ago Filipino workers who wanted to organise an independence day parade that would take them through the Orchard Road shopping district were forced to cancel after being targeted with vitriolic abuse, apparently for giving themselves ideas above their station.

Behind this tension is an anxiety about the increasingly precarious lives of ordinary Singaporeans. Singapore's fortunes are built on its embrace of globalisation, but as costs have risen, many of its traditional industries have laid off workers. Imagine being a Singaporean engineer made redundant from an electronics factory which has decided to cut costs and move production to an Asian country with lower wages. Since Singapore has no automatic unemployment benefits, if the redundant engineer cannot get another job in the same industry, he may be forced into driving a taxi or working in a shop. He may not envy a migrant earning low wages in construction, but the other kind of migrant – the wealthy global elite of which I was a part – attracts significant resentment. It is a persistent complaint that companies favour foreign professional hires over skilled local talent. The ostentation of some of these hires rubs salt in those wounds.

The video footage of Ma Chi's final moments shows his red sports car hurtling through an intersection before ploughing into the back of a taxi. Ma, who ran through a red light at over 100mph, died in the accident. So did the driver of the taxi and his passenger. Ma, a financial adviser, had been at the wheel of a US$1.4 million limited-edition Ferrari that he'd bought for his thirtieth birthday the year before. The cabbie, Cheng Teck Hock, was fifty-two and the sole breadwinner in his family, leaving behind a widow and three children.

The fatal accident lifted the lid on a resentment that had been seething below the surface in Singapore. Ma had been reckless, and was clearly living a far wealthier and more privileged life than Cheng. But it was the fact that Ma was a migrant from mainland China that provoked fury. A government minister attended the taxi driver's wake, while the Chinese embassy issued an unusual statement urging their citizens to have respect for human life and abide by Singapore's laws.

In part, as the tragic Ferrari crash showed, the tension is driven by economic competition. Wealthy migrants, and mainland Chinese in particular, are blamed for pushing up property prices and placing strains on essential infrastructure; Singaporeans often complain that there are too many foreigners on the subway. But there is a racial and cultural edge too. Singaporeans frequently look down on mainland Chinese as uncouth and cliquish, while mainland women are accused of pursuing married Singapore men. As imagined by Singapore's tabloids, the mainland Chinese temptress is often a 'study mama' – a mother accompanying a child who has moved to Singapore for their primary or high-school education.

In turn, mainlanders complain of hostility from Singaporeans. Sun Xu, a Chinese student studying on a Singaporean government scholarship, blogged about 'gangster Singapore uncles' who stared coldly at him when he brushed past them in the street. 'There are more dogs than humans in Singapore,' he added. His university fined him, revoked his scholarship for his last semester and ordered him to perform three months of community service.

Chinese Singaporeans may have an ancestral kinship with the mainland, but their identity is also coloured by generations spent in Southeast Asia. A neighbourly dispute a few years ago highlighted this, when a mainland Chinese family took offence at the aroma of curry wafting from their Singaporean Indian neighbours' house and cooking smells became a national talking point. A freelance writer, Florence Leow, launched a Facebook campaign encouraging Singaporeans to 'cook and share a pot of curry'. Singapore's ethnic groups might have their own racial prejudices, but they banded together against this foreign assault on their shared cuisine. Cooking curry became a celebration of Singapore's hybrid culture, in the face of a perceived threat from narrow-minded outsiders.

Officially, Singapore accepts the need for greater migration, but it remains an intensely delicate subject. In a white paper published in January 2013, the government anticipated a population that could reach 6.9 million by 2030, of whom just over half would be citizens. Its publication prompted a rare public demonstration, with around 4000 turning out to a rally at Speaker's Corner in Hong Lim Park. The white paper and that December's Little India riot bookended a year in which the conversation on migration in Singapore turned. The government had already tightened controls on migration, but the restrictions were widened to include professional jobs.

Both having babies and encouraging migrants nevertheless remain vital to securing Singapore's future. At a conference in 2019, the prime minister Lee Hsien Loong aimed at a fertility rate of 1.3 or 1.4 births per woman, envisaging a society that was two-thirds native-born Singaporeans with the shortfall topped up by migration. This, Lee suggested, would mean the 'core' of society would remain distinctively Singaporean. Ministers say they calibrate both the pace and profile of migration to maintain the current ethnic profile of the country. But this racial balance is likely to come under increasing pressure.

There is one exception to the overall decline in fertility. The birth rate among the island's ethnic Malay minority has climbed in recent years, and is now nearly twice the Chinese-Singaporean rate. While the reasons for this are unclear, the trend suggests that one distinctive feature of Singapore, its ethnic Chinese majority in a region that is predominantly Malay and Muslim, may be diluted in years to come. Meanwhile, South Asia, where the demographic outlook remains favourable, is the most likely source of the new migration that will replenish Singapore's labour force.

These demographic changes are unlikely, by themselves, to bring significant cultural or political changes. The country's political and business elite will probably remain dominated by a Westernised group of ethnic Chinese, as it has been since independence. Robert Kang, business director of a chemicals company, moved to Singapore from Beijing in 2019. He was dazzled by the 'small but mightily developed city' the first time he landed at Changi airport and took a taxi to the city centre. 'Seeing the big trees along the expressway and modern buildings gave me the impression of an orderly and disciplined city, yet one that is constantly upward-moving and on the rise,' Kang said. It struck him as the ideal country for his daughter Kang Ning to grow up in, where she could be exposed to Western culture without losing touch with her Chinese roots.

Kang, a tall, well-built, middle-aged man with a full head of dark grey hair and an affable smile, thought Singapore had held onto many of the best aspects of traditional Chinese culture. Much of this heritage had been lost in the 1990s, Kang believed, when China began opening up to the world and became increasingly Westernised. 'In 2002, I visited Singapore to attend my good friend's wedding,' he recalled. 'To my surprise, everything was executed following the old customs, including the couple kneeling to serve tea to the parents. I was truly shocked and touched. China is the source

THE DEMOGRAPHIC CHALLENGE

of these traditions, yet in the big cities we have all but forgotten about them, preferring Western culture instead.'

Though it is true that Singapore observes time-honoured customs such as sweeping ancestors' graves and burning 'hell money' to tide restless spirits on their way, it would surprise many to hear themselves described as less Westernised than mainland Chinese. The city state's English-speaking elite and a younger generation educated largely in English and Mandarin struggle to communicate with their grandparents, who still speak Chinese dialects such as Hokkien and Teochew. Kang said he had heard of mainlanders encountering prejudice in Singapore, but had never experienced it himself. Newcomers who fail to assimilate may bear some responsibility for the prejudice they face, he suggested. 'There are mainland Chinese who continue exhibiting uncultured behaviour in Singapore – speaking very loudly, disturbing the peace and otherwise breaking social rules and ignoring how others think of them. And why wouldn't it irritate the locals? Even I, a fellow mainlander, feel ashamed.'

As Singaporeans step out of their air-conditioned offices for a lunchtime bowl of soup noodles, they will pass construction workers, often men from Bangladesh or southern India, napping at the roadside to escape the worst of the noonday heat. The divide has echoes of Singapore's past, when blue-collar workers battled employers for better pay and shorter hours. Plenty of other advanced societies have outsourced low-skilled jobs in manufacturing, or brought in cheaper hands for humdrum work such as fruit-picking, but there are few societies quite as reliant on cheap labour as Singapore.

Economists disagree about the extent to which it has fuelled Singapore's miraculous growth. In a famous 1994 essay, *The Myth of Asia's Miracle*, the Nobel Prize-winning economist Paul Krugman argued that Singapore's economic achievement was based more on sweat than ingenuity, mobilising resources of labour and capital rather than growing through increased efficiency. The claim mattered because, while countries can achieve short-term growth by adding more workers or bringing in foreign investment, long-term growth relies on making more efficient use of labour and capital. Such gains often come from applying innovative technology, such as making greater use of robots to perform routine manufacturing tasks like welding and painting.

Singapore's leaders were stung by Krugman's remarks, but they also took heed. Lee Kuan Yew himself conceded the point in 2010, when he said: 'We've grown in the last five years by just importing labour. Now the people feel uncomfortable, there are too many foreigners.' The country tightened rules on hiring foreign workers and pushed businesses to invest in technology. Hospitals began using robotic transporters to ferry supplies, while food manufacturers pasteurised fresh noodles to give them a longer shelf life. At a café near one of the universities I encountered a dish-collecting droid that trundled around chirping: 'Could you help me to clear your table?' The introduction of labour-saving innovations has paid off. Officials say that economic growth has increasingly been driven by productivity gains rather than growth in employment in recent years. Still, more than half the workforce in Singapore's construction sector are low-paid migrants, which keeps costs down and discourages companies from seeking greater efficiency.

But economics alone offers us an arid perspective on Singapore's future. One of my earliest memories of Singapore is arriving at Changi and seeing curling Tamil script on the airport's liquid-crystal display panels. An alphabet I had only ever seen as handwriting or in dusty books on my parents' shelves was part of the modern world. When we lived there, I learned to recognise the subway announcements that rattled through station names in multiple Asian languages; Botanic Gardens was rendered in Tamil as 'Flower Hill'. In recent years, politics in Singapore has taken an uncomfortable turn, entrenching the rights of the native-born population in the face of the growth in migration. Singaporeans appear to want three impossible things: fewer babies, fewer foreigners and low taxes.

But countries are always more complex and subtle than their political rhetoric. Singapore remains a proudly multi-cultural society, and one in which there are many ties of affection and understanding between citizens and outsiders. The pandemic compelled Singapore to recognise its migrant workforce, not just the professionals who are accepted into the upper echelons of society but the labourers on its roads. The government footed their healthcare bills, a gesture of solidarity in a crisis, while citizens raised funds to buy masks, hand sanitiser and data top-ups for foreign labourers. Seen in a different light, Singapore's demographic crisis offers an opportunity. The country is short of labour and surrounded by nations with surpluses of manpower. But the current set-up, in which workers are tied to specific employers, leaves them vulnerable to exploitation. Each year dozens of companies are found to have breached overtime limits. And because foreign workers are seen as cheap hires, who will soon return home, there is little incentive to train them. Giving the lowest-paid migrants a route to settle, and ultimately a right to claim citizenship, would change this calculation. It would create a new source of skilled talent for the country.

Singapore still has time on its side. On current trends, it is only by the 2030s that its workforce will shrink. That gives businesses time to adapt to new technology, workers time to acquire new skills and society as a whole a chance to rethink its attitude to migration. A nation built on hope, with ancestors who were often illiterate labourers escaping rural poverty, could revive its future by remembering its past.

15

The Future

When Lee Kuan Yew died in 2015, one of his grandsons delivered a eulogy which turned from personal reminiscence of an affectionate grandfather to a deeper reflection on the statesman who remade Singapore. History is full of plans for the total transformation of society, said Lee's grandson Li Shengwu. 'Few plans succeed and many cause more bloodshed than happiness.'

Singapore is an engineered society, perhaps the only example in history of an efficient and prosperous society that has been created from the top down. There are tensions between its rulers and their people, and an uncomfortable divide between its richest and poorest. But being a citizen of Singapore remains a privileged birthright.

As Li Shengwu noted, there are no monuments to his grandfather in Singapore, no streets with his name, no airport named in his honour, no statues. 'His legacy is not cold stone, but a living nation,' he said. (The younger generation of the family have changed the spelling of their surname from the more anglicised 'Lee'.) The most significant achievement of

Singapore's founders was to create a system that has outlasted their own lives. This was done by forging a network that extends beyond government into the civil service and military, creating a businesslike state coordinated on the objective of nation-building.

Six months after I moved to Singapore, Britain voted to leave the European Union. The decision was greeted with merriment by Singaporean friends. Britain's shadow still loomed large, as the former colonial power, but the UK seemed to have taken leave of its senses. Behind the laughter, there was consternation. 'The economics and the politics seem to be working in opposite directions,' a senior government official suggested to me, politely summing up the Singapore elite's bafflement that Britain seemed bent on a course of action with such negative economic consequences. Singapore is a political hybrid, combining features of a democracy such as regular elections with strict controls on dissent. Its leaders have always feared the consequences of untrammelled democracy and believed that a disciplined society was more important than a democratic one for their nation's development.

Curiously, Singapore has emerged as a role model for the UK's post-Brexit future. The seed of this fascination was planted in 2012, when it featured in *Britannia Unchained*, a book written by five Conservative MPs. Four of them went on to be cabinet ministers under Boris Johnson, the prime minister who led Britain out of the EU in 2021, including Priti Patel, who became home secretary, and Dominic Raab, who was foreign secretary. The book plucked lessons from around the world, admiring Singapore's maths teaching, alongside the regulation of Canada's banks and Israel's state encouragement of the venture capital market for hi-tech start-ups. Over time, the other countries faded into the background and Singapore became a shorthand for the kind of country Brexiters wanted: with lower taxes and less regulation (despite the fact that Singapore intrusively manages many aspects of its citizens' lives).

The term 'Singapore-on-Thames' was initially coined as a warning by British chancellor of the exchequer Philip Hammond, who suggested that the country might transform its economic model if it was shut out of the single market. The threat was aimed at EU leaders, who were urged to avoid the risk of Britain becoming a lightly taxed and regulated competitor on their doorstep. Instead of a warning it became a slogan for Brexiters, a mantra that summed up their optimistic view of the future. The reaction to this in Singapore was a mixture of pride and confusion, as Singaporeans absorbed the compliment while pointing out the significant differences between the two countries. This unlikely embrace by Britain's Eurosceptics was a reminder of Singapore's magnetism, and the appeal of a system which seemed to hold out the hope of greater stability and security, even if that came at a price.

As climate change highlights a global system of consumption which appears out of control, despairing environmental campaigners have even suggested that authoritarian states may be the only ones that can deal with the crisis. The pragmatic engagement of Singapore's leaders with the climate emergency, acknowledging the gravity of the threat and taking steps to mitigate its risks for their country, are in stark contrast with some democratic leaders who have denied the human contribution to global warming or downplayed the scale of the challenge.

The Covid-19 pandemic battered Singapore's economy and exposed a critical weakness in its society around the treatment of migrant workers. But its efficient management of the crisis underlined its reputation for stability. I visited Singapore in the early weeks of the pandemic, when the contagion appeared under control. There were no restrictions in place. The subway was crowded, and food courts were packed with diners. While I was there, one of the earliest migrant workers to contract the disease was admitted to hospital. But Singapore had already closed its borders with China and distributed masks to every household.

Returning to Heathrow, I found a government that seemed blithely unconcerned at a distant crisis. Britain's prime minister, away at his country retreat with his pregnant fiancée, skipped meetings of the UK's national crisis committee, the *Sunday Times* reported. The contagion has exposed the limitations of the illiberal populist governments that have won power around the world. In Britain and the US, leaders dismissed the views of experts, declining to wear masks and continuing to shake hands. By May 2021, the US death toll from Covid-19 had reached almost 600,000 and nearly 130,000 lives had been lost in the UK. Singapore had one of the lowest mortality rates in the world.

It was clear that Singapore had one of the most effective regimes for dealing with the outbreak, combining testing capacity with the ability to trace contacts. But it was not the only country that had kept the virus at bay; New Zealand, Taiwan and South Korea have all proven effective at testing and tracking to identify weak points where the disease is spreading fast, and then isolating cases to curb further transmission. This points to something significant. It is not Singapore's authoritarianism that is key to handling a crisis well, nor its people's supposed willingness to submit to authority.

Singapore works because it appoints diligent and talented people to positions of leadership. The system roots out corruption. Its leaders are unashamed about stealing effective ideas from elsewhere, while sticking to their own distinctive course when they are convinced this will be most successful. Among its politicians, there is a strong emphasis on managerial ability rather than effectiveness at campaigning or winning battles of ideas. Goh Chok Tong, who succeeded Lee Kuan Yew as prime minister, was drafted into politics after turning around the fortunes of a state-owned shipping company.

As well as far-sighted strategic moves such as building a container port, there was a perfectionist attention to detail, which could sometimes take an absurd turn. Weekly reports on the state of the airport's washrooms crossed Lee's desk. The prime minister even enquired about the water pressure of public fountains in the 1960s. This could seem petty, but it ensured that officials lower down the hierarchy stayed focused on their tasks.

Singapore's rulers have never been predatory. In other countries, elites have exploited mineral wealth and enjoyed lives insulated from the troubles of their citizens. Without any resources apart from its people, Singapore had to emphasise health, education and housing as the preconditions for a workforce that could build an industrial society. Once the left had been defeated, there was little significant opposition to Lee Kuan Yew's plan to reshape the country. Since then the government has dominated both political and economic life. There are no powerful businessmen with an interest in influencing politics in the way that corporate titans in the West have lobbied against climate change or the European Union. In its early years, the country's leaders disciplined their people with the fear of economic disaster or foreign invasion. The Singapore dream offered material comfort in exchange for the sacrifice of freedom. Now it is prosperous and safe, these levers are less effective. A bargain that has held for six decades is unravelling as a wealthier and more sophisticated population is increasingly defying its leaders. The government has failed in attempts to persuade Singaporeans to have more children, or to accept apparently unrestricted migration. Among those born between 1940 and 1949, who were young adults when the country won independence, just 7 per cent have a degree. For the generation born between 1970 and 1979, 44 per cent are graduates.

Discipline mattered when Singapore needed to establish its reputation. It is harder for Singapore's leaders to bully or cajole an educated population. They must be won over by force of argument. In recent years, the system has become more flexible. Social media, sidestepping the straitjacketed domestic press, has forced the government to accept a level of public criticism that would have been unimaginable in a previous era.

Singapore's challenges are substantial. Some can be measured. The country is greying rapidly and the population is reluctant to reproduce or to embrace immigration. While China has become the world's manufacturing heartland, and the US leads the growth of the global technology industry, Singapore is struggling to carve out a new economic niche. An increasingly assertive Chinese military prowls around its borders and – allegedly – probes its cyber defences. Climate change presents a looming threat to a low-lying island in the tropics. Nearly a third of Singapore's surface area is 5 metres or less above sea level. Vital infrastructure will need to be built higher above sea level, while insect-borne diseases are likely to become a more frequent occurrence as the island warms.

The melting of polar ice presents a combined risk and, in a grotesque fashion, an opportunity. In 2013, Singapore was granted observer status on the Arctic Council, the club whose full members are nations with territory inside the Arctic Circle. An increase in shipping through the melting north could divert maritime trade away from Singapore. This is a remote threat at present, as navigating the ice and fog of our northernmost seas remains an impractical and hazardous option for container shipping. Though it may slice into seaborne trade, any growth in use of Arctic routes presents a commercial opening for Singapore's industries, particularly shipbuilding and engineering. *Varandey* and *Toboy*, the first icebreakers to be built in Singapore – indeed the first such ships built anywhere in the tropics – were delivered to a Russian crude oil producer in 2008.

Other challenges are less tangible. The country lacks a sense of fun. The atmosphere in its bars can sometimes feel as illusory as a film set. The elements of glamour and danger in the city's early history have been erased, replaced by an emphasis on eating out and shopping as the primary entertainments. Formula One, the world's dullest and most expensive sport, is the chief sporting attraction. The writers and artists who display the most verve and originality, like the novelist Catherine Lim and the cartoonist Sonny Liew, are still the ones most likely to attract official disapproval. Economies driven by low-skilled manufacturing can thrive without creativity. It is much harder for restrictive societies to succeed when knowledge is the engine of growth. Singapore has prospered from globalisation, opening itself up to investment and trade in the 1960s and 1970s when other countries favoured protecting their economies. Now, the trend of a more globally interconnected economy seems to be going into reverse, a risky moment for a small, open trading nation.

At the same time, the leadership that confronts these challenges looks weaker than ever before. Since Lee's death, his family has splintered. The eldest child, Lee Hsien Loong, a Cambridge graduate like his father, became Singapore's third post-independence prime minister in August 2004. He has faced repeated criticism from his younger sister, Lee Wei Ling, a neurologist, and brother, Lee Hsien Yang, a former chief executive of the telecoms provider SingTel. The dispute was triggered by the fate of the family home, a bungalow on Oxley Road that Lee wanted demolished after his death. Publicly, he gave the practical reason that demolishing the house would allow the building of a high-rise, increasing the value of the land. He may also have feared the creation of a cult of personality: the younger siblings have accused their older brother of conspiring to maintain the house, in defiance of their father's wishes, in an attempt to draw on the patriarch's legacy. The prime minister's sister has also accused him of wanting to establish a dynasty. In a statement to parliament, the premier rejected his siblings' claims. He has withdrawn from government discussions about the fate of the house, and said that his son Li Hongyi has not been pushed to enter politics.

This kind of public infighting at the apex of Singapore's society is unprecedented. Foreign newspapers that make claims of nepotism or dynastic politics usually end up in court facing a defamation suit. But the Lee siblings have, so far, not been sued.

Few countries in the world are so intimately bound up with the fortunes of a single family. In a city which has gone through constant and sometimes turbulent change, the Lee family has been a constant presence in public life. When the elder Lee stepped down as prime minister in 1990, he stayed on in cabinet for another twenty-one years, first as Senior Minister and then as minister mentor, a guide to the younger generation. This is an unprecedented degree of continuity in leadership for a democratic state's government, and one more reminiscent of a family business – with a founder staying on as chairman even after his heir takes the reins. As Singapore's family businesses know, the handover to a third generation is typically the moment of vulnerability.

The Lee family earned the nation's loyalty by delivering good jobs and security. Few leaders in history have matched Lee Kuan Yew's achievement of propelling a country in such a short time to the front rank of the industrialised world. His son's record in office is more uneven. Under the younger Lee, voters have grown increasingly critical of overcrowding on public transport and the dramatic rise in immigration. The enduring power of the Lee name sits uncomfortably with Singapore's insistence on meritocracy. If the next generation of leaders does not include a member of the clan, it will send a reassuring signal that Singapore has a wider pool of governing talent.

Lee Hsien Loong was due to retire by 2022, but put this off indefinitely when Covid-19 hit. In April 2021, the transition to a new leader was thrown into disarray when Lee's designated heir, Heng Swee Keat, stepped back, saying a younger politician should take his place. Heng is widely regarded as a capable but dreary bureaucrat and is unpopular with voters, scraping through in his constituency at the 2020 general election. The disarray over succession suggested a party in need of renewal, and a spell in opposition might be what the PAP needs to find its voice again.

There are plenty of reasons to be optimistic about Singapore's future. Its location at a maritime crossroads remains a powerful advantage, and the country has exploited this to the full, becoming one of the world's busiest ports and a hub for fossil fuels in the region. Clean, reliable and well-governed, it offers a convenient entry point into Southeast Asia both for Western multinationals and, increasingly, for Chinese companies. A second great advantage is the fact that it is both small and sovereign. This makes the pursuit of difficult decisions easier. Singapore's brief experience of a merger with a larger country, when it was part of Malaysia, illustrated the conflicts that can arise between an entrepreneurial city and a larger nation with different goals. At a time when Hong Kong's pro-democracy movement is being crushed by the Chinese government, Singapore's ability to steer its own course is more vital than ever.

The third and most essential advantage is its people. Highly educated and hard-working, fluent in English and some of the most widely spoken languages in Asia, Singapore's citizens have always been its most valuable resource. The crowds that gathered to welcome the swimmer Joseph Schooling home from the Rio Olympics, a mix of races and classes unified by a sporting triumph, were a reminder of this strength. Schooling's victory in the 100-metre butterfly – Singapore's first Olympic gold – felt like the nation's historic achievement writ small, an illustration of the success that is possible through determined application of talent. Now Singaporeans themselves are pushing back against the limits of the system and demanding a greater say in how they are governed. The time has come to offer the country a new deal.

The outlines of a more progressive Singapore could be discerned during its response to the pandemic. The government provided cash handouts to households, and subsidised wages to protect jobs in the private sector. It is a short step from here to a more generous welfare state that would give Singapore greater resilience in a downturn. A state-funded backstop of this kind may well help foster a more entrepreneurial culture. During the crisis, the state acknowledged the important role that migrant workers played in building Singapore, accepting that this foreign element was an essential part of society. It should go a step further, offering a route to citizenship that would build a living connection between Singapore and its Asian neighbours.

There is a pervasive myth that Singaporeans are not interested in politics. But the history of recent elections shows that passion for politics runs high when Singaporeans believe that change is within their grasp. The success in the 2020 election of the opposition Workers' Party in gaining ten of the ninety-three elected seats in the legislature was built on a platform that opposed a tax increase, and called for a national minimum wage and unemployment insurance. For the first time in its history, Singapore's prime minister granted the head of the opposition party the official title of Leader of the Opposition. Relaxing its draconian attitude to free speech and permitting more alternative voices is enabling Singapore to build a more inclusive future.

From its foundation, tiny Singapore has told a global story. In the nineteenth century, it was the exemplar of a successful society built on migration and a collaboration between a Western imperial power and Asian entrepreneurs. In the twentieth century it became a pioneer of globalisation, weaving together the resources of its people and Western investment to become one of the world's great economic success stories. In the twenty-first century, it must walk the line between populism and authoritarianism, allowing its people's voice to be heard and embracing its place at the heart of Southeast Asia.

Epilogue

I should have realised from the age gap between us that I didn't know everything about Dad's life before he had me at forty. This was late for a South Asian man of his generation, though not unheard of, especially in cases where a man started out poor and made the money to provide for a family through years of bootstrapping, as my father had done.

News trickled out on the family grapevine. My father's younger brother kept a picture of a South Asian woman wearing the finery of an Indian classical dancer. One day, when asked who she was by one of my younger sisters, he gave a teasing answer about the family resemblance: 'Do you think she looks like you?'

Dad was born in 1932 in the north of Sri Lanka, then the British colony of Ceylon, in a family so desperately poor there was often too little food to go round. His birth certificate lists his father's occupation as a tea stall vendor, but this seems likely to be a euphemism for someone whose work was irregular. Running a tea stall requires none of the outlay involved in owning a shop but sounds respectable enough to adorn a birth certificate. As a teenager, my dad stowed away on a ship bound for Singapore, then also a British colony, emerging from his hiding place when the ship was out on the open sea. I was never entirely clear about the timeline, but he later told me stories of seeing Japanese bombers flying in the skies over the Straits of Johor, which separate Singapore from neighbouring Malaysia.

Chitra was around a decade older than me, and had been a little girl – aged three or four – when my dad left for Britain. Dad told me little about why his first marriage had fallen apart; only that his first wife was domineering, a portrayal that did not quite square with the genteel, sari-clad woman I met at my sister's apartment. Through her adult life, Chitra had only seen our father on a handful of snatched occasions. He would visit her discreetly when we came to Singapore on holiday as children. She had insisted that he return to take part in her wedding ceremony, an obligation he accepted.

My sister and I had spoken on the phone briefly to set up that first meeting. I had addressed her using the Tamil word for older sister. She had politely but firmly asked me to use her name, and used mine in return – a relatively unusual move between members of a Tamil family, but a fitting marker of the distance between us.

We met on a day that had been turned muggier than usual by a burst of tropical rain. My wife and I were staying on one of the lower floors of a compact modern hotel, a rectangle painted as white as icing and located just off Singapore's main designer shopping street, Orchard Road. Chitra had met my younger sisters already, and was cautious about meeting me. She had been told that I was the 'mother's pet' – in her version of the story, an ally of the woman who had turned her father's heart against her. She was accompanied by her husband, Mahendran, a Singaporean Tamil who worked in municipal government. She had noticed him at a Hindu temple and asked him out. She had consulted our dad about the match: when Dad asked how dependable he was, she had retorted that he wouldn't abandon her as her father had done.

The four of us went for lunch. I wasn't sure how conservative my sister would be. But she was wearing Western clothes and when we sat down – at a local food court – she ordered a prawn-topped pizza while I had a Singaporean dish of stir-fried rice strips and seafood. My dad was quiet when I told him we had reconnected, but obvious pleasure radiated from his face.

Food was central to our family memories of life in Singapore; there's a picture of my dad, holding a pair of chopsticks loosely in his left hand, a crab claw – his favourite – in his right. My youngest sister is next to him, her mouth and dress sticky with food. There is a cornucopia of Chinese food spread out on the table in front of them. Another picture from the same evening shows my mother in a Malaysian gown, her hand reaching for a melamine dish laden with noodles.

Yet another picture frozen in my mind is my elder sister's wedding portrait. Both sets of parents are behind them. My dad, father of the bride, stands next to a woman I don't recognise, his first wife. Chitra's mother is a Brahmin, the priestly caste at the top of the social hierarchy in India and northern Sri Lanka. Her mother's family home was part of a temple complex. My father never told us what caste he was, but it wasn't the same. For a Brahmin woman to marry out of her caste is difficult even now. In 1950s Singapore it must have caused shockwaves. The marriage would have been a controversial one – and the break-up the perfect opportunity for family recriminations about marrying beneath yourself.

Like many imperial subjects, my dad was raised with the belief that England was his mother country. When he arrived in England in the 1960s, he thought he was coming home, an illusion that quickly dissolved in early conversations about sport. Englishmen simply assumed that he would support a subcontinental team at cricket, he recalled in disbelief.

Back in Singapore, the letters from him to his first wife slowed to a trickle and then petered out. They had no news of his whereabouts. In her eyes, they were still married. When he came back to Singapore and visited his daughter, his wife would go to the market to buy his favourite fish for supper.

My mother, born and raised in southern Malaysia, had studied biochemistry in India and was then sent to London by her family for postgraduate training. She came to stay with my dad, who she knew through a family connection. I later heard from her side of the family that they had never expected love to blossom between my parents. According to one of my uncles, when the family came looking for her, they found her with a little boy – me – in her arms. It's hard to imagine in a world of instant contact, but communication between far-flung relatives could easily dwindle to near zero in the early 1970s, especially if there was an unexpected romance to hide.

Growing up on the outskirts of west London, we knew that Sri Lanka was the place we came from, in some fuzzy, distant way. Our parents spoke Tamil in the house and we ate Sri Lankan food. But after civil war broke out in Sri Lanka in 1983, when I was ten, the way back there seemed barred forever. Singapore and Malaysia were the places we headed back to every few years for the musky heat of a grandparents' bedroom, a dose of tropical sunshine and durian, the pungent Southeast Asian fruit. As I grew older, Singapore seemed to become glitzier; when I went back as a young man the office towers had gone from low-rise to high-rise, the hotels had grown in scale and the malls were more glamorous than the ones I remembered from my childhood. Singaporeans weren't just buying Gucci handbags. People who lived on a flat, sweltering island were buying designer snow gear for Alpine holidays. I sometimes wondered about the counterfactual life I might have had if I had grown up in Singapore.

In Britain, being of Sri Lankan Tamil descent meant being a minority within the wider British Asian minority. Singapore offered an Asian edition of the modern world I knew; a place where you could come home from a day's work as a financial journalist and jump off the public transit train at Tekka market, where a Tamil-speaking butcher would hack up a goat carcass for the evening's curry. The data connection would be strong enough for you to check the news on Twitter as you picked up a box of Alphonso mangoes from the grocer. Outsiders sometimes scoffed that this was 'Asia-lite', 'Asia for dummies' or the 'suburbs of Asia'. But it was also a place where you could live a comfortable, middle-class life in a stable and well-run country. Singapore is imperfect, but it is also a place which has kept much of Asia's traditional culture intact – from the noodle hawkers selling *char kway teow* to the worshippers at the temple of the Hindu mother goddess Sri Mariamman – while making the most of Western technology. Britain was my home; a country I loved and identified with. But Singapore felt like a glimpse of an alternate existence in which my Asian heritage could coexist with my desire to live a modern life.

It was a difficult place to work as a journalist, someone whose professional life is driven by the need to uncover juicy morsels of information. The country's politicians and businessmen were masters of the art of eloquently saying very little. Its officials are rarely indiscreet. I never quite got used to the Singaporean habit of policing their own minds. I made Singaporean friends, who could be refreshingly frank about their country's flaws, from racism to the occasional government ineptitude. But many ordinary Singaporeans seemed conditioned to obedience. I remember an encounter with a middle-aged taxi driver, who gave me a candid account of his long hours and low earnings. But he ended the conversation blaming himself for his inability to get a better job, rather than concluding that he deserved a fairer deal from his employer.

Six years after that first meeting with my sister, our father died. He had a brain tumour which we had known about for a few months. But in the end his passing was very swift; internal bleeding meant he went from sitting out in the garden one morning, with the family making plans for a barbecue, to fading away in a hospital bed the next day. It was late autumn in London but the weather turned as balmy as the tropics for those few days. Chitra came to London for the funeral, her first trip to England. During the service she was literally floored by grief, collapsing in front of his open coffin.

It sometimes feels to me now as if impersonal forces had picked us all up like chess pieces and moved us around the world – the poverty that pushed my father from Sri Lanka to Singapore, the war that kept any of us from returning to Sri Lanka for a generation. And, set against these forces, there was the personal magnetism of love – which had torn my father's first marriage apart and then, at the end of his years, pulled his first child all the way around the world to see him depart.

Acknowledgements

My thanks to Andrew Yeo, Michael Syn and Lim Hsuen Elaine, Sheryl Lee Tian Tong, Shashank Bengali, Stefanie Yuen Thio and Thio Shen Yi, Kirsten Han, Sri Jegarajah and Deepa Balji, Dhevarajan Devadas, Chitra Manickavasagar and Mahendran Murugesan, Lionel Barber, Roula Khalaf, Alec Russell, Victor Mallet, Josh Spero, Sara Kalim, Jan Royall, Toby Mundy, David Bamford and friends in Singapore who can't be named here. Thanks above all to my mother Devi, Vidya Manickavasagar White, Priya Manickavasagar Askew, Roshan, Nila and Meera.

Endnotes

Introduction

not having a great run Interview with deputy prime minister Tharman Shanmugaratnam in October 2016, https://www.ft.com/content/bcee463e-9674-11e6-a1dc-bdf38d484582

A great commercial emporium Raffles, letter to Colonel Addenbrooke, 10 June 1819.

We decide what is right Lee Kuan Yew National Day Rally speech in August 1986. Marcos had fled the Philippines in February 1986, https://eresources.nlb.gov.sg/newspapers/Digitised/Article/straitstimes19870420-1.2.26.13

Trade boomed George Bogaars, 'The effect of the opening of the Suez Canal on the Trade and Development of Singapore', *Journal of the Malayan Branch of the Royal Asiatic Society*, March 1955.

We don't have Interview with Lee Kuan Yew *International Herald Tribune*, August 2007, https://www.nytimes.com/2007/08/29/world/asia/29iht-lee-excerpts.html

now home to twelve billionaires Credit Suisse Global wealth report, October 2020.

1 Emporium of the East

messianic mission *A History of Singapore*, C. M. Turnbull

Justin Trudeau 'Trudeau traces family links to Singapore at Fort Canning', *Straits Times*, November 2018, https://www.straitstimes.com/singapore/trudeau-traces-family-links-to-singapore-at-fort-canning

The wharfs were absolutely crowded George Windsor Earl, *The Eastern Seas* (W. H. Allen, 1837).

Their habitations may be James Brooke, diary for July 1839.

Tan Kah Kee See the Tan Kah Kee foundation's biography, https://www.tkkfoundation.org.sg/biography

Today Singapore stands unrivaled 'Singapore to be new link in British defense chain', *New York Times*, 8 February 1925, https://www.nytimes.com/1925/02/08/archives/singapore-to-be-new-link-in-british-defense-chain-far-eastern-base.html

people bowed to passing cars Gregg Huff and Gillian Huff, 'The Second World War Japanese Occupation of Singapore', *Journal of Southeast Asian Studies*, June 2020.

Elizabeth Choy See her obituary in *The Times*, 5 October 2006, https://www.thetimes.co.uk/article/elizabeth-choy-kxc2qkk8ld3

mass graves https://eresources.nlb.gov.sg/newspapers/Digitised/Article/straitstimes19620301-1.2.100

various tortures 'Lee foils bid to spark off trouble at rally' *The Straits Times*, 26 August 1963.

2 Blood Will Flow

He was agnostic Interview with the *New York Times*, 1 September 2010, https://www.pmo.gov.sg/Newsroom/ transcript-minister-mentor-lee-kuan-yews-interview- seth-mydans-new-york-times-iht-1

If you have two white horses The quote is from *Hard Truths to Keep Singapore Going*, a book of interviews with Lee.

This proclamation today Lee Kuan Yew speech, 31 August 1963.

without being granted them constitutionally 'Singapore's claim not valid', *Straits Times*, 4 September 1963, https://eresources.nlb.gov.sg/newspapers/ Digitised/Article/straitstimes19630904-1.2.5

In peacetime they were all friends Interview with Zainul Abidin Rasheed, Institute for Societal Leadership, Singapore Management University, January 2016, https://ink.library.smu.edu.sg/cgi/ viewcontent.cgi?article=1044&context=isl_dna

3 The Engineered Society

MacDonald House 'Terror bomb kills 2 girls at bank', *Straits Times*, 11 March 1965.

Israeli advisers 'A Deep, Dark, Secret Love Affair', *Haaretz*, 16 July 2004.

by 1978 that figure Women in the labour force. Cheng

Siok Hwa, 'Recent trends in female labour force participation in Singapore', *Southeast Asian Journal of Social Science*, 1980.

'eliminate the communists' Lee Kuan Yew tribute to Albert Winsemius, https://www.nas.gov.sg/archivesonline/data/pdfdoc/090-1996-12-06.pdf

eighty banks 'Singapore emerging as major banking center', *New York Times*, 6 July 1978.

men had to wear formal attire 'Discos tighten up entry rules after warning by minister', *Straits Times*, 23 October 1973, https://eresources.nlb.gov.sg/newspapers/Digitised/Article/straitstimes19731023-1.2.106

licences to serve alcohol withdrawn 'Discos lose liquor permits', *Straits Times*, 18 November 1973, https://eresources.nlb.gov.sg/newspapers/Digitised/Article/straitstimes19731118-1.2.8

eased a few years later 'Restrictions eased. Govt eases curbs on nightclubs and discos', *Straits Times*, 15 February 1975, https://eresources.nlb.gov.sg/newspapers/Digitised/Article/straitstimes19750215-1.2.51

'pay the highest penalty' Lee Kuan Yew statement in parliament, January 1987.

British historian Arnold Toynbee See Michael Barr, *Lee Kuan Yew: The Beliefs behind the Man*, for more on the Toynbee connection.

act of folly 'The UK knew China was planning a massacre at Tiananmen Square', Quartz, 42017, https://qz.com/878627/the-uk-knew-china-was-planning-a-massacre-at-tiananmen-square-in-1989-two-weeks-before-it-happened/

4 The Singapore Dream

'You take a poll' Quoted in Han Fook Kwang, Warren Fernandez and Sumiko Tan, *Lee Kuan Yew, the Man and his Ideas*.

2. Analysis by the *Straits Times*. As quoted in a Reuters report, 'Income gap tears at Singapore social fabric', January 2007.

Employers were reluctant to hire Eng Fong Pang, 'The Economic Status of Malay Muslims in Singapore', ghttps://ink.library.smu.edu.sg/cgi/viewcontent.cgi?article=1437&context=lkcsb_research

excluded from sensitive positions ... Singapore bans the wearing See the Singapore government-commissioned Suara Musyawarah Report, published July 2013.

women held 16 per cent Council for Board Diversity, March 2020, https://www.councilforboarddiversity.sg/statistics/as-at-dec-2019/

Monica Baey, a student 'Change has finally come': Monica Baey on NUS handling of sexual misconduct cases, Channel News Asia, May 2019, https://www.channelnewsasia.com/news/singapore/monica-baey-sexual-misconduct-nus-university-instagram-11494822

heart, soul and spirit 'The PAP and the people – a great affective divide', *Straits Times*, September 1994.

5 The Model City

The creation of new land https://data.gov.sg/dataset/total-land-area-of-singapore

world's biggest sand importer 'Boom in global sand

trade fuels fears over conservation', *Financial Times*,
30 December 2019, https://www.ft.com/content/
aa614ec6-21ae-11ea-b8a1-584213ee7b2b

killer litter 'Singapore's high-rise littering problem – out
of sight, out of mind', Channel News Asia, September
2019, https://www.channelnewsasia.com/news/
singapore/hdb-killer-litter-high-rise-nea-yishun-nee-
soon-ang-mo-kio-11930078

most intrusive social policy Tharman Shanmugaratnam
at the Singapore Forum, 2015, https://www.mof.gov.
sg/news-publications/speeches/Dialogue-with-Mr-
Tharman-Shanmugaratnam-Deputy-Prime-Minister-
and-Minister-for-Finance-moderated-by-Mr-Ho-
Kwon-Ping-Executive-Chairman-of-Banyan-Tree-

the pride quickly soured 'Singapore Industrial Park
Flounders: A Deal Sours in China', *International Herald
Tribune*, October 1999,
https://www.nytimes.com/1999/10/01/business/
worldbusiness/IHT-singapore-industrial-park-
flounders-a-deal-sours.html

People in Suzhou want This is the account Lee gives in
From Third World to First.

the partnership was scrapped 'Andhra Pradesh
project with Singapore to develop the Indian state's
new capital cancelled', *Straits Times*, November
2019, https://www.straitstimes.com/singapore/
amaravati-city-joint-project-officially-terminated-mti

inhospitably hot Jeremy Pal and Elfatih Eltahir, 'Future
temperature in southwest Asia projected to exceed
a threshold for human adaptability', *Nature Climate
Change*, October 2015.

6 Authoritarianism with Gucci Handbags

a believer who refused to give up Lee Kuan Yew, *From Third World to First.*

realised also An account of Cheng's confession is given in 'The Communist Conspirators', *Index on Censorship*, 1987, https://journals.sagepub.com/doi/pdf/10.1080/03064228708534303

A hedge of laws More on this in Jothie Rajah, *Authoritarian Rule of Law.*

an outlet for dissent Interview at Davos in which Lee discusses the idea, https://archive.nytimes.com/www.nytimes.com/library/opinion/safire/022299safi-text.html

charged with solicitation 'Amos Yee pleads not guilty in US court to child pornography and grooming', Channel News Asia, 25 November 2020. https://www.channelnewsasia.com/news/singapore/blogger-amos-yee-pleads-not-guilty-in-us-court-trial-child-porn-13633110

7 Fighting Disease: From TB to Covid-19

We owe the foreign workers Tommy Koh, 'Letter to my grandchildren in a time of pandemic', *Straits Times*, 18 April 2020, https://www.straitstimes.com/opinion/letter-to-my-grandchildren-in-a-time-of-pandemic

a British doctor, William Simpson. W. J. Simpson, *Report of the Sanitary Condition of Singapore* (London: Waterlow & Sons, 1907).

among the first in the world 'Singapore claims first use of antibody test to track coronavirus infections', *Science*,

27 February 2020, https://www.sciencemag.org/
news/2020/02/singapore-claims-first-use-antibody-
test-track-coronavirus-infections

more than 50,000 people had signed. https://www.
change.org/p/singapore-government-singapore-
says-no-to-wearable-devices-for-covid-19-contact-
tracing

In China, this figure Johns Hopkins University,
mortality analyses, https://coronavirus.jhu.edu/data/
mortality

8 'No one owes Singapore a living'

maths teacher Kho Tek Hong 'Ex-teacher Kho Tek
Hong solved Singapore's maths problem', *Straits Times*,
24 November 2014, https://www.straitstimes.com/
singapore/education/ex-teacher-kho-tek-hong-solved-
singapores-maths-problem

Admiralty Secondary School 'Why Singapore's kids are
so good at maths', *Financial Times*, 22 July 2016,
https://www.ft.com/content/2e4c61f2-4ec8-11e6-
8172-e39ecd3b86fc

Donations came in 'Nanyang fund is over $10
mil.', *Singapore Free Press*, 19 May 1954, https://
eresources.nlb.gov.sg/newspapers/Digitised/Article/
freepress19540519.2.47

suspected involvement in communist politics '3am
crackdown: 51 held at Nanyang', *Straits Times*, 28
June 1964, https://eresources.nlb.gov.sg/newspapers/
Digitised/Article/straitstimes19640628-1.2.2

restricted the use of dialect Singapore government
press release, 17 October 1988, https://www.

languagecouncils.sg/mandarin/en/-/media/smc/
documents/goh-minister-lee-hsien-loong_smc-launch-
speech_031088.pdf

the local patois is 'fun' Speech by Second Minister for
Education Indranee Rajah, 2019, https://www.moe.
gov.sg/news/speeches/speech-by-second-minister-for-
education--ms-indranee-rajah--at-the-speak-good-
english-college-west-2019

9 Taming the Internet

complex relationship with the internet For more
on the internet and its impact on political speech
in Singapore, see Garry Rodan, 'The Internet
and Political Control in Singapore', *Political Science
Quarterly*, Spring 1998.

blogger Roy Ngerng 'A butterfly on a wheel', *The
Economist*, 13 June 2014.

He was cross-examined 'Minister grills researcher, says
he is not an objective historian', *Straits Times*, 30 March
2018.

For his YouTube video questioning the law 'Issuance
of Correction Directions under the Protection from
Online Falsehoods and Manipulation Act to New
Naratif and Mr Thum Ping Tjin', Singapore Ministry
of Law press release, May 2020.

possession of child pornography 'Amos Yee Indicted
on Child Porn Charges in Illinois', *Straits Times*, 6
November 2020.

10 Singapore Inc

My father believed in Asia 'Chinese Buyers Try to
Avoid Overpaying, As Japanese Did', *Wall Street
Journal*, February 1997

prospered during the Japanese occupation Hong
Leong Foundation and Asian Civilisations Museum
press release, April 2009, https://www.nhb.gov.
sg/acm/-/media/acm/document/about-us/media/
press-releases/2009-10.pdf

stripped of his Singapore citizenship 'Citizenship
move against magnate', *Straits Times*, 23 September
1963, https://eresources.nlb.gov.sg/newspapers/
Digitised/Article/straitstimes19630923-1.2.4

BHP Billiton 'Miner BHP to pay $390 million in
Australian tax dispute over Singapore hub', Reuters,
November 2018, https://uk.reuters.com/article/
uk-bhp-tax/miner-bhp-to-pay-390-million-
in-australian-tax-dispute-over-singapore-hub-
idUKKCN1NO0DT

No one wants to get their hands dirty 'Can Singapore
rely less on foreign workers?' Channel News Asia,
June 2020, https://www.channelnewsasia.com/
news/singapore/singapore-foreign-workers-reliance-
challenges-12806970

average monthly salary From Singapore in Figures
2019, https://www.singstat.gov.sg/-/media/files/
publications/reference/sif2019.pdf

In Singapore's financial sector Parliamentary answer
given in September 2020.

11 Asian Values

Bear with us 'Remarks by Secretary Mattis at Shangri-La Dialogue', June 2017, https://www.defense.gov/Newsroom/Transcripts/Transcript/Article/1201780/remarks-by-secretary-mattis-at-shangri-la-dialogue/

bought precious time Lee Hsien Loong, 'The Endangered Asian Century', *Foreign Policy*, July/August 2020, https://www.foreignaffairs.com/articles/asia/2020-06-04/lee-hsien-loong-endangered-asian-century

Google deleted thousands Google Threat Analysis Group bulletin, September 2020, https://blog.google/threat-analysis-group/tag-bulletin-q3-2020/

Beijing made an official protest 'China protests to Singapore over military ties to Taiwan', *Financial Times*, November 2016, https://www.ft.com/content/5459aaba-b54f-11e6-ba85-95d1533d9a62

an instrument of political pressure 'A Bleak Assessment as Rights Declaration Nears', *New York Times*, April 1993, https://www.nytimes.com/1993/04/25/world/a-bleak-assessment-as-rights-meeting-nears.html

The forty-two-minute film 'North Korean film on Kim's Singapore trip reveals new focus on economy', Reuters, June 2018.

strengthening its defence ties 'India and Singapore deepen defence ties with naval agreement', *Straits Times*, November 2017, https://www.straitstimes.com/asia/se-asia/india-and-singapore-deepen-defence-ties-with-naval-agreement

have fired shots in anger just once 'Commandos storm airliner, kill Pakistani hijackers', Associated Press, March 1991.

It was really surgical Interview with Fred Cheong, 'As a Special Forces soldier, he stormed a hijacked Singapore Airlines plane. Now he's a monk', Channel News Asia, July 2019.

Belt and Road Initiative 'Belt and Road. Can China Turn the Middle of Nowhere Into the Center of the World Economy?', *New York Times*, January 2019.

this settlement, called Forest City 'Chinese-backed Forest City rises above the sea', *Financial Times*, February 2017.

12 The Art of Resistance

Sam Lo 'Strict Singapore divided by arrest of its own Banksy', *Observer*, 10 June 2012, https://www.theguardian.com/world/2012/jun/10/sticker-lady-strict-singapore-divided

The tickets were sold 'The Struggle: Late theatre doyen Kuo Pao Kun's play finally staged after 1969 ban', *Straits Times*, https://www.straitstimes.com/lifestyle/arts/the-struggle-late-theatre-doyen-kuo-pao-kuns-play-finally-staged-after-1969-ban

the theories of Richard Florida Richard Florida, 'Cities and the creative class in Asia', 17 November 2011, https://www.bloomberg.com/news/articles/2011-11-17/cities-and-the-creative-class-in-asia?sref=CXarFWFz

have been growing faster From 1986 to 2000 creative industries grew by an average of 17.2 per cent per annum, compared with average annual GDP growth of 10.5 per cent. 'Economic contributions of Singapore's creative industries', Ministry of Trade and Industry, 2003.

comparable to exactly what we are doing 'Using the Force: Lucasfilm opens Singapore creativity centre', Reuters, January 2014, https://uk.reuters.com/article/us-singapore-lucasfilm-idUKBREA0F09N20140116

stealing innovation 'Responding Effectively to the Chinese Economic Espionage Threat', speech by Christopher Wray, FBI director, https://www.fbi.gov/news/speeches/responding-effectively-to-the-chinese-economic-espionage-threat

13 Sin City

transvestite street performers were banned 'No transvestite shows for Bugis Street', *Straits Times*, April 1992.

Three traffickers were convicted 2020 Trafficking in Persons report: Singapore. US Department of State, https://www.state.gov/reports/2020-trafficking-in-persons-report/singapore/

even if the sites are hosted abroad Ministry of Home Affairs press release, October 2019, https://www.mha.gov.sg/newsroom/press-release/news/first-reading-of-women-charter-amendment-bill

more than 1400 foreign women 'More foreign women nabbed for online vice, police concerned with vice activities in residential estates', *Straits Times*, 2 November 2019, https://www.straitstimes.com/singapore/courts-crime/vice-activities-increasingly-moving-into-residential-estates-police

a problem gambler Lee Kuan Yew, speech in parliament, April 2005, https://www.nas.gov.sg/archivesonline/data/pdfdoc/2005041902.pdf

petition against the casinos 'Singapore is likely to lift casino ban', *Wall Street Journal*, April 2005.

key element 'Moving Away from the Death Penalty: Victims and the Death Penalty', September 2016, https://www.mfa.gov.sg/Newsroom/Press-Statements-Transcripts-and-Photos/2016/09/MFA-Press-Release-Transcript-of-Minister-Vivian-Balakrishnans-Intervention-at-the-HighLevel-Side-Eve

Booze is heavily taxed 'Singapore ranks 6th most expensive city for beer in the world, 2nd in Asia', *Straits Times*, July 2015, https://www.straitstimes.com/singapore/singapore-ranks-6th-most-expensive-city-for-beer-in-the-world-2nd-in-asia

14 The demographic challenge

More stupid Lee Kuan Yew, National Day Rally speech, 1983

The emphasis on graduate fertility 'Graduate mum scheme to go', *Straits Times*, March 1985, https://eresources.nlb.gov.sg/newspapers/Digitised/Article/straitstimes19850326.2.2

Singaporeans are staying single Population in Brief 2020, https://www.strategygroup.gov.sg/media-centre/publications/population-in-brief

Ma Chi's final moments 'Ferrari crash fuels Singapore anti-foreign sentiment', Yahoo! News, May 2012, https://sg.news.yahoo.com/ferrari-crash-fuels-singapore-anti-foreign-sentiment-193659157.html

Ministers say they calibrate 'Grace Fu: proportion of Malays in citizen population will not shrink', *Straits*

Times, February 2013, https://www.straitstimes.com/singapore/grace-fu-proportion-of-malays-in-citizen-population-will-not-shrink

15 The Future

perfectionist attention to detail 'The boss' attention to detail', *Straits Times*, October 2014.

Climate change presents a looming threat National Climate Change Secretariat, https://www.nccs.gov.sg/faqs/impact-of-climate-change-and-adaptation-measures/

the first icebreakers to be built Keppel Singmarine – Ice Class Vessels, http://www.keppelom.com/en/content.aspx?sid=2581

Further reading

Michael Barr, *Lee Kuan Yew, the Beliefs Behind the Man*,
 Richmond, Surrey: Curzon Press, 2000
Chua Beng Huat, *Liberalism Disavowed*, Ithaca: Cornell
 University Press, 2017
Cherian George, *The Air-conditioned Nation*, Singapore:
 Landmark Books, 2000
Ho Kwon Ping, *The Ocean in a Drop*, Singapore: World
 Scientific, 2015
Lee Kuan Yew, *From Third World to First*, New York:
 HarperCollins, 2000
Sonny Liew, *The Art of Charlie Chan Hock Chye*, Singapore:
 Epigram Books, 2015
Jothie Rajah, *Authoritarian Rule of Law*, New York:
 Cambridge University Press, 2012
C. M. Turnbull, *A History of Singapore*, Kuala Lumpur:
 Oxford University Press, 1977

Index

Abdul Rahman 55
Acemoglu, Daron 67
acronyms, widespread use of 172
activism 4, 11–12, 15, 19, 48, 52–3,
    125–37, 141, 142–9
    detention without trial 56–7, 63,
        87, 126–7, 132–3, 134–5,
        136, 141, 147, 148
    gay activism 144–5, 187, 191
    online 189–94
    see also strikes; student activism;
        trade unions
air conditioning 119, 140
alcohol, attitudes to 261–2
Alfreds, Ravi 227, 229
Amaravati 118
Ang, Jaelle 176
Anglo-Chinese School 173, 174,
    186, 208
Anglophone society 96, 168, 171,
    208, 275
Apple 75, 203
aquaculture 107
Arab Spring 183, 184
architecture 119–20
    HDB flats 113–14
    new towns (planned
        communities) 114
    resilience 123
    sustainability 121, 122

    see also housing; urban
        transformation
Arctic Council 285
*The Art of Charlie Chan Hock
    Chye* (graphic novel) 241–2,
    243–4
artificial intelligence 181
arts 232–46, 285
    censorship 234, 235–6
    festivals 236, 237
    films 87–8, 244
    performing arts 234–7
    political thread 240, 241–2, 243
    public 232–3
    Renaissance City initiative
        238–9
    state subsidies 238–9, 242
    street art 233–4, 245
    trophy value 236
    videogames 244
Asian dollar market 76
Asian Values ideology 77–8, 221,
    225, 229, 230, 236
Au, Alex 184–5, 190–1, 194
Aung San 43, 49
authoritarianism 3, 4, 11–12, 16, 81,
    136–7
    see also conservatism

Balakrishnan, Vivian 160, 161, 261

banking 75–6, 84, 141–2, 199,
        209–11
    scandals 209–11
Barings Bank 207, 209
Barisan Sosialis 55, 73, 125, 126
Bay, Jason 160
Belt and Road Initiative 229–30
beriberi 156
Bhutan 222
billionaires in Singapore 9
birth rates 17, 139, 264, 266–7,
        273–4
    births outside marriage 248
    Chinese Singaporeans 268–9
    declining 220, 266, 268–9
    Malay minority 273–4
    state incentives 266–7
Bittner, Maximilian 179
books, censorship of 137–8
Bose, Subhas Chandra 43, 49
Brazil 116
Britain
    Brexit 4, 136, 280–1
    colonialism 6, 7–8, 22–3, 25–6,
        27–50, 51–8, 155–7
    Covid-19 pandemic 163, 282
Britannia Unchained 280
Brown, George 219
Brunei 215, 218
Bruner, Jerome 166
BSI bank 209–11
Buddhism 1, 25, 91
Bugis Street 249–50
Bukit Brown 142–3
Bukit Timah 85, 113, 170
bumiputra 59
business 196–213
    alignment of politics and
        business 199–206
    business elite 196–9, 207–8
    exchange of gifts 203, 204
    family businesses 197–9, 200, 211

state capitalism 205–6
    see also entrepreneurship;
        startups; and specific sectors

capital punishment 2, 259, 260, 261
car ownership 86–7, 120
Cathay Building 37, 40, 49
Cavenagh Bridge 94
censorship 11, 137–9, 147, 183–4,
        188, 234, 235–6, 249, 256
Central Provident Fund (CPF) 99,
        111, 117, 189
Chan Poh Meng 173
Changi airport 2, 75, 123, 276
Cheang Hong Lim 142
Chee Soon Juan 141
Chen, David 179
Chen Wen Hsi 238
Cheng Teck Hock 271, 272
Cheng, Vincent 131, 133, 135
Cheong, Fred 227
Chew Kheng Chuan 87, 129,
        130–1, 132, 133, 134–5, 136,
        139–40, 148–9
chewing gum ban 2, 4–5
Chia Thye Poh 125, 126–7, 128,
        132, 147
China 15, 16, 23, 35, 163, 245
    anti-US espionage 219
    Belt and Road Initiative 229–30
    capitalist conversion 216
    China–Singapore relationship
        18–19, 116–17, 122–3, 203,
        216–18, 230
    military might 215, 216, 217,
        284
    'One China' principle 218
    and the Singapore model 224–5
    Singapore-based propaganda
        217–18
    Sino-Japanese conflict 38–9
    Tiananmen Square 81, 229

Chinatown 61, 95
Chinese High School (Hwa Chong
    Institution) 168, 170
Chinese New Year 84
Chinese Singaporeans 7, 8, 18, 24,
    25, 33, 34–5, 47, 58, 96, 217
  birth rate 268–9
  clan associations 95–6, 169
  Confucian ethics 220
  festivals 1–2, 84
  languages and dialects 8, 12, 96,
    170–1, 275
  secret societies 33
  social tensions 272–3
  Straits Chinese 49
  time-honoured customs 22, 203,
    217, 274–5
  World War Two 39–41
cholera 158
Choo Wee Khiang 96–7
Choo Zheng Xi, Remy 186–7, 191
Choy, Elizabeth 41, 43
Christianity 25, 91–3
city states 13–14, 115
civil servants 68, 171, 172, 180, 203,
    204
civility, lack of 100
clan associations 95–6, 168
cleanliness, public 112–13, 158
climate change 105–6, 118–19,
    123–4, 281, 284–5
Cold War 216, 219–20, 229, 243
colonial Singapore 6, 7–8, 22–3,
    25–6, 27–50, 51–8, 155–7
commodities trading 201
communism 47, 48, 55, 56, 57, 58,
    64, 69, 229, 238
  Singaporean anti-communism
    62, 63, 128–9, 130, 192,
    216, 241
computer industries 75
concubines 73–4

Confucian ethics 219–20
conservatism 76–7, 146, 221, 222,
    225, 248
container shipping 74
contempt of court charges 190–1
convict labour 29–30
corporal punishment 2, 137, 233
corporation tax 18, 202–3
Corrective Work Orders 112
corruption 68, 78, 85, 283
cosmopolitan Singaporeans 221,
    225
Covid-19 pandemic 18, 83, 93, 106,
    121, 147, 150, 151–5, 157,
    159–64, 208, 218, 277, 281–2
  communal solidarity 162–3, 277
  global comparisons 163, 164
  government strategy 157, 281–2,
    288
  mortality rate 163, 282
  surveillance technology 159–62,
    163
Crazy Rich Asians (film) 14
crime rates 14
Criminal Procedure Code 161
critical faculties, numbing of 140–1
cultured meat production 107
currency trading 202
cyberattacks 218–19

Dalforce 40, 41
Daniel, Rosa 243–4
dating 263–4, 266, 267–8
deep technology ventures 181
defence force 66–7, 71, 97, 225–9
  combat experience 227
  national service 53, 82, 97, 227
  personnel and resources 226
  ties with other countries 217,
    225, 230
  total defence doctrine 226
  training exercises 226

demographics 17–18, 264–78
  ageing society 17, 18, 264, 269,
    270, 284
  life expectancy 158, 264
  population growth 22, 273
  racial balance 139, 273
  see also birth rates; ethnic
    diversity; migrant workers
Deng Xiaoping 15, 81, 224
Dhanabalan, Suppiah 135–6
disease
  colonial death rates 156
  see also Covid-19 pandemic; Sars
    epidemic; and specific diseases
domestic service 85, 154–5, 173
driverless cars 3, 120
droughts 106
drug trade 2, 7, 255, 259–61
  legal penalties 2, 259–61
Dutch traders 25–6, 27
dynastic politics 138, 286–7

early history of Singapore 7–8, 24
  see also colonial Singapore
East India Company 27–8, 31
economic growth 9, 66, 69–70, 73,
    275–6
  slowdown in 17, 88
Edible Garden City 104–5, 108
education 9, 10, 15, 16, 17, 30,
    165–81
  Chinese-language 35, 47, 53, 77,
    138, 168, 169, 170
  competitive 89, 172, 174–7
  elite schools 173–4
  English-language 35, 50, 78, 82,
    96, 168, 169, 275
  grade anxiety 174–5
  graduate numbers 284
  maths teaching 3, 166–7
  primary education 168, 175
  private tuition 99, 173

  PSLE exam 175, 176, 177
  reforms 176–7
  scholarships 89, 172
  science teaching 167–8
  social studies 178
  Special Assistance Plan 170
  T-score 175–6, 177
  universities 169
  see also student activism
elections 4
  1959 53
  1968 72, 73
  2006 184–5
  2011 17, 102, 185
  2020 102, 148, 208, 288–9
electoral system 80, 134
  minority representation 80
elite, Singaporean 16, 78–9, 84–5,
    86, 90, 146, 172–4
  business elite 196–9, 207–8
  high net worth individuals 9, 197
  'old money' 84–5, 91
  overseas trophy purchases 196,
    208
  Westernised 96, 168, 208, 274,
    275
  see also family businesses
emigrants 101
employment
  full employment 73
  older workers 189, 269, 270
  shrinking workforce 277–8
  unemployment 8, 10, 14, 73,
    98–9
  women 74, 98, 205, 266
  see also migrant workers
engineered society, Singapore as 279
entrepreneurship 67, 69, 120, 178,
    181
  deep technology ventures 181
  science-based 201
  start-ups 178–80, 181

Equator Art Society 238
ethnic diversity 6, 8, 24–5, 58, 95,
    96–7
    see also Chinese Singaporeans;
        Malays; Tamils
ethnic violence 59–60, 61, 66
eugenics 50–1, 265–6
export-oriented industry 9, 69, 70,
    200

Facebook 83, 184, 191, 194, 195, 205
fake news law (Pofma) 192–3, 194
family businesses 197–9, 200,
    211–13
    clan wealth 198
    younger generations 211,
        212–13, 287
family planning 264
family values rhetoric 144, 248
Farquhar, William 28–9, 30, 31
Fay, Michael 137
film industry 87–8, 244
    censorship 249, 256
financial centre 9, 36, 75–6
    see also banking
financial crisis (2008) 141–2
5Cs 86, 100
Florida, Richard 244
Foo Chee Chang 93
food
    domestic production 107–8
    imports 106, 107
food hawkers 12, 75, 157–8, 251
foreign currency controls 76
Forest City 230
free speech, restrictions on 4, 17, 19,
    187, 190, 194, 289
future challenges for Singapore
    283–8

gambling 30, 255–9
garden city 113

Gardens by the Bay 122, 123, 223
GDP 10
Geylang 32–3, 248, 250, 251, 253
Gibson, William 2
globalisation 9, 20, 83, 271, 285,
    289
Goh Chok Tong 88, 89, 101, 134,
    173, 283
Goh Keng Swee 51, 55, 60, 68, 70
Goh Lay Kuan 235
Goh, Michelle 263–4, 268
goods and services tax 18
Google 83, 145, 203, 217–18
government and leadership
    anti-corruption 68, 78, 85, 283
    authoritarianism 3, 4, 11–12, 16,
        81, 136–7
    dynastic politics 138, 286–7
    one-party politics 4, 19, 80, 148,
        186
    political salaries 68, 87, 88
    surveillance technology 120–1,
        159–62, 163, 207
    see also Lee Kuan Yew
Government of Singapore
    Investment Corporation
    (GIC) 205
Grab 179–80
graffiti 137
Grant Associates 122–3
group representation constituencies
    (GRCs) 80

Hamid, Yusuf Abdol 93, 94
Hammond, Philip 281
happiness, national 87
Hassell, Richard 105, 120, 123
healthcare 16, 17–18, 98
    funding 158–9
    political hybrid 158–9
    see also Covid-19 pandemic; Sars
        epidemic

heartlanders 221, 225
heat island effect 118–19
Hendrickson, Mason 134
Ho Ching 205
Ho, Vanessa 253, 254, 255
Hokkien Huay Kuan 169
home ownership 99, 110
    see also housing
homelessness 10
homosexuality 101, 143–5, 221–2,
    256
    criminalisation of 12, 101, 143,
        187, 252
    gay activism 144–5, 187, 191
Hon Sui Sen 70
Hong Kong 3, 9, 11, 71, 86, 91,
    106, 200, 203, 218, 222, 287
Hong Lim Park 141, 142, 144, 145
Hoong, Kimberly 104, 108–9
housing 10, 18, 79, 93–4, 109–11,
    113–15
    depreciating asset 115
    ethnic quotas 95
    HDB flats 90, 95, 110, 113–14,
        121
    high-rise 90, 110, 111
    'landed houses' 90
    for migrant labour 153–4, 155
    mixed development 110–11, 114
    multi-generational 269
    public 93–4, 109–11, 113–15
    single people 114
human rights 11, 222, 224
    see also activism
Hungry Ghost Festival 1–2, 22

Ibrahim, Yaacob 194
Ilo Ilo (film) 87
immigration
    from China 32, 96, 219, 270,
        272, 275
    from India 32

policies 17, 19, 273, 276
public unease 17, 185, 208, 270,
    271, 273, 276, 284
racial profile 96
see also migrant workers
import substitution 70
in vitro fertilisation (IVF) 143, 267
income tax 18
independence 23, 58, 146, 253
India 23, 53, 82, 117–18, 222, 225
individualism, challenge of 76, 220,
    221, 236
Indonesia 21, 26, 53, 66, 105, 215
industrialisation 8, 16, 54, 70, 71,
    75, 201
infant mortality 158, 266
Infectious Diseases Act 157
intellectual property protection
    244, 245
Internal Security Act 126, 138, 235
Internal Security Department 130,
    135
Islamic Revolution 134
Islamism 97–8
Ismail, Ishak 228
Israel 66–7

Japan 17, 34, 222, 225, 264
    Japan–Singapore relationship 44
    occupation of Singapore 38,
        39–43, 44, 49–50, 198
    Sino-Japanese conflict 38–9
Jeyaretnam, Joshua 79
Johnson, Boris 280, 282
Jurong Island 202

Kagame, Paul 223–4
Kampong Glam 96
kampongs 109, 114
Kampung Admiralty 121
Kang, Robert 274, 275
karaoke bars 204

Kassim, Ismail 97
Kazakhstan 223
Kennedy, Kathleen 244
Kho Tek Hong 166
Khoo Teng Chye 121
kiasu mentality 177–8
Kim Jong-un 15, 223
Koh, Tommy 155
Kong Hee 92–3
Krugman, Paul 276
Kuik Shiao-Yin 178
Kuo Jian Hong 235
Kuo Pao Kun 234–5, 237
Kwa Geok Choo 10–11, 55
Kwek Hong Png 197–8
Kwek Leng Beng 196

Lambreghts, Stefaan 123
land nationalisation 109
land reclamation 105
'landed houses' 90
Law Society 131
'lazy native' stereotype 80–1
Lee Hsien Loong 79, 172, 185, 186,
    205, 219, 228, 249, 273, 286,
    287
Lee Hsien Yang 286
Lee Kuan Yew 15, 19, 44, 57, 59,
    64, 68, 69, 71–2, 79, 80, 86,
    87, 112, 116, 117, 119, 138,
    140, 146, 165, 172, 173, 220,
    223, 225, 241, 265, 283, 286,
    287
  and activists 12, 141
  anti-communism 62, 128–9, 130
  anti-corruption 68
  authoritarianism 5, 50, 81
  and the break with Malaysia 6,
    60–1, 63
  co-founder of PAP 51–2
  and Confucian ethics 219–20
  death of 6, 82, 182, 279
  education 49
  elected prime minister 6, 54–5
  and end of colonial rule 58
  on ethnic communities 8, 80, 81
  and eugenics 50–1, 265
  governmental career 82, 286
  lifestyle 10–11, 78
  on migrant workers 16, 276
  opposition to gambling 256
  pragmatism 49, 50
  predictions for the future 82–3
  public demeanour 11
  trade union legal adviser 48, 51
  World War Two 42, 49–50
Lee Wei Ling 286
Leeson, Nick 207, 209
Leow, Florence 273
Leow, Vernon 258–9
Li Hongyi 286
Li Shengwu 279
libel suits 11, 79–80, 138, 188–9, 190
liberal democracies 4, 245
liberation theology 130
Liew, Sonny 241, 242, 243, 285
Life Beyond Grades campaign 176
life expectancy 158, 264
Lim, Andrew Koay 92–3
Lim, Catherine 101–3, 285
Lim Chin Siong 48, 55, 57, 168,
    241, 242
Lim, Ivan 228–9
Lim, Jeremy 163
Lim, Jui 181
Lim Tzay Chuen 239–40
littering 112–13
  'killer litter' 111
  penalties 5, 111, 112
Little India 32, 62, 96, 97
Little India riot 153, 207, 262, 273
Lo, Sam 233–4, 245–6
location of Singapore 6–7, 21, 33–4,
    287

long-haired males, discrimination
        against 76–7
Low, Jho 210
Low, Vincent 192
Low, Wilson 161, 162

Ma Chi 271–2
MacDonald House bombing 65–6
MacRitchie Reservoir 113
Mahbubani, Kishore 152–3
Mahizhnan, Arun 236, 237
Malacca 28, 29, 31
malaria 156
Malaya 34, 48
    communist insurgency 47, 55
    ethnic mix 58
    independence 55
    nationalism 58
    Singapore's union with 55, 57–8
Malayan Emergency 48, 129
Malays 8, 24, 25, 59, 60, 96, 97–8,
        139
Malaysia 21, 37, 105, 186, 206, 215,
        259
    formation of 57
    split with Singapore 6, 8, 60–2,
        63–4, 66, 70
    terrestrial link with Singapore 37
male-dominated society 98, 205
Mandarin 12, 18, 79, 96, 170–1,
        208, 275
Marcos, Ferdinand 5, 130
Marina Bay 95, 223, 257–8
marriage
    age at 268
    arranged marriages 267
    dating 263–4, 266, 267–8
    state promotion of 266
'Marxist conspiracy' 130, 131
Mass Rapid Transit (MRT) 5, 115
material aspiration 86, 87
Mattis, Jim 216

May, Liang 175
media
    censorship 11, 138–9, 183–4, 188
    foreign newspapers 138
    see also social media
Medisave 158–9
Medvedev, Dmitry 222
meritocracy 12, 63, 88–9, 90, 172,
        253, 287
Merlion 239–40
middle class, growth of 37, 47, 85,
        110, 172
migrant workers 16–17, 147, 153–4,
        173, 206–7, 219, 270–1
    citizenship and 270, 277, 288
    Covid-19 153–4, 162–3, 277,
        288
    housing 153–4, 155
    low-paid 154–5, 206, 207, 208,
        275–6
    migration controls 273, 276
    professionals 3, 154, 207, 270,
        271, 273
    proportion of population 270
    public unease over influx of 185,
        208, 270, 271, 273, 276,
        284
    reliance on 16, 17, 154–5, 206,
        275–6
    sex work 253
Minchin, James 138, 241
mixed martial arts 245
money-laundering 211, 259
Mountbatten, Lord Louis 43
Muhlinghaus, Herman 35
multinational companies 8, 69, 71,
        75, 83, 144, 202–3, 204, 221
music, modern 77
Muslim headscarves 97–8
The Myth of Asia's Miracle (Paul
        Krugman) 276

Nanyang Technological University 169, 224
Nanyang University (Nantah) 169
national anthem 54
National Day 63, 88, 267
National Gallery 237–8
national identity 96
National Pledge 63
national service 53, 82, 97, 227
National University of Singapore (NUS) 169
National Wages Council 72–3
Nazarbayev, Nursultan 223
nepotism 80, 89, 90, 199, 227–8, 286
new towns (planned communities) 114
Ngerng, Roy 189–90, 191, 194, 225
night soil collection 156
North Korea 223
nouveau riche 91
Nye, Joseph 141

oil and petroleum 9, 34, 36, 37–8, 54, 201–2
'old money' 84–5, 91
One North 120
One Raffles Place 75
Online Citizen 187, 188
Operation Coldstore 55–6, 193, 241
Operation Snip Snip 76
Operation Spectrum 129, 132–6
opium trade 7, 30, 32, 77, 260, 262

Padang 95
Palay, Seelan 147
Parliament House 82, 94
Patel, Priti 280
People's Action Party (PAP) 11, 17, 54, 55, 77, 125, 148, 241, 243
  electoral performance 17, 73, 102
  founding of 51–2

'permanent residents' 24
Philippines 130, 215, 216
Pillai, Naraina 29
Pink Dot 144, 145, 225
plane hijacking 227
plastic waste 113
police 60
Political Study Centre 68
polygamy 74, 266
population growth 22, 273
poverty 93, 94, 189
  see also wealth inequalities
productivity growth 16, 17, 269–70, 276
property taxes 112
prosperity gospel churches 91, 92–3
prostitution see sex work
Public Order Act 137, 146, 147
Pulau Brani 35–6
Pulau Bukom 36, 37–8
Pulau Semakau 113
Putin, Vladimir 222

Raab, Dominic 280
racism 96–8, 205, 272
Raffles, Sir Thomas Stamford 7, 22–3, 25–8, 29, 30, 31, 69
Raffles Institution 23, 30, 49, 173, 174
Raffles Place 21, 23, 141
rainforest 113
Rajaratnam, Sinnathamby 51, 55, 78
red light districts 247–8, 249–50, 253
  see also sex work
religion 25, 91–2, 191–2
  religious scepticism 221
  see also specific faiths
Remaking Singapore committee 100
Renaissance City initiative 238–9

retirement income, inadequacies of 189

retirement savings scheme, compulsory 99

Rewcastle Brown, Clare 210

Rexadvance Technologies 206–7

rice imports 108

risk aversion 81, 180, 181, 262

robotics 167–8, 276

role model, Singapore as 116–18, 122–3, 124, 223–5, 280, 281–4

rubber industry 7, 34, 36, 58, 75

Rwanda 223–4

Sarker, Raju 153, 163

Sars epidemic 88, 150–1, 153, 154, 157, 187

Schleicher, Andreas 167

School of Design 119

Schooling, Joseph 288

sea level rises 123, 124

Seah, Irvin 115

Seah, Nicole 185

Sedition Act 137

self-governing status 53, 73
  see also independence

self-reliance doctrine 9, 99, 159, 181

self-sufficency in water and food 106, 107–8, 120

Sentosa 127–8, 248

Seow, Francis 133–4

sex change surgery 145

sex trafficking 251, 253

sex work 78, 247–8, 249–55
  foreign workers 253, 254
  illegal brothels 253–4, 255
  physical assault 255
  state regulation 250–1, 253, 254

sexual attitudes, conserve 248–9

sexual harassment 98

shaming, public 5, 112, 137

Shanghai 3, 74

Shangri-La Dialogue 214–16

Shared Values statement 221

Shaw, George Bernard 191

Shell 36, 37, 38

Sherqueshaa, Sherry 251–2, 253

shophouses 37, 47

Simpson, William 155–6

Singapore Airlines 23, 75, 205, 206, 227

Singapore dream 85, 86, 88, 89, 99, 283

Singapore Dreaming (film) 87–8

Singapore-on-Thames 281

Singlish 25, 171, 232, 233, 270

size of Singapore 90

skyscrapers 37, 75

slavery 30

Smart Nation project 120–1

social change movements see activism

Social Development Unit 266

social inequalities 89, 90, 173–4
  see also meritocracy; wealth inequalities

social media 182–95
  criticism of government 182–3, 189, 284
  government constraints 183–4, 188, 194–5
  new spaces for debate 184, 186, 195
  news websites licensing schemes 188
  OpenNet Initiative 184

solar energy 121

'solarpunk' 122

Solomon Islands 222

Sook Ching massacre 40–1, 43–4

South China Sea 18, 19, 217, 218

South Korea 9, 11, 16, 71, 82, 132, 222, 264, 282

Speak Good English movement 171
Speak Mandarin campaign 171
Speakers' Corner 141, 142, 186, 190, 273
spitting, criminalisation of 5, 157
Spot (robotic dog) 159–60
squatter colonies 109, 125
Sri Lanka 53, 291, 294
startups 178–80, 181
    foreign entrepreneurs 179–80, 181
    home-grown 180
status anxiety 87
sterilisation policies 264–5
Strait of Malacca 6–7, 27
Straits Times 57, 70, 89, 97, 101, 126, 134, 138–9, 155, 205, 235
strikes 12, 51, 52, 69, 72, 207
student activism 53, 76, 130, 132, 138, 169
Suez Canal 7, 13, 34
Suharto, President 186
Sun Ho 92, 93
Sun Xu 272
Supreme Court 94–5
Surbana Jurong 116–17
surrogacy 144
surveillance technology 120–1, 159–62, 163, 207
Sustenir 108
Suzhou 116–17
Sword, James 35

Taiwan 9, 11, 16, 18, 71, 82, 199–200, 215, 218, 222, 264, 282
Tamils 8, 24, 25, 96
Tan, Alex 194
Tan, Anthony 180
Tan Che Sang 29
Tan Cheng Eam 109, 110
Tan Chin Tuan 49
Tan Hooi Ling 180

Tan Kah Kee 34–5, 37, 39, 41, 53
Tan Lark Sye 109, 169, 200
Tan Wah Piow 130, 131
Tanglin Club 91, 207–8
Taoism 1, 25, 91
taxation 18, 70, 72, 112, 202–3
Tay, Eugene 143
Teh Cheang Wan 78
Temasek 24, 136, 204–5, 206
Teo, Kelvin 178–9, 180
Teo Soh Lung 131, 133, 148
Teo You Yenn 90
terrorism 65–6, 227
Thailand 206, 259
Tharman Shanmugaratnam 114, 136
theatre 234–5, 236–7
Thum, P.J. 193, 194
Tianjin 122–3
tin industry 7, 34, 35–6, 58, 75
Tochi, Iwuchukwu Amara 260–1
Toh Chin Chye 55
Toh Thiam Chye 167, 168
Total Defence Day 44
tourism 201, 257
Toynbee, Arnold 80, 81
trade unions 4, 8, 14, 16, 48, 51, 52–3, 55, 66, 72
transgender people 145–6, 250, 251–2
Trump, Donald 4, 136, 196, 215, 223
tuberculosis (TB) 156, 157
Twitter 184, 195
typhoid 158

unemployment 8, 10, 14, 73
    welfare provision 98–9
United States
    Covid-19 pandemic 282
    defence cooperation 217, 230
    investor in Singapore 75, 203, 216

United States – *continued*
  military influence in the region 215, 216
  US–Singapore relationship 18, 71–2, 203, 208, 226
universities 169
University Socialist Club 76
urban farming 104–5, 107, 108–9
urban transformation 19, 109–10, 111–12, 115–24, 200
  overseas cloning of Singaporean model 116–18, 122–3, 124
  see also housing

vandalism 2, 233
videogames industry 244
Vietnam 118, 215
Vietnam War 5, 34, 72, 125, 129, 137, 216
vulnerability and insecurities, national 14, 19, 44–5, 82, 177–8, 192, 193–4, 217

waste treatment 113
water supply 106, 139
waterways 21, 122
wealth inequalities 8, 79, 94, 97, 279
wealth management business 202
Wee family 84–5, 198–9
Wee Cho Yaw 198
Wee Ee Cheong 198
Wee Teng Wen 173, 212–13
welfare provision 10, 98–9, 159, 288

Western youth culture 76–7, 78, 235–6
Wham, Jolovan 147
wildlife 113, 122
Winsemius, Albert 69, 70, 74, 75
women
  in the labour force 74, 98, 205, 266
  unmarried 266
  women's rights 9, 73–4, 254, 266
Women's Charter 74, 254, 266
Wong Kan Seng 251
Wong, Lawrence 146
Worker' Party 131, 148, 185, 289
workfare 99
working hours 15, 81
World Economic Forum 163–4
World War Two 38, 39–43, 49–50, 198

Xing Han Jiang 230–1

Ye, Gang 179
Yee, Amos 182–3, 184, 191–2, 194
Yeo, Dickson 219
Yeo Jiawei 210, 211
Yeo Oi Sang 46–7, 48, 56–7
Yong Ser Pin 234
YouTube 185, 193, 217–18
Yu, Runze 231

zero waste goal 113
Zhang Xinsheng 116
Zhang Yong 211–12
Zheng He 237